Mediating the Global

Mediating the Global

Expatria's Forms and Consequences in Kathmandu

Heather Hindman

Stanford University Press
Stanford, California

Stanford University Press
Stanford, California

This book has been published with the assistance of The University of Texas at Austin.

Printed in the United States of America on acid-free, archival-quality paper

Library of Congress Cataloging-in-Publication Data

Hindman, Heather, author.
  Mediating the global : expatria's forms and consequences in Kathmandu / Heather Hindman.
     pages cm
  Includes bibliographical references and index.
  ISBN 978-0-8047-8651-5 (cloth : alk. paper)
  1. Foreign workers--Nepal--Kathmandu--Social life and customs. 2. Professional employees--Nepal--Kathmandu--Social life and customs. 3. International agencies--Officials and employees--Nepal--Kathmandu. 4. International business enterprises--Nepal--Kathmandu--Employees. 5. Labor and globalization--Nepal--Kathmandu. 6. Culture and globalization--Nepal--Kathmandu. I. Title.
  HD8670.9.Z8K374 2013
  331.6'2095496--dc23   2013025716

  ISBN 978-0-8047-8855-7 (electronic)

Typeset by Bruce Lundquist in 10/14 Minion

Contents

Acknowledgments

THE DEBTS THAT ONE ACCRUES as part of the process of thinking about, researching and writing a book are diverse and innumerable. It was only midway into the process of this book that I began to understand its genesis in my grandparents' expatriate experiences. Robert and Ethel Stewart lived in many locations, places I came to know through stories of life in Switzerland, the Netherlands and Japan, and later through trinkets and coins brought back from short trips to Asia, Africa, Europe and South America. While I long credited my grandfather for my wanderlust, I did not understand why I was drawn to understand Expatria until the project had already taken over my life.

This project and its intellectual merit, if there is any, developed from the rich intellectual communities I was embraced by, first at Reed College and later at the University of Chicago. The workshop culture at Chicago and the friends I developed out of it were the incubator, if not always a nurturing one, for this project. Colleagues in the workshops and coerced readers were invaluable in helping me to cohere the ideas that evolved into this book, including Anne Bartlett, Beth Buggenhagen, Kathleen Fernicola, Liz Garland, Sean Gilsdorf, R. Scott Hansen, Jenny Huberman, Matt Hull, Chris Nelson, Marina Peterson, Clare Sammells, Tara Schwegler, Amanda Seaman, Evalyn Tennant and Emily Vogt. I was also lucky to have a cohort of Nepal colleagues who were a source of comfort and challenge in two continents: Mary Cameron, Tatsuro Fujikura, Greg Grieve, Susan Hangen, Genevieve Lakier, Lauren Leve, Geeta Manandhar, Peter Moran, Katherine Rakin and Abe Zablocki. Jim Fisher, David Gellner, Mark Liechty and Kamala Visweswaran offered support in ways which will leave me always in debt. As a counterbalance for all the pain endured while in graduate school, the prodding of brilliant faculty is something

I long to recapture, and I aspire to live up to my mentors, including Dipesh Chakrabarty, Barney Cohn, John Kelly, Rashid Khalidi, Saskia Sassen, David Scott and M. Rolph Trouillot.

Fieldwork incurs a special form of indebtedness, one that is more difficult to publically acknowledge. Workers at USAID and other aid organizations, members of the Rotary Club, various women's organizations and interest groups welcomed me and answered my questions with generosity and honesty. Many of those who were both friends and "informants" appear in pseudonym in this text. I hope "David," "John," "Dianne" and others will see this book as one that honors their lives and struggles. Research also brings financial debts, and I am grateful to the Social Science Research Council for funding much of the initial research of this project, and subsequently to the Committee on Southern Asian Studies at the University of Chicago and the Northeastern University Department of Sociology, as well as the South Asia Institute, the Mossiker Fund, the Co-op and the Vice President for Research at the University of Texas. Many valuable comments and ideas came from four anonymous reviewers and my supportive editors at Stanford, Michelle Lipinski and Stacy Wagner.

The institutions that have served as my home since Chicago have also provided important interlocutors, especially John Cort, Jill Gillespie, Chris Gilmartin, Whitney Kelting, Veve Lele, Sita Ranchod-Nilsson and Bahram Tavakolian. Andrea Hill and Leandra Smolin offered research assistance at key moments. At the University of Texas, the support of Kamran Ali, Craig Campbell, Kaushik Ghosh, Madeline Hsu, Sofian Merabet, Martha Selby, Snehal Shingavi, Nancy Stalker and Katie Stewart have been invaluable.

My mental health, such as it is, has been sustained in this process by Bob, Shirley and Jen Oppenheim, Lilith and Sally Hindman. If there are merits to this book, they are most likely due to the generosity of people I met in Nepal and Rob Oppenheim, whose partnership, challenge, support and love have made this adventure possible and at times even enjoyable. I cannot thank those who have supported me enough, while I accept that all shortcomings of this text undoubtedly trace back to the author.

Mediating the Global

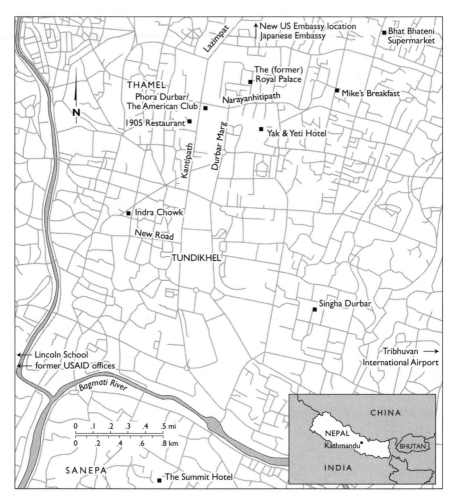

Map of Kathmandu

Introduction

Expatria in Nepal

SITTING AROUND THE HOTEL GARDEN, Iris and I were among the few remaining at the table by mid-afternoon from the group of expatriate women who met for lunch at least one Thursday a month. Much of the day's conversation had centered on recent fluctuations in the value of the Nepali rupee against Western currencies and how this might affect the costs of goods and services. Concerns about this economic event had touched off a wider conversation about other financial worries shared by foreigners working abroad, including changes in home leave policies of employers and the distinct likelihood that several families soon to depart Kathmandu would not be replaced by new expatriate arrivals. After lunch, women began to drift away to run errands, pick up children or fill volunteer shifts until only the two of us remained. Iris had a rare free afternoon and seemed eager to talk about anything, from her daughter's academic problems to her anxiety about her husband's contract not being renewed. After an hour of conversation, she worried that she was keeping me from important tasks, preventing me from doing my research. When I said that talking to people was a big part of what anthropologists did, she tried to clarify, asking why I was wasting time talking to her "when there is so much culture all around us."

She gave herself little credit for a fascinating life. Iris had lived in nearly a dozen different countries. She had grown up betwixt and between, her German father having married an Irish woman, and the family shuttled between the two countries when she was a kid. She had married an Irish mechanic when she was young, just out of high school. Her life took an unexpected twist when he was offered a job in Indonesia for a substantial amount more than his starting salary, just a few years into the couple's marriage. Although in her own

Garden of the Summit Hotel after the Wednesday Farmers Market. Author photo, February 2000.

words her life had been "never dull," she could not see it being of interest to a scholar. During our conversation, she told stories of her family's adventures on three continents, but she would claim they were only the tales of a housewife and common to so many of the wives who had been at the lunch. Why would an anthropologist be interested in her, she wondered, when Nepal presented more culture of interest to anthropologists?

In 1994, Iris's question was one I was working through myself. I was in Kathmandu on a fellowship to develop my Newari language skills and explore a possible dissertation topic examining Newari linguistic and cultural revival groups as well as the emerging Janajati movement, which was seeking rights for minority groups often underrepresented in the government and other spaces of power. During that visit, I was learning about the culture and language of Kathmandu's long-standing population of artistic and business elites, the Newars, as well as attending Newari rituals and talking to community leaders. My days were spent following the young women who had adopted me as a part of their group to Newari religious festivals, as well as more mundane events like movie viewing parties. Other times, I was trying to practice my Nepali and Newari (but often quickly being converted to English) in meetings with male community leaders about their concerns over dying Newari practices. Many of the community leaders were ambivalent about allying with Janajati activists, whose fight for linguistic and cultural acknowledgement by the government was centered on claims to exclusion from zones of power, claims that could not be shared by Newars. Janajati and Newari culture movements resonated with the issues of anthropology in the 1990s concerning nationalism and invention of tradition, as well as the rise in ethnic politics in Nepal during that period. Neither my advisors in the United States nor the Nepalis I spoke with found anything odd in an anthropologist studying these topics; it was Iris who was an unexpected anthropological subject. It was a coincidence that my conversation with Iris occurred at about the same time as a discussion that would dramatically shift my research, putting Iris at the center of the story.

Just a few days previously, I had attended a Newari festival celebrating the first rice eaten by a child (see Levy 1992: 661). This *macha janku* was somewhat unusual, as the honoree was the child of a Westerner doing research in Kathmandu. The official ceremony over, the guests sat down to what was for us the highlight of the activities, an elaborate Newari *bhoj*, or feast, with dozens of traditional dishes and *aila*, a homemade rice liquor. Conversations mixing Nepali, Newari and English were taking place in the courtyard and servants with new dishes kept arriving for hours until it was nearly dark. At this point, several Western academics adjourned to the parlor of the host's rental house, a former royal palace, and continued our conversation. I spoke with a senior scholar attending the event about some of the unusual dishes, such as fish gelatin with the head and tail extending from the serving tray, which, I noted, was delicious but also would provide me with good stories to take back home. She remarked that it was no more disgusting than the processed meat parts that went into the hot dogs served at the American Club in Kathmandu. This provoked a good laugh about the unusual world of the expatriates who populated this space and discussions of how their behavior could be incomprehensible to the outside observer, either Nepali or Western academic. I cannot replicate the exact exchange which followed, but I do distinctly remember the question being raised as to why no anthropologist had studied this unusual community, about the impracticality or unsuitability of expatriates as an anthropological topic, and the final proclamation of the most senior scholar present. There was nothing inherent in anthropology that said that this could not be a legitimate topic for research, and in fact, someone should do it, she declared. It took me several years to fully take up this challenge, but this book is an attempt to engage that task.

In the nearly twenty years since that initial question, I have searched for something like "expatriate culture in Kathmandu"—culture that might parallel more conventional ethnographic subjects like Newari heritage protectors and Janajati activists. In the process, I have found both a more complex and a more simplistic sense of an "expatriate culture" and, like many other anthropologists of the twenty-first century, come to question the value of the concept of culture. The presumptions of uniformity and stability that were necessary for culture to be captured, as if in an ethnologic zoo, were never particularly illuminating, sometimes strategic and often objectifying (cf. Handler 1988; Anderson 1991; Malkki 1992).[1] Although my research on the "strange foreigners" of Kathmandu's expatriate community initially relied on these past codifying anthropological models of culture, subsequent research with this unusual ethnographic subject highlights the lacuna that such approaches encode as well as the difficulty of escaping the culture concept. To destabilize this framework and keep readers conscious of the constructed nature of all ethnographic subjects, I have resorted to the neologism *Expatria*, a polity that this study grounds in Kathmandu. Yet before trying to triangulate what shapes the network of associations called Expatria, I need to return to Iris's provocation and ask why expatriates are a difficult topic for anthropological study, perhaps particularly in Nepal.

The invisibility of expatriates to ethnographers has not always been the case; in the 1970s two manuscripts on the topic were written by scholars who went on to be key figures in the anthropology of tourism, *A Community in Limbo: An Anthropological Study of an American Community Abroad* (Nash 1970) and *Expatriate Communities* (Cohen 1977).[2] Yet, it is not until the rise of "mobilities" scholarship (e.g., Urry 2007) that interest in expatriates as an ethnographic subject appeared again, albeit often under the rubric of "transnational mobile professionals" (e.g., Beaverstock 2005; Walsh 2006; Fechter 2007; Nowicka 2007). The often ambivalent reaction of anthropologists to expatriates (and vice versa) stems in part from their having very different relationships to "the field" as well as ideas of "home" and "away." The challenges presented by an ethnography of expatriates in Nepal are encapsulated in two encounters I had with people frustrated with expatriates. In two very different venues, nearly the same phrase of exasperation about "those people" erupted—a phrase laden with contempt and a lack of cultural relativism rarely explicit in settings with a mission of cultural acceptance. Seven thousand miles apart, the problem of studying expatriates became apparent as they were deemed horrible in one venue and insane in another. In Boston, the question was "how can you stand those people?"

In Nepal, it was "why are those people so crazy?" Either "those people" were an irrational group—a community not worthy of contextual understanding—or there was something more to this story.

The Difficulty of Studying "Those People"

The first question about "those people" was put to me by an audience member at an academic conference where I was presenting some initial research on the expatriate community in Kathmandu. The inquirer, a fellow ethnographer, could not comprehend how I could "stand" to spend time with a population of foreigners who showed little interest in "local culture" and spent all their time at American clubs. She "knew those people" from international schools and social events she had been to when she was in the field, and although she occasionally had been "forced" to enter the world of expatriates, she described how eager she was to escape to the more real world of fieldwork. Her tone was sympathetic towards me, suggesting that it was a great sacrifice to work with such a population, although she remained contemptuous of my research subjects. Such denigration seemed out of place, given the general inclination of anthropology towards cultural relativism and appreciation of all humankind.[3] Her disdain licensed a communal outpouring of frustration among other audience members, who interjected with their own anecdotes about lazy wives who appeared to spend all their time on tennis lessons, spoiled children with local servants who picked up after them and men who played golf all day. There arose in the room a general exasperation at the lack of knowledge about local customs and language demonstrated by people who had lived for two years in a foreign country. One commenter expressed jealousy, exasperated at how fortunate these expatriates were able to spend years in "his" field site while he was only allowed a few weeks away from his family and university teaching responsibilities every other summer. While he struggled to get a few moments off to visit Nepal to keep up his contacts and research interests, these expatriates were wasting their opportunity. In part, it was his job that compelled him to go to Nepal as well, but what was the exasperating distinction for this anthropologist between his work-related relationship to Nepal and the work done by the expatriate other?

The content of my presentation became superfluous during responses to the panel, overwhelmed by the collective effervescence of a community sharing repressed anger. Later I was able to reflect upon the contempt cast on these mid-level workers in development and business who lived in Nepal—condemned as people of leisure, lacking the appropriate interest in the local—particularly in light of one of the examples I had given in the paper. It was one expatriate's story of trying to get a job in Nepal, a place he had asked to be posted on several occasions. Many years previously, he had done a tour in the Peace Corps in rural Nepal that had allowed him to study Nepali and gain some familiarity with the country. For several rounds of overseas assignments his application to be posted to Nepal had been rejected for fear that he might "go native." As the human resources professional had explained to him, they wanted to be sure that his loyalty was to his home country and to the employer—that he did not simply desire to be in Nepal.

Why Are "Those People" Crazy?

The second question about "those people" was put to me during a visit to a rural area of Nepal where a Kathmandu friend's schoolmates lived. In an attempt to escape the dusty heat of the city, we went for a few days of rural life and to enjoy the jackfruit currently ripe in the area. During one late-night conversation (although it was probably only eight o'clock—with no electric lights it seemed later), we became embroiled in a discussion about *bikas*, or development.[4] My Nepali companions were far more educated on the changing theories of aid work than I, but they hoped I could answer one question that perplexed them, why were the foreign aid workers they met "crazy"? Insanity was the only explanation they could find for the constantly changing organizations and practices that invaded their community every few years. One year the project was rural electrification, the next, irrigation, the following year brought the removal of the old irrigation system under a new agenda of sustainable agriculture. The cast of foreigners rotated in and out even more quickly than the policy changed, and the urban Nepali managers stayed even less time in their village than foreigners. For this relatively wealthy area of Nepal, it was a source of amusement—what are the crazy foreigners going to come up with next? Although part of my goal in this trip was to practice my language skills, what I found was a much larger problem of translation.

Upon returning to Kathmandu, I began to investigate what promulgated the "crazy" behavior of expatriate development workers. What I found was a world driven by shifting intellectual and economic fashion. Governmental and nongovernmental aid agencies would generate new calls for proposals—requesting bids for aspects of a given project—every few months. Aid workers were constantly chasing the shifting priorities of granting agencies. Even permanent employees of aid organizations worried about how they might be affected by each new directive, especially one expatriate worker who described his current job as "spin doctor." This task required that he change the language of the program materials every six months to claim that the work they were doing in Nepal was precisely in line with the agency's new emphasis on "women and children" or "the environment" or "democracy." This had gone from being a small part of his job to taking up most of his time and he lamented that he had gotten into this line of work to help people, rather than to write reports.

This "spin doctor" and other direct employees of aid agencies and governments were the main expatriates I encountered in Nepal in the 1990s, families on three-year tours to various countries in the Global South. By the new millennium, there was a different paradigm—many of the "crazy aid workers" did not identify with the job title of "aid worker"—they did not self-identify as development professionals. They were subcontractors, brought in for a specific job, asked to design a bridge or an irrigation system. Employed by third-party organizations to fulfill the objectives of development projects, these technical specialists were unconcerned with the constant changeover in aid priorities, they were just doing a job—and might be doing the same work in a few months in Des Moines or Accra. This process further separated the work of aid from politics or local context, as they continually focused on building the next bridge or democracy project, which required networking with other subcontractors rather than concern over the local impact of their labors (Ferguson 1994; Hindman 2011). This left me only more confused. Who are (or were) "those people"? And what was happening abroad that drove their "crazy" behavior in Nepal? This book is an attempt to answer these questions by taking seriously the transformative power of global middlemen, those people trapped between central policies and local conditions, all the while trying to conduct a mobile life.

Expatriates and Expatriate Packages

In Kathmandu in the 1990s, who was an expatriate seemed self-evident. It was an explicit term of self-reference—expatriates were who other expatriates identified them to be. Nepal presents some unusual boundary-making challenges for expatriates. Given the large numbers of tourists who visit Kathmandu, the city teems with Western (and more recently East Asian) faces, some seeking the spirituality associated with the location, others the natural wonders and some just to participate in the continuing hippy trail and low cost of living (Moran 2004; Liechty 2005a). Nepalis varied in their capacity to distinguish between tourists and expatriates, as well as their interest in doing so, depending upon the nature of the encounter. For expatriates, the distinction that was most salient in defining who was a part of their self-understood community was the receipt of an "expatriate package." Expatriate package contracts defined for families the reason and conditions of their presence in Nepal. For employees, such contracts described a particular set of payments and services provided as part of their overseas posting, distinguishing package-employed personnel from other foreign workers in Nepal. Yet "packages" also produced the community by creating regimes of consumption that drove the social habitus of those who identified with the category expatriate. From an employer point of view, an expatriate package was a financialized list of compensations, such as hardship allowances and moving expenses, incurred to post a worker to a location abroad. The variety and nature of these compensations were important to expatriates as recompense and distinction-making, but equally important was what having these packages communicated about the relationships between workers, their families, the employers and the home and host country locations. Expatriate packages made expatriates and brought them to Nepal; and although this would change in the new millennium, in the late twentieth century the majority of foreigners were employed under this model.

For many, having an expatriate package meant that one had a career that happened to bring one to Nepal. Kathmandu was, for these people, not an intentional destination but one they came to as a result of the demands of their job. Foreign Service personnel, development workers and those businesspeople who ended up in Nepal all shared an understanding that they had undertaken positions that would require them to move every three to five years where their services were needed. Although they might assert some influence on where and when those moves would be made, they realized that moving was an assumed part of the job. This perspective reconfigured many of their significant relations. It made their home nation not only a place they would live in infrequently but also a reference within the package regarding the right to "home leave" and the currency with which they were paid, thus making it more distant yet at times more important than to a permanent resident[5] foreigner living in Nepal. Home became, in part, a bureaucratic category, one that might require a family to return to Australia, if that is where the company and employee were based, even if the family's relatives and friends were in Britain. Home also served as a performative category for expatriates, for example when families demonstrated where their home was through their choice of dress on "International Day" at the local school for expatriate children.

The displacement entailed in a package expatriate position reconfigures the worker-employer relationship; in displacing the worker, the employer assumes new responsibilities for the employee's life outside the workplace, in ways both supportive and intrusive. Most dramatically, the expatriate package entails a reconfiguration of the family, drawing spouses and children (but not other extended family) into the work of the employee. The employer takes on responsibility for finding housing for the family, supporting the schooling of children and providing services that might otherwise be offered through the state or on the public market. Concretely, the work of one family member—when displaced thousands of miles over multiple years—transforms the lives of all other members of the family. Thus, in pointing to the expatriate package as a central defining feature of expatriates in Nepal, I take the word "package" in two senses, first as a descriptor of worker compensation, but also to exemplify how it "packages" a set of actors, connecting workers to their family and their employer in a novel way.

One of the key outcomes of the "expatriate package" is the production of a group of people with a distinctive style of movement. The routines of packing and moving to a new city every few years are common points of experience for expatriates, and as they move, it is frequently sharing the challenges of this style of movement that brings people together. What becomes clear, although often not until people cease this style of motion, is that institutions, like international women's organizations and national clubs, make this life more comfortable for those who participate in it for multiple circuits than a stable life in a single country—than life at home. The expatriates I spoke with in the 1990s in Nepal described how they followed a network of similar organizations and familiar practices as they moved around the world. I had the opportunity to observe these parallel institutions myself. Taking advantage of graduate school colleagues doing research around the world, I visited several countries in Asia and Europe and had no difficulty discovering SIWA (Seoul International Women's Organization) based on my experience with UNWO (United Nations Women's Organization of Nepal). As expatriates I had spoken to in Kathmandu described, it was easy to walk into a group in Seoul or Berlin and find a welcoming atmosphere to newcomers as well as personal connections to people I knew in Nepal; these were people who had been posted to the same place or participated in the same club when they were in Dhaka, or Delhi. Both in Nepal and in its wider global formation, Expatria shared many of the characteristics of a small town—everyone knew everyone else, even at a distance of thousands of miles.

Expatria, although a product of the package expatriate labor system, depends less on the actual nature of the work that expatriates do and more on these institutional and bureaucratic frameworks, and thus there is limited discussion of the everyday work of expatriates in this book for two reasons. First, there is a problem of anonymity. Given that many of the people I spoke with were connected to either governments or nongovernmental organizations, information on their work is readily available online. Thus, were I to describe the work of a Canadian health care worker involved in a maternal health improvement program in the late 1990s, it would be very simple to attach a name to that story with a little online research. The other challenge is that the work that expatriates in Nepal do is quite standard across what are traditional divides, such as government, development and private sector business. Regardless of the industry, many expatriate workers find themselves spending much of their time on computers, writing reports or doing research, not unlike what similar workers might do at a home office. There was also a significant amount of time devoted to meetings with local officials, experts and expatriates in other agencies. The field site visits that one might imagine being the main labor of expatriate workers—visiting or exploring project sites outside of Kathmandu—were occasional breaks from the far more common routine of paperwork and consultation between agencies. Particularly as political tension and violence erupted in the rural areas of Nepal in the late 1990s, trips outside the Kathmandu Valley became increasingly rare for foreigners. When I visited the offices of workers and followed them throughout the day, more than half of their time was devoted to writing reports, sometimes short casual emails to a home office about recent activities but more often long and formal missives required by their employers, which were structured to allow comparisons across sites and to provide quantifiable data about projects. This format of daily labor held true to a large extent across various industries. The workers and families I describe in the book came to Nepal with the assistance of many different industries: career diplomats for European, American and Asian countries, professional aid workers for both private and government agencies, and businesspeople involved in import-export concerns, alternative energy products, and banking and finance. Thus, on the same day, two expatriates might be writing reports on the potential of solar energy in Nepal, one employed by an aid agency, the other for a solar panel sales company, and later in the day these same individuals might meet to collaborate and discuss the aid agency's interest in buying solar arrays from the company. The drama of movies like *The Constant Gardener* about aid and development work have little resonance with the piles of paperwork that command much of the time of the mid-level expatriate in Nepal.

The small town feeling of shared work and social life depends on a common experience of employment and mobility as well as a cohort of those sharing the same pattern of movement. By the time I was back in Kathmandu conducting research in the 2000s, the clear boundaries of the expatriate community were fading. Thus, one of the issues this book explores is the nature of the expatriate community, or Expatria, in its instantiation in Kathmandu, but also its potential demise, or at the least transformation, in the present day. The initial chapters of the book present "package expatriates" in their most typical form, the middle chapters show a time of transition, as expatriates, institutions and employers are changing their approaches to overseas labor, albeit often in conflicting rather than coordinated ways, while the concluding chapter points to a new era of expatriacy, one not predicted by experts but a result of local contingencies and global conjunctures. As a community created and dependent upon a particular structure of global labor and employment policies, changes that produce deskilling and outsourcing among expatriate workers transform the experience of those who work abroad as well as their families, eroding long-standing support networks as well as shared practices. While the expatriate community in Kathmandu in the 1980s and 1990s largely consisted of Western families staying in-country for several years, this population is declining. Instead one sees more single Westerners working in Nepal for only a few months, some as volunteers occupying formerly professionalized jobs and others as highly paid consultants. In addition, greater numbers of aid workers and business people are arriving from Japan, South Korea and China, some of whom adopt the expatriate package model, while others are employed under a variety of new models of elite overseas work.

The package and packaging of expatriates, both in its older forms in Nepal and the more recent processes, places work at the center of the life. Whereas the rigid divide between work time and leisure time is by no means transhistorical, the disciplining of work time, even in the age of flexibility, is still very strongly instantiated in much of the world (Thompson 1967; Lefebvre 1991: 29–42). Leisure and work are, as Lefebvre and others argue (29), mutually constitutive, yet expatriacy introduces space into the equation in a way that entangles work in private realms in an unusual way. The radical physical displacement necessary for expatriate employment extends far beyond the time and task of the employee to the entire life-world of the family. The result is the incorporation, to use Callan and Ardener's phrase (1984), of entire families in the work of one member. This experience—of incorporation and displacement as a result of work—is shared by all expatriates. It is not merely the long hours demanded of expatriate employees that erode the private sphere, but the necessity of doing that work thousands of miles from home and displacing one's family as a result.

While Expatria is a global phenomenon, it is often less cosmopolitan than one might imagine. Despite the many moves made by most package expatriates, the infrastructure of Expatria itself provides familiarity and insulation from many encounters with the Other. The ethics of development often espouse a universalism that projects the obligation for care and understanding beyond the bounds of the nation-state, yet the practices of expatriates are often those I call "enclavic cosmopolitanism." As with gated community dwellers or business travelers, movement and superficial forms of diversity need not extend to complex or sophisticated interest in Others (Iyer 1998; Low 2003). Expatria exists at the intersection of what has been described as strong and weak (Friedman 2005; Foster 2008) or rosy and dark (Appadurai 2006) forms of globalization. Scholars of globalization, either in celebrating it or in accusing it of destroying local cultures, often slip into a conceptually and spatially flattening rhetoric.

My argument here is that expatriates are often able to live what one might call "provincial" lives, even while they move through many spaces. Thus, what one observes in the mobilities of expatriates, particularly those hired under the package system, is a despatialized community, albeit one that shares similar places where "transnationally organized circuits of capital, labor, and communications intersect with one another and with local ways of life" (Rouse 1991: 16). Similarly to James Clifford's concept of "discrepant cosmopolitanisms" (Clifford 1997: 36), which opens up the disjunctures and frictions that exist in the global flow, enclavic cosmopolitanism questions if mere mobility brings about understanding. Even this caution is not enough, as cosmopolitanism threatens, as Timothy Brennan argues, to occlude history and economic inequality in order to seek hope in a world always in tension (Brennan 1997). To call expatriates cosmopolitans would neglect their particular embeddedness in enclavic places as well as within institutions like the United Nations, which could easily gloss over the inequalities of globality in favor of its liberatory potential (cf. Kelly and Kaplan 2001).

Expatria is thus a community defined by a unique labor structure above all other features. While the development workers, diplomats and business-people who make up the majority of the expatriate community in Nepal may have very different job titles, those who share the experience of being under an expatriate package have a great deal in common. Conversations about hardship allowances, the relative quality of local schools and the problems of keeping in contact with the home office during power outages are shared by those who come to Nepal for work with an embassy, an aid agency or a multinational corporation. Exploring what makes expatriates in Kathmandu define their own boundaries nearly always led to the structure of employment rather than to the employer. An individual aid agency, particularly in recent years, might employ two or three Western expatriates as well as a dozen or more Western interns, consultants and volunteers, who are often not a part of the social milieu of their package-employed colleagues. The central role of institutions like women's clubs, church organizations and school groups creates a divide between those who are in Nepal for an extended period of time with a family and those only passing through for several months, who sometimes find more in common with the tourist population.

Spaces of Expatria

Doing ethnographic research with people who move every three years presents challenges, but it is the solutions that expatriates themselves use to overcome the a mobile life that provided me with my pathway into the community. Although I was able to undertake brief trips to Nepal in 1994, 2007, 2010 and 2012, the bulk of the research for this book was conducted in two longer trips to Nepal, in 1997 to 1998 and 1999 to 2000. Each time I visited, I was able to find some families who had been in residence since my last visit, but often my first stop was the same as for many expatriates, a visit to one of the frequent "Newcomers Coffees" that are sponsored by local women's clubs. At these events, I was able to see who was still in town, learn about events and institutions, and meet new people. The inherent challenges of studying moving populations were undercut by the common experience of being a new arrival.

At these meetings, the lack of a spouse whom I was trailing or a history of expatriate experience was rarely a topic of conversation. In part, my appearance as a young white Western female fit me into a known position, even if my career did not, and my relative youth made many of the women quickly assign me honorary daughter status, with concern about my well-being and that I was alone. With time, the challenge became to remind people of my research agenda and my work as an ethnographer, which I often reiterated explicitly in moments of more intimate conversation and tried to emphasize by publically taking notes. Western researchers were not unknown presences at expatriate clubs, and despite the protestations of my anthropologist audience member, Kathmandu's foreigners clubs often saw academics, Fulbrighters and Peace Corps volunteers as visitors. Time was one of the most useful attributes that contributed to my involvement in expatriate life; the ability to say yes to the many activities that followed from formal events both allowed me access to other parts of daily life, and marked me as someone without daytime office-work responsibilities. Beginning with events that were designed for new arrivals, I was able to build connections with other organizations, participate in the lives of expatriate families outside of formal social events and visit workplaces of the employed members of families. Also, through contacts at an organization that trains Nepalis to work in the homes of expatriates, I was able to speak to housemaids and drivers about their experiences working for Western foreigners, although these conversations, even when conducted in Nepali, were undoubtedly influenced by my status as a foreigner and thus potential employer.

My "ethnographic sites" in Kathmandu were eclectic and I went to meetings spanning every possible interest, participating in an amateur theater production, learning to quilt and attending sophisticated costume balls. I also visited two-room offices as well as elaborate embassies to see expatriate workspaces and enjoyed lunches and dinners at people's homes or local restaurants. I became a fan at the local international school basketball games and learned to read bulletin boards to find out about and attend Norwegian Day or meetings of the Hash House Harriers. The size of the expatriate community in Kathmandu was such that there was one overarching social circle, and once people became aware of my interests, they were eager to suggest other people I might want to meet. Many important conversations occurred in the back of the white Jeeps that are the predominant mode of transportation for expatriates. A trip across town from a club meeting to the grocery store might take as long as an hour if traffic were particularly bad or if a political protest blocked the path through town. My experience of workplace life for expatriates often stemmed from connections with women who would introduce me to their employed husbands and open up opportunities to observe life in aid and diplomatic offices. Businessmen working in Nepal often had more ambiguous workplaces, some attempting to establish new enterprises, working largely from home or a rented office space, while others had established relationships with local companies or agencies and worked from within their offices. My own foreignness was a distinct privilege as well as a limiting factor in these settings: it allowed me access to restricted spaces and permitted my easy acceptance as a potential new employee or newly arrived spouse, while making conversation with Nepalis a hierarchical challenge predetermined by my race. Often I had the most success in talking to Nepalis about their experiences with expatriates in settings where I was already known from my previous research on Newars. Thus, the limits of this research go beyond the difficulty of working with mobile populations to my own presumed position in the structure.

What I learned in Kathmandu in the 1990s showed me that this story extended beyond the confines of Nepal and even the various cities in which expatriates resided, to the structures and institutions that produced expatriate lives in a particular form. Between trips, I was able to fill in this aspect of the expatriate puzzle through investigating the employment practices and training programs that I had heard discussed in Nepal. Although much of my research on how expatriates are managed as employees and the perception of families' impact on overseas laborers was conducted via published sources, I also spoke to cross-cultural trainers and several expatriate services professionals about their jobs. This U.S.-based "fieldwork" was necessary to gain a perspective on how the structures of expatriate employment were built and understood away from their sites of implementation. Through tracking how workers in Nepal experience their employment, exploring fields of scholarship devoted to culture contact and transnational elite labor management, and talking to those who were responsible for translating scholarship into policy, I came to better understand lives of expatriates and what made them appear crazy from several different angles.

Mediation and Globalization's Middlemen

What emerged from this combination of on-the-ground ethnographic research in Kathmandu and contextualizing investigations of ideas of transnational employment policy is a book that places labor at the center of the story, not only the work of expatriates but the work done to make them expatriates. The commonalities of expatriate life draw from the way in which their labor is structured by their employers, and the extension of these workplace logics into the everyday lives of foreigners resident in Kathmandu. Thus, the unifying aspects of Expatria in Kathmandu stemmed from the mediating character of the labor and the expatriate packages that governed not only workers' presence in Nepal but also to a large extent the behavior of their families. Workers posted to Kathmandu are often at the midpoint of their careers, and their jobs are to connect metropolitan goals to local conditions. What appeared to be changing between 1990 and 2000 was that expatriates in Kathmandu were starting to experience negative effects of business efficiency, rhetorics of global flatness and neoliberalism, even as they were engaged in promoting similar ideas in Nepal. Thus, although economically far better off than their Nepali counterparts, expatriates in Kathmandu are globalization's middlemen—in the sense of being neoliberalism's advocates and its objects as well as being mediating forces connecting Nepal and elsewhere. In their lives, one can see advocates of new forms of financialization being negatively impacted by the policies they promote.

Philosophically, Expatria indexes mediation as a role beyond the extremities workers and families might be seen to be mediating among. In the claim to the special role for global middlemen, one is continually thrown back into the idea of a global-local duality, threatening to make real the constructs that it is the job of expatriates to negotiate or negate. The work of expatriate middlemen may be assumed to be transmitting a message between two parties, but more often they are mediating among a diverse set of actors not simply defined by global versus local.[6] Expatriates participate in a complex and transformative process of translation, one of mediation, wherein they are "endowed with the capacity to translate what they transport, to redefine it, redeploy it, and also to betray it" (Latour 1993: 81). For Latour, the key distinction is to be made between intermediaries and mediators, with the former presumed to be neutral actors who emit consistent and predictable results while the latter are more agentive and transformative.[7] The process of implementing a development project or negotiating a trade agreement is rarely predictable, and yet the agency and intervention of the expatriate middlemen is rarely given attention. Expatria is an attempt to (temporarily) capture and ethnographize this type of labor and to focus on "amongness," rather than here and there, as itself a possible field of study (Oppenheim 2007). Thus, "the goal is not to *replace* the cultural figure 'native' with the intercultural figure 'traveler.' Rather, the task is to focus on concrete mediations of the two, in specific cases of historical tension in relationship" (Clifford 1997: 24).

More specifically, Expatria describes a world of moving-without-moving, where geographical displacement is trumped by social coherency. I intend Expatria to be a destabilizing term—one that acts as a continual reminder of the problematic rooting of people in place (Malkki 1992: 26; Appadurai 1988: 37) and the practices that are made invisible by the expectation of stability. It also is intended to mark the possibility of spatially discontinuous community, not unlike what Roger Rouse calls a "transnational migrant circuit" (Rouse 1991: 14). Expatriates live in many places, deeply linked in ways that allow everyday life to be conducted in multiple spaces simultaneously, if not evenly.[8]

It is a place with both its own characteristics and a complex set of internal and external social rules, rules that are changing as the employment policies that create them are changing. I aim for this book to be not merely an ethnography of expatriates in Kathmandu; such a project would threaten to succumb to "the anthropological gambit" (di Leonardo 1998: 57), a particular danger, as the anthropological fieldworker often lives side-by-side (albeit hostilely) with the expatriate scene, thus presuming to know the world of "those people." Instead of an exclusive focus on expatriate Nepal, I look also at the intersecting structures that govern practices in Expatria and demand historical context and particularity, rather than mere exoticism. I use Expatria as an intentionally troubling concept to loosely frame the field and produce more than a description of a strange people and their customs, focusing attention on the many rules and structures that dictate the changing logics of expatriate lives. Yet, I strive to avoid describing Expatria as a culture because of the role that "cross-cultural communication" will come to play in subsequent sections of this book. In addition, over the course of the book, it will become clear that Expatria is changing, or even collapsing: its fragility becomes apparent as the distance between elite international laborers as people and as quantifiable units grows. In order to delineate between the shared ideas of expatriates and their obligations to "represent" national cultures in their role as mediators, it is necessary to disentangle the question of a possible expatriate culture from strategic deployments of culture as part of the job of those charged with moving between cultures. The word *culture* will be most often deployed as an emic term of art, rather than one of anthropological description of a people, with the implied scare quotes that entails.

The Structure of the Book

In endeavoring to write a book about abstract ideas such as mediation and "amongness" within globalization using the concrete example of expatriates in Nepal, I attempt to tack between different positions, as global mediators do. Often, what I am describing are misrecognitions that result from the abstraction of labor and care. Early in my research, an expatriate aid worker said, in describing his frustration with the bureaucracy of his organization, "rules make you stupid," and this has been an important motto for my research since then. What follows is a story of rules, sometimes governing expatriate employment, sometimes governing the work that they do, which, when translated across thousands of miles and dozens of contexts, become stupid—even if in the abstract they make sense. The initial chapters of *Mediating the Global* explore the structures and institutions that influence the deployment of mid-level global workers overseas and the implications of these policies for expatriate life in Kathmandu. These employment policies for package expatriates exemplify scientific management and "best practices" approaches that are widely accepted among business professionals, but when investigated through the lens of actual mobile professionals and their families living in Nepal, the unconsidered assumptions of these abstracted audit cultures are revealed (Strathern 2000a). For expatriates, procedures about travel, compensation and employment condition the social reproduction of global elite labor—and cause the changes that are occurring in the last few years. It is these regulations that ultimately produce expatriates themselves and determine how they live in Nepal. Taking a perspective from Kathmandu, central chapters of the book examine how local—but often transnationally connected—institutions and practices shape expatriate lives but are also changing with new employment practices. The last dozen years have seen dramatic changes in these structures, as well as shifts in work and gender, that are echoed in expatriate life; thus this is also a book about the fragility and transformation of Expatria in the twenty-first century.

In "Conjunctures of Mediations," I provide historical context for the present-day form of overseas employment, the internationalization of Nepal and foreign business in the region. The necessary background for *Mediating* is a genealogy of the intimacy of foreign employment in relationship to various spatialized political and social economies. The contemporary intersection of Expatria and Kathmandu must take into consideration both the changing structures governing what is entailed in working in a foreign land and Nepal's own historical reception of international funds and people. The changing practices of the British Empire in India offer a social history of the intersecting dimensions of race-based domination and prescribed relations for both rulers and ruled, especially in the iconic figure of the *memsahib* and the strategies of family deployment, which conveyed to both a metropolitan and local audience the level of imperial commitment (Hutchins 1967; McClintock 1995; Stoler 2002; Burton 2003). Thus, although Nepal was never colonized by a European power, the influence of British colonialism across the border is a reference point for Nepalis and expatriates alike. Nepal's own history of interaction with other countries also tells a story of mutual transformation and the intertwinings of political ideology and bureaucratic implementation. The 1950–51 revolution in Nepal opened the country to Western influence and produced it as a site for Cold War friction that was played out on the ground through the presence of foreign experts and equipment. The incorporation of Nepali domestic politics in global narratives is also seen in the present, as the Maoist conflict and subsequent Maoist leadership of the government has made Nepal a location for the deployment of guns and money in the War on Terror, as well as causing governments in the West and Asia to find ways to engage a democratically-elected Maoist government. Between these two sea-change events, Nepal has seen large flows of foreigners and their capital, yet the numbers of people and money have vacillated depending not only upon geopolitics but also upon trends like the popularity of Tibetan Buddhism in the West and mountaineering as a hobby in East Asia. While the complexity of Nepali foreign relations is beyond the scope of this book (see Mihaly 1965; Pokharel, Shakya, and Dahal 2009; Einsiedel, Malone, and Pradhan 2012), I focus on the 1950–1951 moment as one that set the tone for contemporary diplomacy and development. Yet it is necessary to go beyond politics, to reflect upon postcolonial forms of international employment and compensation as they structure the experience of contemporary expatriates in Nepal and elsewhere. An exploration of Shell Oil, a major expatriate employer of the past and present, takes the story from colonialism to multinational companies and up to the present, examining how employers have understood their responsibilities to transnational employees. This chapter illuminates the history of international diplomacy and development in Nepal as well as relevant moments of "culture contact," and how they are structured by bureaucracy, geopolitical coincidence, and epistemologies of difference—all contexts that contribute to the changing experiences of expatriates in Kathmandu.

The chapters in the body of the book are framed by the dynamic relations between mechanisms and actions, or systems and practice. In each chapter, I combine describing general policies of expatriate deployment with explorations of everyday life for expatriates in Nepal. In "Families That Fail," the focus is on the mechanisms that employers use to minimize the cost of employing expatriates while maximizing the potential that they will succeed in their appointed task. The technologies and methodologies of the field of international human resources management are marshaled to generate a cost-benefit analysis of various methods for sending workers abroad. Through metrics borrowed from psychology and economics, companies and governments research how to get the most value out of the high costs of deploying expatriate workers. The results suggest that expatriates who "fail" do so because of their families. There are many reasons why families generate worker "failure"—a condition defined by the inability to meet centrally determined productivity goals or leaving the country before the duration of expected overseas deployment. Families, rather than any intrinsic element of working overseas, thus become the targets of intervention. Spouses are often called into service to engage in social activities that research suggests will make their employed partners happier, but these remedies are unable to account for individual families or local conditions in Kathmandu. The prescription that families bond through taking drives in the countryside neglects to consider Nepali petrol shortages, the poor condition of most roads, employer bans on workers driving themselves and road closures due to political strikes. Although expatriate families find many creative ways to support each other and to socialize with other expatriates, the proclamation that "families make expatriate workers fail" circulates through the community, creating new anxieties and demands, as spouses worry that a child's misbehavior at school might count against her and label the family as a potential failure.

Blaming families for worker failure and the associated creation of new labors for family members to avoid failure is replicated in the policies that govern compensation and employment in the form of expatriate packages. In "Market Basket Economics," I examine a key practice that is designed to erase, or at least occlude, the difficulties of living abroad. Cost-of-living allowances are given to many expatriates as compensation for living abroad, in particular to allow them to purchase the same commodities that they would purchase at home. Through salary supplements, moving allowances and school fee payments, the hope is that workers will be able to live "as if" they were in their home country, even while moving every three to five years. Behind these financially lucrative practices is a great deal of labor required to quantify the costs of displacement across the globe, work that is often displaced onto families. The practical implications of these financial incentives produce new problems, as the ability to consume as if at home is read by many as a requirement. Thus, expatriate spouses scavenge the shops of Kathmandu seeking to fulfill what they are informed are the "best practices" of overseas living, such as generating a set of "normal" commodities, a process which is often very time-consuming and entails the appointing of an idealized "home" that could exist nowhere and leaves little room for Nepal.

The great expense that is entailed in cost-of-living allowance payments and expatriate failure has produced a movement within international employment circles to eliminate expatriate employment, not in practice but in rhetoric. Taking their cues from certain discussions of globalization that claim global spread of people and goods will erase difference (Friedman 2005), some researchers propose moving to an "international citizen" model of employment, wherein workers would not be associated with any home country but would reside "globally" and thus not require any support designed to mitigate separation. In "The Protean Expatriate," I explore how employers deploy their own understanding of culture and difference in configuring overseas employment and expatriate lives. Research on the desire of employees for flexibility combined with a perception of increasing global homogeneity gives justification for moving away from the "expatriate package" to short-term employment and forms of both hyperskilling and deskilling. While rhetorically, these new policies of employment are anticipated to provide expanded opportunities for minorities and women in the workplace, for expatriate workers in Nepal, they hinder the career opportunities for exactly these populations. The shift from the family-wage policies of older forms of expatriate employment to an expectation of short-term, independent contractors produces an influx of single white men into the expatriate community in Kathmandu. Although the dissemination of a "protean" career philosophy (Hall 1976) rather than the older company-man model is promoted as a tool to improve worker success and happiness, this chapter suggests that in Nepal it radically transformed the very nature of Expatria as it moved into the new millennium, changing who occupies expatriate offices and homes.

Culture is a central component of how expatriates frame their social engagements, and the difference in employer and expatriate considerations of culture is the subject of "Saving Business from Culture." Second only to families, "culture shock," or other forms of cross-cultural miscommunication, is seen as central to the difficulties encountered by expatriate workers, especially in places deemed "exotic" such as Nepal. Preparing workers and families for cultural difference presents unique challenges to the logics of outsourcing, as presumably each encounter is unique and requires training particular to their home and host locations. This chapter explores the ways in which cross-cultural communications research tries to overcome these disjunctures. Through the development of generalizable approaches to "culture shock" and the transformation of national difference into a kind of personality test for cultures, groups can be prepared for an encounter with "the Other" regardless of context. I compare this approach with the interest in culture of the expatriate community in Kathmandu. Culture is of great interest to many foreigners living in Kathmandu, but it is made to take a very uniform shape. At parties and community events, nationals are encouraged to "represent" the culture of their home country, leading to an array of booths, one per country, highlighting the clothing, food and holidays of different places. These two practices, culture shows and "culture-general training," highlight a ghettoization of culture wherein diversity is a cause for celebration, but only when it takes particular forms. In issues of business or economics, culture is presumed to be inapplicable, and expatriates and locals alike are presumed to share certain assumptions about "best practices."

In "Living in Expatria," I turn away from the externally produced understandings of community to look more directly at the institutions that frame expatriate social life in Nepal and the continuities they create with other posting locations. The ability to play tennis, join a Christian church choir or act as a hospital volunteer in countries around the world often makes the transient way of life of the expatriate seem more like stability than life at "home." Through international schools, activity-centered groups, national clubs and civic associations, expatriates generate continuity in their lives. Within these common institutions, families can maintain not only a similar schedule of activities across space but even a common set of acquaintances. These despatialized affiliative organizations are also the means of perpetuating life in a location, passing on traditions and practices across the various departures and arrivals. Expatriates have depended upon these organizations to provide familiarity in spite of the constant movement, yet these groups rely upon and anticipate a particular demographic, a population of men busy during the week, wives with flexible daytime schedules and children in local international schools. For example, the international women's organization, the mainstay of expatriate life in Nepal for many years, is changing. With nuclear families and male wage-employees no longer dominating the expatriate population in twenty-first-century Nepal, this institution finds fewer Western "trailing spouses" at its meetings. Single men, male trailing spouses and short-term visitors all benefit from some of the organizational work of groups like the United Nations Women's Organization of Nepal, but they have limited interest in attending coffee hours or serving on the board. Thus, I speculate on how management practices of efficiency and new geopolitical mappings of international engagement are transforming Expatria into a new social entity and what influence this might have on the labor of a new generation of overseas elite workers.

Within this story of Expatria and its configuration through certain structures and institutions, there are frameworks and practices with wider relevance for social science, business and understandings of difference in a global world. I explore these links in the Conclusion, subtitled "Kathmandu's Twenty-First-Century Expatria." As a result of their mediating tasks, as well as the liminality of Nepal in many global circuits, the transformation of expatriate labor and expatriate laborers illustrates a perspective on global labor, gender and bureaucratization that escapes other frameworks. Globalization, interpreted in a myriad of ways, has been proclaimed to be producing new forms of labor, especially for women. "The End of Men" issue of *The Atlantic Monthly* suggested that the rise in service jobs, greater demands for emotional intelligence and the rising numbers of women with advanced degrees in the United States was causing the economic downturn in the United States to hit men particularly hard (Rosin 2010). While this piece focused on women's success in well-compensated positions in the West, another strain of literature has seen a rise in the demand for women in low-paid positions in global manufacturing, reinforcing the "nimble fingers" paradigm that accompanied the outsourcing of factory labor to maquiladoras and factories in East and Southeast Asia (Freeman 2000; Ehrenreich and Hochschild 2002; Salzinger 2003; Brennan 2004). While few writing about gender and globalization saw a story of unmitigated empowerment for women, most saw a transformation in gendered labor roles, sometimes in ways that brought more opportunities to women, other times in ways that harmed them. In the transformation of expatriate life in Nepal, I have observed a decline in women in positions of power, a decline brought about not by explicitly discriminatory policies but by mundane transformations couched as efficiency mechanisms. A similar phenomenon can be seen in the situation of non-white expatriates and others formerly excluded from lucrative expatriate positions, who are finding their incorporation often comes at the very moment when incentives are declining. Most people in the scholarly community have seen the limits of "the world is flat" (Friedman 2005), but this claim caused many to pursue "globalization" with limited reflection upon what it entails (cf. Ho 2005), leading to repercussions for the experience of expatriates in Nepal.

1 Conjunctures of Mediations

The Historical Logics of Expatriate Nepal

WHETHER IN THE CRITIQUES of development policy or in the denigration of expatriate lives, today's elite international workers are often condemned as practitioners of colonialism in a contemporary form. Trailing spouses are castigated as modern memsahibs and government programs for business and industry promotion are compared to eighteenth-century European trade exploitation. What exactly are the terms upon which this comparative critique is made? Is contemporary international business merely an extension or repetition of European colonialism? Could such a denigration have more substance that a mere ad hominem attack? Furthermore, what do such comparisons obscure? Does this erase the particularities of a place such as Kathmandu in favor of typologizing the Western interloper? Does it erase changes in practices in favor of a colonial-postcolonial dyad?

In this chapter I want to rethink the stakes of such comparisons of contemporary international labor to earlier forms of global business and governance and to explore the history behind the accusations that overseas labor practices are just like some past injustice, in order to investigate if there are more tangible historical and structural connections between expatriates and colonists. In addition, I will bring in particular employers, rather than the generic "colonialism," and particular locations, in this case Nepal, into the story to observe differences as well as similarities between colonialism and contemporary overseas employment. My focus will be on the technologies that underlie the analogized labor forms to shift the question from whether development is neocolonialism to an alternative query about the structural practices shared by these two moments of international work.[1] The question of whether contemporary expatriate spouses are memsahibs allows only a banal yes or no answer and often typologizes both ends of the comparison. In the critique of global business exploitation as colonialism, the question of which colonialism, where and when, is irrelevant, because colonialism in this frame more or less stands for "bad things the West did to the rest of the world," reducing the complexity of both sides of the equation. Exploring the history of the governance of elite international employment permits a more complex narrative of how and why work and families have been shaped by international career structures as well as local context. Simplistic historical analogies threaten only to highlight similarities while obscuring the purpose behind comparison itself (Asad 1993; Scott 2004). In this chapter, comparison will be put in the service of understanding the world of contemporary Western expatriates in Nepal, their mediation by international institutions and the influence of changing political situations in Nepal. What I offer is thus not a linear history of the events leading up to the arrival of expatriates in Nepal, nor a succession of international employment practices, but a series of analytic spaces, each of which suggests something about how the structures that have come to define international elite labor in Nepal have come into being.

There is a second function of this chapter: to introduce the particularities of Nepal and its unique relationship to the rest of the world for the purpose of understanding elite transnational labor. While throughout this book I intend to avoid categorizations such as nation-state or culture, this should not imply that they do not matter. These frameworks are central to the culture-clash approach that predominates in the global business community, often to the exclusion of other important ideas like gender, race or class. As an emic term of global business, culture often becomes a list of rules that essentialize difference in order to simplify the process of translation. Yet this is not to say that national histories and cultural difference are unimportant. Thus I direct attention not necessarily to those events that are significant to national textbooks but to histories of exchange and assumptions that develop and shape the experience of foreigners working in Nepal (cf. Pigg 1992; Onta 1996). In what follows, I look at several key conjunctures: the manipulation of British employment and families during India's colonization, the opening of Nepal to the world in 1950 that shaped the country's engagement with the West and led to its popularity as both a tourist and development site, and the rise of globalisms, initiated by countries and companies that changed what it means to be an overseas worker. These elements set the tone for the production of a new form of global labor and life, Expatria, and its eventual instantiation in Kathmandu.

Is Colonizer to Expatriate as
Empire Is to Transnational Corporation?

In the search for antecedents to contemporary actions of global middlemen and their everyday work and lives in Nepal, colonial India is an obvious site, especially when the subject is the intersection of work and domestic life among international laborers from the Global North to South Asia. Perhaps because of the wealth of information about British domestic life in India during colonialism (Stoler 1989; Procida 2002; Buettner 2004; Blunt 2005) or because of the Raj nostalgia that continues to permeate Western dreams of South Asia (Ward 2001; Bissell 2005; Buettner 2006), the world of expatriate Nepal can evoke images of elephant safaris and elegant tea on the lawn. For a Western audience, visions of white families waited on by South Asian servants echo what all know, or think they know, about colonial India. There is something to be learned from the comparison of expatriate life in Nepal to British colonial life in India, but a different set of insights emerge from the very assumption that this is the appropriate comparison.

Under scrutiny, in the relationship between these two interactions as forms of social life, an unconsidered analogy becomes evident that threatens distortion in the service of finding Expatria's past. With this caution in mind, the information on British colonialism nonetheless provides a rich resource for widening understanding of the intersection of work and domestic life of those living abroad. "Household Guides," which have provided important material to scholars of New Imperial History (Wilson 2004; Levine 2004), show how such domestic texts might be read against the grain to illuminate aspects of power and politics at the highest level. Furthermore, the literatures that exist under the rubrics of postcolonialism and Subaltern Studies provide a theoretical groundwork for understanding current mediations between metropolitan policy and local conditions, but one that demands attention to the historical and contextual discontinuities between the world of eighteenth-and nineteenth-century European colonial traditions and the present.

In the 1980s, Subaltern Studies opened up new methods and, importantly, new materials for understanding the world of those whose lives did not appear in official archives or government records. Meanwhile, scholars of the archives of colonial life were still buried in the papers and ephemera of the Empire, the regimented bureaucratic system of England having translated itself into a recording impulse of the license-permit-quota Raj. By reading between the lines of formal archives and giving attention to materials not generally considered archival (Ghosh 1994; Burton 2003), scholars learned a great deal about domestic life in the colonial outposts, using a vast number of diaries, house-keeping manuals and serialized descriptions of English women's experiences of life abroad. The many published and private advice manuals for women headed to the colonies provided much information about the worldview of colonists as read through domestic concerns, via lists of clothing, health concerns and guidance on the hiring and management of servants abroad (Walsh 2004). The packing manuals and housekeeping guides (Steel and Gardiner 1890; Diver 1909) that served as the manuals on life in the colonies parallel contempo-rary "newcomers' guides" and corporate packing lists.[2] These documents, when combined with research on British colonial policy in India, tell a compelling story of how the work of Empire was carried out by and through the families of those who worked for the East India Company.

Assumptions about a universal and atemporal divide between public and private, as well as the divisions of intellectual labor that often parallel these cat-egories, have kept much of the analysis of such domestic documents separate from examinations of Imperial policy and political practice. Without feeling compelled to survey the history of European involvement in India, I propose that suturing official colonial documents and materials about private lives to-gether will offer a new lens on the Raj, especially illuminating how policies on overseas posting were a part of the official apparatus of political and economic pursuits similar to the way they are for contemporary business in Nepal.[3] The Portuguese officials and British traders who came to the Indian subcontinent in the sixteenth century were single men. The concerns of both the sending governments and local superiors about the domestic lives of their employees centered around Catholic-Protestant tensions (Malabari 1910: 128; Mickelson 1978: xii), and liaisons with local women were often encouraged as a means to avoid crossing this religious barrier or to propitiate local populations of widows created by battles with European powers, thus solving two problems for the foreign powers (Stark 2007: 3–8). As the size of the British population in India increased, the self-contained forts that had served as miniature white bachelor worlds could no longer contain the men sent to outposts of the East India Company. In the mid-seventeenth century, the Company began formal recognition of the large number of British soldiers setting up households with local women and facilitated these relationships with financial sponsorship and official, if unequal, status for their offspring (14–26). The children of the elite Englishmen and local women produced a population of use to the Company, a hybrid progeny that could operate in local contexts and in the world of English bureaucracy. Taking a British bride was unfeasible for most English workers in the eighteenth century, mainly due to the cost of the upkeep of a proper English household that such a liaison was expected to produce (Mickelson 1978: 41). Although it is difficult to ascertain the precise number of Englishwomen in India before 1815 (see Michaelson 1978: x), it was by most accounts quite low (Ghosh 1970: 70).

Several subsequent events changed attitudes about appropriate forms of domestic life and their intersection with political practice in India. British Parliament, through the East India Company Act and later the Charter Acts, made the conjunction between the Crown and the Company stronger and gave official status to the Company monopoly. The Industrial Revolution and the American Revolution brought dramatic change to the English economy and new class divisions. These governance shifts coincided with a greater public interest in overseas activities, and more efficient communication available to those in the UK allowed a greater flow of information about sons and brothers in the subcontinent. The Company used this conjuncture to take on a new role of matchmaker, sending single Englishwomen to India in search of husbands among the Company workers (MacMillan 1988: 16). This small-scale and short-lived practice transformed the social scene of the English in India, as officers hosted parties that were designed to facilitate staff marriage proposals to these imported bachelorettes, a practice which continued even though the "importation" of English women was banned as a part of the Company Charter renewal in 1833. The salaries of most Company officials did not permit the establishment of an appropriately "English" home by any but the most elite, especially given the highly social character of colonial life that developed in this period. The quest for higher status was often a part of the motivation for employment in the colonies, and this, combined with an explicit Company charge to perform "civilized" life for an Indian audience, led to a lifestyle abroad that included elaborate—and atmospherically uncomfortable—attire and formal events. A shift was occurring that moved from the laissez-faire approach to commercial activities that had marked the eighteenth century to a more moralizing rhetoric associated with a rise in central government attention to the colony and a Whiggish approach to the social and political activities of English men and women in India.

Much attention has been focused on English women in India between the 1833 Charter renewal and the 1857 Sepoy Rebellion, especially as English women are often targeted as the instigation of the Rebellion. Their presence, some claim, was seen as a threat to the population of Anglo-Indians who had served as assistants to the colonists and whose very existence was emblematic of the shifting endorsement of sexual relations by the Company. White women were also claimed to be disruptive of a purported "racial harmony" which had developed between English men and Indian subjects/sexual partners (Furber 1948). Yet, what is most remembered is the invocation of the death of white innocents in the Rebellion as a reason for increased violence and militarism by the British Government. Despite the lack of statistics on the number of Englishwomen present in India at a given time, their presence or absence often played a role in arguments about how the Raj should be run. At one moment they would be cited as a way to increase discipline and civility among the male British workers and at another denigrated as immoral creatures representing the worst of English society (Malabari 1910: 128). In the changing attitudes towards gender relations in the colonies and the attendant transformations in understanding racial relations, one can see the Company/Crown manipulation of British family arrangements as a means to other political and economic needs.

It was more than changing migration and employment policies that transformed the project of British Imperialism; it was a change in domestic style as well. The family life of Britons sent to the colonies was a frequent topic of concern for political theorists who worried about the Englishmen's loss of "Englishness" during times when single men were the dominant population. It was this fear and the new endorsement of an ongoing imperial presence in India that produced financial incentives for the establishment of English families abroad (Hutchins 1967). British women were seen as part of a double civilizing mission: on the one hand to the local population they would act as exemplars of civilized life, but on the other, to their own house and British society they would contribute a veneer of normalcy by establishing a more "British" life in India (Strobel 1991; Burton 1994; Jayawardena 1995).[4] Women were explicitly tasked with creating English homes and English recreational activities for the men living in India. There were subsidiary outcomes of this production of "Little Britains," including a new gendered division of space and greater demands for local workers to labor in larger English homesteads. English women's constitutions were seen as incompatible with the crowded world of city life in India, and many British officers moved in the eighteenth century from communal forts in the city to the countryside and "hill stations," thus generating a new suburban lifestyle, perhaps the first instantiation of a familiar form of work-home spatial division that took many years to become common in the Western idea of the suburb (Archer 1997; King 1997; Blunt 2005). This new style of colonial life had men setting out in carriages in the morning while women kept the house running in the cleaner rural environment, creating a suburban style of movement as well as new forms of alienation and affiliation for the British women left behind in the suburbs (Archer 1997: 52–53; Chambers 1997). The enclavic style of compound life produced a call for each house to have individual gardeners, cooks, nannies and a litany of other, largely domestic and feminized labor, work done by both local women and men but which generated new class, caste and gender tensions, of which English employers were often ignorant. The isolation of these new compound-style residences produced a more egalitarian attitude among the British, but also a more hostile attitude towards Indians (Hutchins 1967: 114). This new housing arrangement, encouraged by the British Crown, not only changed the lives of English workers in India but also changed the social hierarchy, the nature of the work day and ultimately the way the labor of colonialism was performed.

Shifts in how British colonial workers were housed in India or whether the families of British men and Indian women were acknowledged and supported by the East India Company are in part stories of changing racial attitudes or medical logics, but they are also moments reflecting changing economic and political realities. Colonial policies about proper lifestyle are read as humorous tales of past prejudices, but they are also policies with an effect exceeding their explicit address. As Company policy changed regarding official permission for British women to travel to India, the Company was making a statement about the nature of the colonial enterprise, its expectations of its male employees and its view of India—at times intentionally, at times not—as captured in the title of a book on the subject, *The Illusion of Permanence* (Hutchins 1967). The moves to hill stations that British officers made are often seen as mere moves to avoid hot summers in the Indian plains, but the effect of moving many of the senior officers away from the center of business and government for a portion of the year did change the way business was done as well as Indian workers' perceptions of their British superiors.

Whether as a result of hindsight or the different attitude taken to the colonial past, the effect of Crown manipulation of mundane aspects of daily British life in India on the official business of colonialism is often easier to see than the effects of similar manipulations by contemporary international employers. One can transfer these lessons from the colonial context to contemporary Expatria, in order to attend to the messages of permanence and dominance encoded within the seemingly benign regulation of domestic life. In retrospect, one can see the role of on-the-ground agents as transformative actors in moments of encounter and the value of placing examinations of economic and political policies in dialogue with understandings of the daily lives of those who implement those policies. With the example of British colonialism in mind, I now turn to the contemporary lives of foreigners in Nepal, and how they came to take on what seems to many an anachronistic appearance reminiscent of white picket fences in suburban America, and how this condition may have been grounded in a 1950s moment when Nepal became a player in modern international politics.

Producing Foreignness: An Encounter History

While there are colonial echoes in the lives of contemporary expatriates in Nepal, those are often visual reminders of Raj nostalgia—elephants and tea-time—in a country that was never formally colonized. To understand what structures the presence of professional and tourist visitors to Kathmandu, one must explore the particularities of Nepal's engagement with the world. Rather like the jump to colonialism, Nepal's history is frequently seen as entwined with its dominant neighbors to the north and south, India and China, or more particularly, Tibet. Although the histories of these large nation-states in the context of transnational and regional politics have been influential on the small country of Nepal, it has its own unique set of foreign engagements that has led to an unusual collection of Western and Asian visitors to Kathmandu. Nepal is often said to have been closed to the world before 1950 when it "catapulted out of its medieval coma into the bewildering stream of twentieth-century existence" (Joshi and Rose 1966: x), but this is both an overstatement and one focused on the presence of Western goods and people (Fisher 1990; Liechty 2005a). Kathmandu itself has been a central node in north-south trade routes for many thousands of years and both the southern and northern boundaries of contemporary Nepal have long been fluid. Geography, including the malarial plains of the south and high mountains of the north, as much as anything else, has dictated who moves where. Even the militarized unification of much of what is now Nepal by Prithvi Narayan Shah in the mid-eighteenth century had limited impact on areas distant from the capital. It was the subsequent rule of the Rana family starting in 1846 that curtailed the power of the Shah dynasty, and which was responsible for limiting the interaction of ordinary people with the world outside the region. During this period, leaders like Jang Bahadur Rana sought to unify the diverse groups of Nepal, often through tools that gave power and legitimacy to the domination of the Rana clan (Höfer 1979; Whelpton 1983). The 1950s moment when Rana rule ended is merely the beginning of the most recent phase of Nepal's international engagement with the world, but it is the one most salient to shaping the contemporary world of elite foreign workers in Kathmandu.

The events of 1950 transformed Nepal from a country with a government actively resisting outside influence into one deeply enmeshed in a number of global circuits (Hindman 2002). The exclusion of transnational commodities from Nepal was an intentional project of Nepali political leaders (Liechty 1997), and the negation of those policies in the early 1950s generated a distinctive intersection of historical events that structured contemporary practices as a result of the conjuncture of policies and processes that would otherwise seem unrelated (Sahlins 1981; Sewell 2005: 221). Here I want to explore some of the events that were set into motion in 1950 that contributed to new structural networks and enabled the contemporary practices of international employment, structures that will be central to understanding how international work is produced in a particular way in Nepal. While each of these events may also be read as part of the story of Nepal's emergence as a modern nation-state (Onta 1996), as a side story in Cold War politics (Khadka 2000; McGranahan 2006), or as a part of U.S. domestic pursuits (Hindman 2002), the events of 1950 also helped shape the current world of Expatria in Kathmandu.

What happened in the early 1950s had its most immediate effect on international presence in Kathmandu through the expansion of diplomatic and development activities beyond the interventions of India and China. The departure of King Tribhuvan through a strategic self-exile to India in 1950 was the first of what have been many subsequent attempts to transform Nepal into a modern democratic nation-state. This dramatic beginning of a new era in Nepali history intersected with leftist and independence movements in India, tense India-Nepal relations and internal tension within the ruling Rana family that offered an opportunity for the king to make demands on the Ranas, asserting his claim as legitimate representative of the people. His return to Nepal and resumption of power after he had obtained concessions from the Ranas was seen as the beginning of a new era for Nepal, rather like the new beginnings anticipated by many decolonized nations in this period. This "New Nations" phenomenon coincided with European economic troubles produced by the end of World War II and new U.S. agendas to provide aid to the non-West as well as Europe (Geertz 1963). Tribhuvan's demands for openness to foreign goods and financial support as well as more democratic governance structures have been read alongside Cold War politics, both pro- and anti-Indian sentiments, anti-colonial hostility to Europe and internal tensions between powerful factions in Nepal; but looking less at these big narratives and more at the bureaucracies

and structures they produced gives insight into the production of contemporary roles of foreigners and expertise in Nepal.[5]

As the first Western country to establish an aid agreement with Nepal and
one of the first to establish diplomatic relations with the country in this period,
the United States was strongly positioned to play a role in a modern Nepal, yet
these formal firsts were undercut by practical delays, political difficulties and
personality conflicts within the U.S. Mission staff (Mihaly 1965). China
and India were significant players in shaping modern Nepal, but they were also
dangerous allies due to their proximity, and were often used as foils against one
another by Nepali leaders or political parties seeking foreign support (Rose
1960). The exchange between the United States and Nepal was deeply shaped
by the domestic concerns of each country, with the U.S. emphasis on technical
assistance and Cold War rhetoric influencing aid and diplomatic relations with
Nepal and producing a distinct character to the newly forming U.S. expatriate
scene in Kathmandu (Hindman 2002). The rhetoric of U.S. involvement often
overreached what those in-country were actually accomplishing. The United
States took nearly eighteen months after establishing the U.S. Technical Co-
operation Mission to Nepal to begin its first project. All the while, Nepal was
undergoing political turmoil, which meant that finding who was responsible
for a given aspect of policy was difficult and establishing diplomatic relations
was challenged by the frequent turnover in government offices in the 1950s
(Mihaly 1965: 30–31). Post 1950s Nepali governments worked with both India
and China while keeping their thinly veiled interventionist agendas in mind.
The British, in addition to coping with their own economic woes at the time,
faced resistance from the new government due to their past support of the Rana
regime. The conjuncture of the "opening" of Nepal in 1951 with the interest of
the United States in Nepal as a Cold War borderland gave the United States a
several-year lead over other Western nations in establishing a presence in Nepal.

Alongside these political challenges were problems less discussed in formal historical and diplomatic texts. Several books were written by Westerners in Nepal in these early years of expatriate presence, including Hugh
Wood's *Nepal Diary* (1987) and Nancy Dammann's *We Tried* (1995), which
bring together the social and structural problems faced by the newly arrived
American families. Alongside these, *Tiger for Breakfast* (Peissel 1996), *Erika
and the King* (Leuchtag 1958) and the thinly fictionalized *The Mountain Is
Young* (Suyin 1999) describe the social lives of newly arriving foreigners and
the emerging milieu that brought together Nepali royalty, American engineers
and hard-drinking Western reporters at the Royal Hotel, founded by the for-

mer Diaghilev dancer Boris Lissanevitch. These early years of Nepal's opening shaped the nature of life for foreigners in Kathmandu in ways that continue to the present. For example, as the Ranas were deposed from power and facing potential loss of income, many needed to sell their large palaces at the same moment the U.S. government was seeking housing and offices; thus the palace built by Bir Shamsher Jang Bahadur Rana became the American Embassy Club (Dammann 1995: 73; Poudel 2003). In Dammann's account of her time with the U.S. Information Service in Nepal, she describes the intersecting political and social tensions in the small American community as well as the practical problems of working in Nepal under the unyielding U.S. government expectations. For example, she describes Washington complaints about poor margins on official forms and the inability to procure typists and typewriters in the midst of the U.S. Mission's abundance of equipment designed for Nepal's betterment, much of which often lay deteriorating on the tarmac. The first leader of the U.S. aid program in Nepal, Paul Rose, found himself in an impossible position produced by the conjuncture of conditions in Kathmandu and the expectations of Washington bureaucracy. The strict and frequent demands for quantifiable accountability regarding development project progress imposed on the U.S. Operation Mission reflected inattentiveness to the more mundane problems faced by this new operation: problems of not being able to acquire gas to power vehicles needed to reach project sites and the arrival of experts and equipment inappropriate to the situation in Nepal (Skerry, Moran, and Calavan 1991: 10). Through these early texts on professional and social lives of expatriates in Nepal, one sees a set of rationalities coming into view which would influence where foreign officials would live, what their housing would be like, the development of social circles, the production of ideas about who should be posted to a site like Kathmandu, how labor would be divided within foreign families and what use would be made of local staffers, both in newly arrived foreigners' homes and workplaces. Both Wood and Dammann, given the opportunity of time and reflection, vent their frustration with Washington and Kathmandu. They describe the many connections between the professional demands of their jobs and the everyday social interactions of an expatriate community that still numbered less than one hundred, one which celebrated the monthly mail pouch deliveries and saw the arrival of any visiting foreigner as reason for a party.

While it is Cold War politics, decolonization and the Chinese Revolution that are often used to frame Nepal's arrival on the global stage, many mundane bureaucratic proclamations were required to respond to these large-scale events. It is these texts that have shaped international business, foreign policy and the intertwining of public and private lives of foreigners living in Nepal. For example, the "Agreement for Technical Co-operation," which established U.S. aid in Nepal, contained the core thematics of President Truman's Point IV statements dictating the philosophy of U.S. aid while deferring specifics about implementation through statements such as "[p]articular technical coopera-tion programs and projects will be carried out pursuant to the provisions of such separate written agreements or understandings as may later be reached by the duly designated representatives . . ." (U.S. Department of State 1951: 490). Yet the document contains remarkable specificity in "Personnel," which states the following: "[E]mployees and members of their families shall receive exemption with respect to the payment of customs and import duties on per-sonal, household and professional effects and supplies including one personal automobile" (492).[6] Personnel must precede projects, and determining not only what type of aid programs the United States would work with Nepal to provide but where its employees would live, what they would be paid and where their children would go to school occupied much time and energy during this early period of Nepal's entrance into a Western diplomatic, development and business scene.

The character that foreign employment was to take in Nepal was shaped in these early days by local problems such as the "feud between Bob Rossow and Paul Rose" (Dammann 1995: 72) and the staff that consisted of the "worst of the personnel attracted by TCA's high salaries" (110). The lease of two Rana palaces by the U.S. government for use as both homes and offices for all of its employees meant that "there was little opportunity to get out of each others hair" (106). Dammann suggests that it was employment perks, health care and school situations that shaped who sought jobs in this newly opened nation. This framework, established in the 1950s by the U.S. government but soon taken up by other foreigners, has had repercussions in the present, influencing how international business and government workers are able to do their jobs and shaping their work–family relationships.

A history of bureaucratic rationalities of international labor, rather than of either "big men" or "little people," makes visible a new set of structures and constrictions on life in expatriate Nepal. Conducting such a history often re-quires reading not only the official policy but also the accounts of secretaries and mid-level bureaucrats like Nancy Dammann, who describe the work they must do to navigate between centrally dictated assignments and the facts on the ground, such as of interoffice fights and a lack of typewriters.

The World Comes to Nepal: Tourism and Virtual Tibet

Expatriates in Nepal coexist with a vast number of foreigners in Kathmandu for other reasons. Tourism and development are two of the most significant foreign income providers in the city and both populate the streets of Kathmandu with non-Nepali faces. At the center of the city is an intersection that epitomizes the diverse foreign populations. Standing at the corner of Kantipath and Narayanhitipath, two institutions face each other—the high concrete walls of the American Club, Phora Durbar, on one side and the tall steel fence of the former Royal Palace on the other (see map on page x). To the west is the budget tourist zone of Kathmandu, Thamel, while to the east is one of the toniest shopping streets, Durbar Marg, as well as some of the older high-end hotels, including the successor to Boris Lissanevitch's Royal Hotel. Just north of this crossroads, Kantipath becomes Lazimpat, home to many of the major embassy offices in the city. Further north and east, on the outskirts of the city around the Ring Road, are important Hindu and Buddhist temples, and this quadrant of the city attracts some long-term resident foreigners, who can better access Boudhanath and clearer mountain air from that section of town. One must go south and west of the crossroads to find Indian and Chinese businessmen who work in the area around New Road, another upscale shopping area, albeit dealing more in appliances and tailor-made suits than the foreign fashion and gems on Durbar Marg.[7] Further south along Kantipath and a few jogs to the east, one crosses the Bagmati River and enters the second city of the Kathmandu Valley, Patan. Although only three miles separate the two barely distinct cities, it can take as long as an hour to drive between the two due to both the difficult traffic and the need to pass by Singha Durbar, home to the Nepali government and thus site of frequent protests. Patan houses the central UN offices, and many aid agencies cluster in this area, taking advantage of the less-expensive real estate and reduced pollution, and many expatriates who do not live in Lazimpat instead reside in Sanepa, a hilly portion of Patan. Even within this geography of foreign presences there are further divisions: those visiting for short-term cultural tours, adventurers in the city preparing or recovering from trekking and long-term travelers enjoying the Kathmandu scene. These groups seek to distinguish themselves spatially, sartorially and economically from one another and to a Nepali audience. The faces in the sea of East Asian and Western foreigners across Kathmandu may appear to blend into one another, yet making distinctions regarding the reasons for various populations' presence in the city has value for Nepalis and visitors alike.

Nepal has a long history as a crossroads for explorers and adventurers: both Western (Liechty 2005a) and Eastern traders and pilgrims visited the valley as early as the fifth century C.E. (cf. Sen 2006). For some, Nepal plays the role of a more convenient Tibet, standing in for the spirituality of its northern neighbor in light of closed borders and political repression. This attraction to Nepal as a more practical Tibet is often accompanied in recent years by an interest in engaging in religious practice with the many Tibetan leaders now resident in Kathmandu, some of whom cater to a Western audience (Moran 2004). Those who are, or seek to be, resident in Kathmandu for a significant period of time for spiritual reasons work hard to distinguish themselves from the many tourists who crowd the streets of Thamel. After one Nepali street vendor received a lecture in Nepali from a long-term Western resident for trying to sell him a chess set, he remarked after the encounter ended that he could not tell the difference between all the various foreigners. Yet, many foreigners in Nepal seek to monitor and clarify the differences between "hippy tourists," "tour bus people," "dharma bums," "mountain gods" and "expats" (Moran 2004: 121). This is but the contemporary manifestation of Kathmandu as a crossroads for traders, religious pilgrims, and those merely curious about a place long seen as mystical. For Nepalis as well, Kathmandu is an important spatial referent, seen in the use of the word *Nepal* to mean the city of Kathmandu, as when someone from rural Nepal will say "I'm going to Nepal" when journeying to the city. Movement from other areas of Nepal to Kathmandu in search of new opportunities has occurred in dramatic numbers in the past few decades but also throughout the country's history, meaning that the city is, for all but the Newar people, a city of migrants. Expatriate workers form a distinct element of that, but are far from unique in being a newly arrived and conspicuous presence in Kathmandu.

It is not merely the concomitants of physical presence in Kathmandu that craft the niche into which expatriates must be emplotted; it is a complex collection of images and mythologies created outside the country. Nepal is a well-known location for visitors to shops such as Ten Thousand Villages or regular readers of *National Geographic* magazine. Whether the attraction of the country is as the location of the world's highest mountain or the site of exoticized religious practices such as those surrounding the Kumari, or Living Goddess, few visitors to Nepal are able to go to the country without a preexisting basket of images and expectations. Likewise, those discussing their time living in Kathmandu must compete with various perceptions of Nepal circulating among their friends and employers. One Canadian assigned to a posting in Nepal for work with a health care organization described the dissonance of her daily meetings before departure regarding the health dangers of living in the country, political violence and everyday hardships—meetings that would be followed by evenings at bon voyage parties discussing how lucky she was to be traveling to such a beautiful land and how many of those she spoke with had hoped to visit the Himalayas themselves.

All of these Nepals, from mountain paradise to terrorist hotspot, can be found. To understand the contemporary world of expatriate workers and families in Nepal requires an understanding of the local conditions of Kathmandu, but also of the city's role through many centuries of encounter and imagination, all of which shapes how expatriates are received today as well as the conditions in which they live and work. The failures of past development schemes haunt contemporary aid workers; the spiritual fantasy of Shangri-la makes many unsympathetic to the challenges of a deployment to Kathmandu; the stories of tourist drug use in the 1960s provoke desire, anxiety and suspicion on all sides. A diverse and disparate history of contact and connection is necessary to tell the story of expatriates, who like "beachcombers," are tasked with bridging between different worlds (Dening 1998: 170).[8] To claim that expatriates in Nepal are conditioned only by the post-1950s world of foreigners working in Nepal ignores other images and narratives that also define them, and reduces the understanding of foreigners in Kathmandu to a story of culture clash. In such accounts they threaten to become actors on an ahistorical stage of bilateral foreign affairs, of national billiard balls bouncing off each other (Wolf 1982: 6–7). Nepal has played many roles in the imaginative world of the West and its neighbors, and the numerous encounters between "locals" and "others" that have occurred in the territory now known as Nepal continue to influence the experience of foreign workers assigned to the area. Thus, although policies of employment and bureaucratic practices attempt to homogenize the spaces in which workers are asked to live, attempting to make expatriate life an undifferentiated series of enclaves, nonetheless, the specificity of place, particularly one like Kathmandu, always overflows the limited opportunities allowed for difference.

The Emergence of Expatria

Colonialism, soft power agendas and the mythology of the Himalayan region have all influenced both the world of international business in Nepal and the interactions between foreigners visiting the country for work and local interlocutors. In addition to these influences, shifts in business practice and management have also affected the work of elite transnational laborers, especially the expansion of a mid-level managerial class. In the last thirty years, new technologies and business attitudes have generated a new format of overseas life, one with similarities to past practices of work abroad but novel in important arenas. It is only in the late twentieth century that speaking about a community of expatriates with durable connections to each other and to a mode of living—an Expatria—comes to make sense. There is no single transformative event or theory that caused this shift, but rather a set of policies and responses by workers, employers and service providers. In this section, I examine three ideas that form the core of this change: an expansion in the number and kind of employers sending workers abroad, a concomitant rationalization of international employment and the emergence of "internationalism" as a skill. The associated technical practices of international employment, while undoubtedly borrowing from colonial regimes, established a distinctive understanding of the expatriate worker, family and package contributing to the generation of Expatria after World War II.

As the discussion of British colonial families in India suggests, employer concern with sending workers abroad has a long history. Yet until recently, the number of employers, employees and locations for overseas employment was limited. One can point to the transnational migration of people for work having a long history, but only the last few decades have seen a widespread expectation that domestic companies, governments and other entities pursue a strategy of globalness. *Globalness*, as described by Karen Ho, refers to an amorphous valorization of "presence" in many different countries and the pursuit of "being global," often without a clear sense of why or what that entails (Ho 2005). It is both a buzzword and an aspiration, one which denotes the positive value of multinationalism in and of itself. While in the past many companies had international offices and some even sent large numbers of employees to affiliate offices overseas, the widespread aspiration to the status of "being global" is a recent phenomenon.

To put this in a specific context, one must consider the shape of international employment before the 1980s. Shell Oil Company has a long history of sending a large number of workers abroad and, through both official corporate pathways and informal institutions, an accessible record of its changing overseas employment practices (Solomon 1996; cf. Gordon 2008). Shell, like many early multinational companies, was focused on locations outside of its corporate headquarters as a result of the natural resources it sought (Wilkins 1974; Stopford 1974; Hopkins 1976). The majority of Shell's international employees were posted to one of a dozen or so overseas enclave communities that were developing petroleum refining plants. Although a move to the use and training of local workers was a mission of Shell,[9] large numbers of foreign—usually European—technical experts were posted overseas. In these locations, entire communities of Shell employees lived, worked and socialized together. As one woman writes about living in a Shell camp in Indonesia, "Your family was the Shell family" (Shell Ladies' Project 1993: 69). For these workers, posting overseas was necessary because that was where the petroleum was and their jobs required the application of their skills in situ. Although culture and language education might take place as a beneficial element of the experience, the mission at hand was not focused on bridging cultural differences or understanding a new market. Families relied on "camp services" for nearly all their needs, doing much of their shopping in Shell commissaries, living in company-provided housing and socializing with other workers and their families. Women referred to themselves as "Shell wives" and families were able to talk to others not only about the shared experience of overseas life but of life in a particular camp—sharing stories about how big the trees had grown over the years at Ras al Hamra, "a modern Shell camp" in Oman (Shell Ladies' Project 1993: 82). This kind of deployment meant that the management tasks unique to employing workers abroad were handled within the company. Instead of a more generalized process of international human resources management, Shell used its own proprietary institutions in camps like Ras al Hamra to support its overseas personnel.

Although Shell has become well known for its expatriate preparation programs, these were developed out of the experience (and complaints) of company employees and offered to those workers whose skills were needed overseas (see Shell Outpost Survey 1993). Before the rise of the cross-cultural testing process in the 1980s, employees were largely selected based on what skills were needed at a job location and an individual interview process discussing their interest in and concerns about going abroad. In joining Shell, most of the engineers who were the core of the company's expatriate staff anticipated that overseas work would be a part of their careers, particularly if they desired advancement. In the "golden era" of Shell's expatriate expansion in the 1960s and 1970s, many of its expatriates were newly married couples and the career considerations of women were rarely discussed. Instead, Shell workers were encouraged to move abroad by descriptions of the high-quality schools, inexpensive household help and recreational facilities. These years of Shell's expatriation process offer several contrasts from the practices that will be discussed in the rest of the book. Although the large population of overseas workers utilized by Shell in the middle part of the twentieth century did require significant corporate resources, those were largely dictated by situational needs and internal considerations. Shell camps were established to resemble military bases: self-contained villages that could supply all the needs of workers and their families without making them venture into the local community.

In the last twenty years, much has changed in how expatriates are employed, housed and compensated. Many more companies are sending workers abroad, even very small organizations that seek to attain globalness, and the same is true of the expansion of the diplomatic corps and nongovernmental development agencies. In a small nation like Nepal, this often means that one or two workers may be an organization's entire presence in the country. Such practices make expatriate support by the employer challenging and many employers turn to specialized agencies for international human resources management, which will be discussed in the next chapters, to fulfill their workers' needs. To outsource worker hiring and family placement requires a distancing and rationalizing process to enable specialized agencies to work with enough companies to make their services viable.

The rise of external agencies to professionally manage expatriate employment and overseas families has intersected with the growth of cross-cultural testing and training to produce new demands—both for specialized services and of workers. "Intercultural skills" begin to take precedence over the technical skills that were the driving force in early overseas employment.[10] Internationalism itself becomes a testable and teachable skill that many involved in human resources seek to institutionalize and understand. This intersects with the outsourcing of expatriate selection and the need to provide quantifiable measures of a service provider's efficacy at a time of rationalization and externalization. The intersection of these phenomena—international employment rationalization and the outsourcing it allows as well as the production of internationalism as a skill—will be the focus of the remaining chapters of this book, but understanding that overseas employment once ran along different logics is necessary to see the transformations that this new form of sending families abroad produces.

This attention to the theory and structure of expatriate employment should not imply that the type of activities pursued by overseas businesses and governments is irrelevant. If early international business focused exclusively on natural resource extraction, in recent decades attention has turned towards generating markets, and even those companies seeking "natural" resources find "cultural" knowledge a necessary component (cf. Petryna, Lakoff, and Kleinman 2006). Likewise, diplomacy and development have changed in character and the fashion for "sustainable development" and "soft power" again entail different skills and forms of engagement with the local. "Emotional intelligence" and cultural knowledge are more obvious expectations when the overseas labor at stake is selling ideas and products rather than extracting from the land, although this shift is also brought about by new ideas about "the Other."

Contemporary forms of expatriate employment also differ from the Shell type in the relationship that exists between employees and employers. While both Shell executives and expatriates were once comfortable discussing "Shell families" and "Shell wives," now one is more likely to read about "flexibility" and "branding yourself" as the outsourcing processes of rationalization are applied to the expatriate worker. Expatriates are encouraged to think of themselves as independent contractors pursuing career goals separate from an individual company. Positions formerly held by career company men are not turned over to host country nationals, but more often to "self-initiated expatriates" who freelance their past successful expatriate positions into consultancies—or become unemployed. The concluding chapters of *Mediating the Global* will explore how this newly emergent contractor class is expanding in the twenty-first century. Between "Shell wives" and "international protean careers" stand several significant shifts of institutions and structures, instituted by expatriates in Nepal and elsewhere but simultaneously defining how expatriate managers themselves live and work.

Nepal's History and the Foreign Gaze

Changes happening in Nepal are also central to how Expatria has been transformed in the almost twenty years this book tracks. The period since the 1990 democratic revolution in Nepal, also known as Jana Andolan I, has been one of great hope and great disappointment as each successive government has failed to bring about anticipated changes. While the bureaucracy that underlies the political system, much of which was constituted in the Rana era—a period in Nepal with paperwork excesses like those of the Civil Services of India—continues, the instability of leadership has led to a state of long-term provisionality. In this state, serious decisions about employment, business and real estate are often deferred in anticipation of a change in the government of the country. While the pursuit of democracy by the people of Nepal and ongoing, vigorous attempts to improve international rights standards have encouraged the investment of money and personnel by foreign governments and businesses, these everyday acts of "global good governance" often have been overshadowed by events less positive in the eyes of the global community.

Nepal's position astride the Cold War front line as a bulwark against China and a neighbor to the always-vacillating India made it a location of great interest for the Soviet Union, China and the United States. While the influence of Soviet educational outreach can be seen in some areas of the country, U.S. investment in development in the post–World War II era has been particularly influential. As discussed earlier, the early 1950s were a period of conjoining American and Nepali interests. For the United States, this was a period that emphasized technological improvements and turned expertise produced during World War II to new aims. The Point Four program, so named for points made in the 1949 inaugural address of Harry Truman, drove the policies of the United States in its early years of involvement in Nepal and meant that most of the investment in the nation was in the form of technical advice as well as machinery for infrastructure building (Hindman 2002). The 1950s were an unsettled time in Nepal, with struggles to build a constitution and establish new government institutions after the long period of Rana rule, which had kept Nepal outside of world events and without practices of electoral democracy or political parties. After the stagnation of the Rana era, King Tribhuvan as well as his son Mahendra, who succeeded him in 1959, pushed for rapid economic development—a goal that fit well with the demands of the eager population as well as the approach of U.S. aid programs. The quick-fix mentality toward both new forms of governance and development proved to be a limited success (Skerry, Moran, and Calavan 1991). Elections held in 1959, won by the Nepali Congress Party, were the beginning of a long series of disappointing adventures in democracy over the last sixty years in Nepal, with the government of B. P. Koirala, which came out of these elections, lasting less than eighteen months (Whelpton 2005).

King Mahendra replaced B. P. Koirala's government with a "partyless Panchayat system" that was designed to distribute power to local polities, in part utilizing long- standing forms of regional governance. Placing some power in the hands of local rulers and village councils, the king nonetheless maintained strict control over the country, unchecked by political parties. Although village leadership was supposed to be independently elected, local elites understood their power was dependent on the whims of the king, and leaders were often high-caste monarchists. While the Panchayat system claimed to return power to both traditional ways and village independence, it was created simultaneously with government attempts to establish greater unity in the country as a whole, with the establishment of Nepali as the national language in 1958 and the development of new educational institutions to promote identification with the nation, a cause that also had a limited audience given the high level of illiteracy in Nepal (cf. Burghart 1993). The devotion of the monarchy and political leaders to a small segment of the population, often an urban, educated elite, pervades Nepali politics even to the present, and shaped the politics of the late twentieth century. This favoring of elites also affected foreigners in the country who, both due to their own inabilities and these established hierarchies, rarely encountered people outside the narrow world of Kathmandu's wealthy and educated. This elite population thus shaped the way these foreigners saw the rest of the country (cf. Pigg 1992).

The 1970s and 1980s saw some resistance to the monarchial dominance, but it was not until 1989 that substantial protest against the Panchayat system arose in response to local conditions of scarcity brought about by Indian embargoes on goods as well as greater awareness of other revolutionary actions taking place around the world (Whelpton 2005: 113). Jana Andolan I (People's Revolution I) began in earnest in 1990, with rallies and strikes in Kathmandu, often by its professional classes (Hoftun 1993). Within the year, King Birendra lifted the ban on political parties and a new constitution was written calling for elections to be held the following year. The Nepali Congress Party was victorious again in 1991, and Girija Prasad Koirala, brother of B. P. Koirala, became the country's new prime minister. As in 1951, there was great hope that this was the beginning of a new era in Nepal, although this revolution was not to bring the hoped for peace, democracy, stability and growth. Foreign governments, international institutions and aid agencies, disappointed by the lack of quantifiable or observable change in the country in previous decades, similarly welcomed the success of the People's Revolution (Seddon 1993). Many inside and outside the country hoped that with democracy would come an expansion of Nepal's historically narrow base of power, outside of Kathmandu Valley as well as beyond the educated, high-caste elites. It was the absence of such expansions of power and wealth that made space for the subsequent Maoist revolution and led to the need for a second Jana Andolan (cf. Onta 2004).

The 1990s were a story of fighting between and within established political parties in Nepal. Democracy was established, but leaders found it difficult to maintain power as they struggled to retain their constituencies and sought support from foreign governments and internal power bases, often leading to charges of corruption and calls for new elections, with eight changes of prime minister in the 1990s alone. In this period, the Maoists, separating themselves from other leftist parties in stages, began to establish themselves as both a political and military force. In 1995, the Communist Party of Nepal (Maoist) was established by Prachanda, the revolutionary name of Puspa Kamal Dahal, who would be joined by Baburam Bhattarai, forming the core of the leadership of the Maoists and establishing the power of the party with a list of forty demands presented to the government in 1996, which led to the launch of the "People's War." The political and military wings of the Maoist party gained a foothold in rural areas of the country, especially west of the capital. In the following decade, there was civil war in Nepal, with much loss of life and hope during the conflict (cf. Hutt 2004; Onesto 2005; Thapa and Sijapati 2005; Lawoti and Pahari 2010). The royal massacre that took place in the midst of this conflict in 2001 not only caused the death of many members of the monarchy but also raised levels of domestic and international tension in Nepal, promoting suspicion as well as causing a decline in foreign aid and tourism (see Gregson 2002). With an unstable government and internal violence, many aid programs cut back their financial and human investment in the country and many nations discouraged travel to Nepal, severely disrupting two of Nepal's major income sources.

Increasing violence, as well as the success of the Maoists in establishing themselves in sections of the country contributed to, but were not the only impetus for, the 2006 democracy movement, also know as Jana Andolan II. Antimonarchist sentiment and frustration with the instability of Nepal's governments led to street protests and strikes, sometimes directed by political parties or established movements, but occasionally arising as spontaneous grassroots eruptions. With the country unable to function, King Gyanendra, who had taken control of the country, having declared a state of emergency, ended nightly curfews and reestablished the House of Representatives and former constitution, only to have the monarchy itself eliminated less than a month later. In 2008, new elections were held for seats in the Constituent Assembly and national leadership. The Maoists (CPN[M]) won a majority of seats in this body, which was to work to write a new constitution, as well as form a new government. Unfortunately, subsequent years have seen familiar political infighting and changes of power, with the Constituent Assembly failing, both in 2010 and after receiving an extension of its mandate in 2012, to agree on a new constitution for the nation.

The political instability of Nepal has caused changes and even suspension of many activities of international agencies and private aid work in the country. Foreign governments called back official staff at several times during the last twenty years and warnings about potential attacks on foreigners came regularly from embassies. Expatriates were often torn in this period between the official anxieties proclaimed by their employers and governments and more immediate and everyday fears. Condemnation of the Maoists as terrorists by many foreign governments simplified a complex political landscape as well as neglecting more everyday forms of violence taking place in Kathmandu. As one Nepali novelist wrote about the complexity of the post-1990 political situation, "[t]he expatriate community was the only one completely bluffed, I thought, or was it that they were never able to grasp the truth that is Nepal" (Shah 2010: 180).

The problem of the dissonance between historical events in this era and everyday experience is mirrored in the chapters that follow. In seeking to understand the precedents for a contemporary Expatria in Nepal, one must look at both geographic and labor contexts. Yet the official are not always parallel to the experiential dimensions of change. Thus, the questions that opened this chapter about the parallels between the current involvement of the West in South Asia and its involvement in the colonial era in India ask that one look beyond the official record to everyday encounters. By this I suggest that there are lessons to be learned from the way in which labor and family management of officials by the British regime in India was itself a political statement, and was read as such by both Indians and Britons. Likewise, when examining contemporary politics in Nepal and labor policies of employers, one needs to look behind the official proclamations to the more mundane bureaucratic practices and their impact on daily life, as well as their reception by various audiences. Thus, even as the U.S. government put the CPN(M) (Communist Party of Nepal–Maoist) on the terrorism watch list, local concerns centered more on the daily traffic disruptions caused by the strikes of various factions and ever-present problems such as lack of electricity, fuel and fear of earthquakes.

Turning back to labor, the rise of employment rationalization has facilitated the capacity of many organizations to "go global" and has also changed the nature of overseas labor. The structuration of employment into systems designed to ensure equity and efficiency has been lauded as an innovation of twentieth-century management practices. The shift to rationalization, as described by Max Weber in both *Economy and Society* (1978) and *The Protestant Ethic and the Spirit of Capitalism* (1992), is a historical moment in the transformation of capitalism that impacts many aspects of human life outside the workplace. The implementation of systems of rationalization allows calculability, such as the pursuit of predictability and techniques of risk management. Much of contemporary globalness relies on rationalization, including the production of

international expectations of financial practice and the generation of a universal vocabulary for measuring corporate efficiency (cf. Maurer 2008). Keeping
the focus on international employment, rationalization in many ways enables
the generation of such a category. Only the production of a system of ratio-
nal management that transcends any particular business or government action
can generate the idea of a good global employee existing apart from the kind
of work they do.

2 Families That Fail

The Mechanisms and Labor of Productivity

ALISON'S HONEYMOON TRIP was her first experience of travel outside of the United States, and it was only the beginning of her journeys. She and her fiancé had moved up the date of their wedding when Jay learned he was to be sent abroad by his company. The first household they would set up together would be in Asia, and Alison, not having lived apart from her parents during her twenty-two years of life, knew she might be in over her head, for now she was going to be an expatriate. When they arrived in Nepal, their assigned country, Jay was very busy with his new job. He had little time to contemplate or experience where they were living, while Alison was at home all day. The wives of Jay's coworkers sought to induce Alison to come out to various events, but she usually resisted, fearing the chaos of the city and potential challenges of communication and transit. One woman did finally convince her to attend a ladies' lunch, and it was there we met. Alison's life before marriage had consisted of working in a clothing shop in a local mall and absorbing herself in the science fiction books that initially brought her and Jay together. She was eager to find others who were young and childless in an expatriate community that was mainly families with school-aged children or empty nesters. As December approached, Alison drew despondent thinking about a Christmas without her parents and younger brother, but she knew Jay's success depended on their successful completion of this and perhaps other international assignments. Alison was concerned that her lack of social interaction was harming Jay's career, marking the couple as a "problem family." As I was returning to the United States for a visit in December, I asked if there was anything I could bring her, and she made two requests: a recently released science fiction book by her favorite author and Saint John's wort, which she had read was useful for treating depression. Although I picked up the book and medicine for her, I was never able to deliver them because by the time I returned, she had left the country. Talk of Alison and Jay's departure circulated within the expatriate community in Kathmandu—several women commented that Alison was too young, not strong enough, that they should never have been sent abroad in the first place. Men, especially Jay's coworkers, speculated about what he could do to redeem his career in the States. They thought it unlikely that he would be considered for another international position, and this negative outcome, it was suggested, would hamper his ability to advance to management. The couple had failed their first expatriate assignment, and friends and colleagues used Jay and Alison's experience to reflect on how close they themselves had come in the past to leaving their post before the end of a contract as well as how obvious, in retrospect, it should have been that Jay and Alison were bad candidates for expatriate life, especially in Nepal.

Jay's coworkers had personal concerns as well: the company had invested a great deal in training Jay for his job, and rumors were that, given this negative experience, the employer might utilize local contractors in the future. Few people had talked to Alison in the weeks before their departure, but many colleagues tried to convince Jay to persuade Alison to stay and to make him aware of how his departure would harm his career. Some suggested that they should have a child, which might give Alison something to do; others proposed bribery in the form of jewelry or vacations. What surprised Jay's colleagues was that he seemed no more invested in staying than Alison. One fellow worker recounted a conversation in which Jay said that he had not wanted this assignment in the first place. Jay's youth and the briefness of his time with the company made him an unlikely candidate for the position he held in Nepal, but he had been encouraged by a mentor in his home office, was receiving a promotion as part of the move and fit well with his employer's push for diversity among overseas employees. One man working on the same project as Jay but through a different employer wondered if the couple had undergone the same battery of tests and counseling that he and his family had undergone before their first posting. Another scoffed at this process, noting that when he had begun working abroad twenty-five years ago, it was just "they tell you where to go and when you are leaving"—no choice or preparation; but, he noted, his generation were used to such things as most had military experience. Nepal itself became part of the debate, as one couple remarked that they would have gone home as well if Kathmandu had been their first posting, but after fifteen years of moving they had developed coping skills for expatriate life, even in a place like Nepal. One woman who had tried to befriend Alison wondered what happened to their belongings, complaining that the company her husband worked for had them already half-packed for a move they were not making for several months. All that Jay's employer would say officially was that he and Alison had returned to the United States for personal reasons.

Learning to Fail at Laboring Abroad

Alison and Jay's unsuccessful venture into the expatriate world exemplifies the concerns of employers of the elite international labor force. The costs of deploying career migrants on expatriate packages include salary supplements, job and cultural training and the expenses of overseas family placement, which add up to several times what the same worker would cost if based in a headquarters office. Beyond economic expenditures, there are intangible losses of credibility and reputation to be endured by the company in the case of worker failure. Thus, elite expatriate deployment is preceded by careful considerations of which workers are most likely to thrive in a given location. This currently involves an external body of quantitative research seeking to predict the demographic profile of those most likely to succeed as expatriate families as well as a collection of specialists who translate this research into helping companies to select workers and facilitating their international placement. As both the scholarship on this topic and the scale of overseas employment has expanded, many companies, governments and organizations are relying on outside agencies to manage this process. As a result of the outsourcing of expatriate selection, the definition of "failure" has had to become a generalizable measure that can be deployed across individual conditions, jobs and family situations. This move to homogenize the transnational elite labor migrant experience produces a genre of scholarship where only a few variables can be taken into consideration before the research becomes too specific to be widely applied.

The research on why expatriates fail must define the reasons for negative outcomes as extrinsic—it cannot be the job itself or a location, like Nepal, that is the problem. Working abroad is the black box assumption that is left uninvestigated in the understanding of expatriate success and failure (Latour 1987). The need to do a particular task away from home is the very precondition of an expatriate deployment and thus the source of failure must be found to be elsewhere. The most frequent variable to which failure is attributed is the one least under the control of the employer—the worker's family. Placing the accusation for failure on non-employee members of the household also aligns with the agenda of specialized service providers who are the primary audience for such research. The close connection of international employment researchers to those who provide training and support services to expatriate families suggests a paradigm where crisis and solution are crafted in tandem (Escobar 1995: 89). As a result, through the system of financial, emotional and physical support mechanisms, spouses and children are incorporated into the employer's domain of concern. Yet this paternalistic approach to expatriate services produces an expectation of certain conformities and the contribution of uncompensated labor by the family.

This chapter looks at the complex web of relations that link families to worker failure through a new mode of technical scholarship about labor, a new knowledge-culture (Knorr Cetina 1999: 7). The field of International Human Resources Management (IHRM) embeds within itself inherent limits in its forms of analysis, limits that become particularly problematic when a family does not fit into the norm, as Alison and Jay did not, or a post location presents unique challenges, as Nepal does. This new regime of managing elite international workers is necessitated by the increasing vertical disintegration of multinational corporations, governments and other organizations and the increasing number of employers seeking to "go global." The testing programs and social support organizations generated by the study of expatriate labor and families often produce auxiliary tasks for the family, thus engendering new obligations and even producing new opportunities for potential failure. Expatriate employers become invested in domestic regulation as a means of producing a better expatriate employee but often produce new hardships for the people they are intending to help. Although Jay and Alison were provided with substantial predeparture training and financial incentives, there was no structure provided for getting them the most recent science fiction book from their favorite author.

Workers Become Resources

Expatriate workers in Nepal did not see themselves as "international human resources" but they felt the effects of the field of international human resources management in their daily anxieties, family responsibilities, and the economic and social support they received from their employer. The centrality of failure could be heard in concern over how Alison's departure would impact her husband's career and in the financial incentives offered to workers who had done well and were able to continue in overseas positions. Workers in locations with large expatriate populations, or those directly employed by governments, might have found institutions and services seeking to prevent early departure or to facilitate worker productivity, but for many foreign employees in Kathmandu the support services they received existed mainly at the inception of an overseas career or new posting rather than as everyday help to which they were able to turn. In Nepal, the intervention of management processes on workers was subtly manifest in the concerns of workers about how they and their families were perceived by superiors. Human resources professionals analyzed their daily lives from afar, a distant gaze that judged their success as a family. In private conversations, parents worried that their child's learning disability might be held against them in future postings and wondered how marriages on the rocks would hold up under the intimate scrutiny of the expatriate community in Nepal. The high costs of expatriate employment, both relative to the local economy and to their peers in the home office, were felt as a pressure by most families, who sought to prove themselves worth the investment.

While some organizations continue to make decisions about overseas postings through personal impressions and casual conversations, dubbed the "coffee-machine" system by one set of authors (Harris and Brewster 1999), most large employers now rely on scholarship and subcontracted evaluations. One expatriate working in Kathmandu described how, although working in India, she had to fly to Europe in order to take a battery of tests on her ability to work abroad. She then participated in a teleconference with the Kathmandu office as part of her job interview. On her return, she lamented the costs the NGO must have incurred for the flight and lodging just so she could fill in a bubble form, and declared how much easier it would have been just to fly her to Kathmandu. Yet such centralized hiring had become the norm by the early 2000s—unlike when she had begun working. It was in the early 1980s that human resources management, which included the study of hiring, compensation and retention of employees, became an important aspect of business school curriculum, and it has grown quickly from these early days.[1] The concept of human resources management was possible only when the relationship between personnel and employers could be conceived independently of any particular industry. Because management and administration were expanding within businesses, they also expanded within the academy and by 1981, human resources management became a mandatory element of the Harvard MBA program (Poole 1990: 2; cf. Kaufman 2008). Following definitions adopted at Harvard, "Human Resources Management (HRM) is seen to involve 'all management decisions that affect the nature of the relationship between the organization and employees—its human resources'"(Poole 1990: 2; citing Beer et al. 1984: 1). It was not long before this field began to address the specific concerns of those managing personnel posted overseas.

Although the successful management of expatriate employees has long been of concern to businesses and government employers, the creation of a scholarly discipline focused on the topic transformed the terms within which it is discussed. Formerly, interest in overseas workers and their likelihood of success came from individual employers—government foreign services, militaries, or private industries such as petroleum—sending significant numbers of workers abroad.[2] With the development of generalized scholarship on international employees, the terms of concern about workers were reversed. What had been money given to expatriates in a concern over their health and happiness became a measurable investment in productivity and financial efficiency. Success became more critically evaluated and the costs of investing in expatriates became the focus of IHRM scholarship. Statisticians began calculating the amount companies spent on expatriate employees and sought to determine if this was a worthwhile expense based on the employees' productivity. Given that salaries and employee expenses are a major expenditure for most industries sending workers abroad, the goal the IHRM authors set was to determine where money for expatriates could be spent most effectively and how to select and place expatriate employees so that the expenses justified employers' goals.

Many levels mediate between the highly quantitative and technical language of this scholarship and the experience of workers on the ground. Academic arguments are distilled into "executive summaries," and further transformed into applied prescriptions by expatriate service providers, who often utilize academics as consultants. The articles in journals designed for an academic audience are often redacted in training manuals for a particular organization's human resources staff, who distill these arguments into attractive PowerPoint-like graphics and a focus on how these theories can be applied. It is from these digested articles that international employment policy is extrapolated, and the most frequent theme is that families are the source of expatriate failure.

Failure is one of the most-discussed metrics by those who write about expatriate employment. As one prominent author states, "it has become almost 'traditional' to open an article on expatriate management by stating that expatriate failure rates are (very) high" (Harzing 1995: 458). Families, as the key source of failure, become a focus of attention and approbation in this research, given the agenda of reducing costs. Scholars in the field produce figures indicating the expenditure for sending an expatriate abroad at around $300,000 per expatriate per year (Fukuda and Chu 1994) or three-to-six times the cost of employing the same individual at the home office by other estimates (Freeman and Cane 1995). These statistics are correlated with estimations of the percentage of expatriate employees who fail, where numbers range from single digits to 79 percent in "developing countries" (Shilling 1993). The link between families and failure is quantified in studies, one of which claimed to find that between 60 and 80 percent of those refusing expatriate assignments cited family as the reason (Munton and Forster 1990), whereas another determined that 80 percent of expatriate failure was due to spouse-related issues (Hawley 2001). The results of these research studies are frequently cited in industry magazines as a call for more research into both reducing expatriate costs and the reasons why families cause failure.

Do Expatriates Fail or Does IHRM?

In many domains of IHRM, the statistics and conclusions that emerge from the scholarship exceed the claims of their initial authors. The study of expatriate failure appears to have its inception in a claim that even its initial author knew was speculative. In an article by a Standard Oil employee relations manager, who had taken time off to assist in the selection of Peace Corps volunteers in 1963, he suggested that companies needed to learn from the rigorous selection process of the Peace Corps, as "30 percent of the people sent overseas by American companies are mistakes and have been—or should have been—sent home," which the author supports through a footnote stating, "I have no precise, comprehensive statistical basis for this 30 percent figure, but from more or less informal data I have been able to obtain it seems to be a conservative estimate" (Henry 1965: 17; also quoted in Harzing 1995: 467). This 30 percent figure nonetheless was taken up by many of the founders of the field, and began what is the now self-reproducing discourse about high rates of expatriate failure and their attribution to the influence of workers' families. Anne-Wil Harzing, an IHRM scholar who has taught in business schools across Europe and Australia, has written several articles critiquing the scholarship on expatriate failure from within the field. "The Persistent Myth of High Expatriate Failure Rates" was her first foray into what has become a larger investigation of how journal ranking systems and a quantity-over-quality mentality produce poor scholarship, especially in her own field of international business (1995, see especially the revealing figure on page 460; cf. Harzing 2002; Adler and Harzing 2009). Although the co-editor of *International Human Resource Management* (Harzing and Van Ruysseveld 1995), Harzing finds much fault with both the content of her fellow IHRM researchers' articles and the incestuousness of the discussion of expatriate failure.

In 2002, Harzing published another article focusing on the generalizations her colleagues engaged in that kept "expatriate failure" a central issue in the field and bemoaning the fact that the erroneous scholarship she had decried seven years earlier remained "a firmly entrenched myth unsubstantiated by any empirical evidence," both undermining the academic credibility of the field of international management and hampering practical efforts in the field of expatriate selection and training (Harzing 2002: 127–28). Although her article is widely cited and referenced, Harzing's campaign has had little effect and her exasperation is expressed in the title of her 2004 article, "Expatriate Failure: Time to Abandon the Concept?" In this argument, she turns away from the problems of data analysis and insularity to the concept itself when she notes the impossibility of a generalized definition of failure and proclaims that "[e]xpatriate failure in itself can be regarded as an empty term, which can only be defined when specific outcomes are related to specific causes within the actual context" (Harzing and Christensen 2004: 625). As a scholar of international human resources and organizational behavior herself, Harzing attacks this research partially from concerns of disciplinary rigor and accuracy but also because she recognizes the potential negative effects of this scholarship on expatriate life.

The scholarly practices Harzing described a decade and a half ago persist, as the same statistics on expatriate failure and its relation to families continue to be cited within scholarship and applied literatures. The claim that the main cause of failure is families persists, as well as the demand for more and better research on expatriate failure and costs, along with the observation that family considerations continue to be misunderstood. As one researcher notes, "the single most frequently reported reason for failure in an international assignment (when defined as premature return) is an inability or unwillingness of the spouse to adapt. Most international firms, however, continue to neglect the spouse" (Andreason 2008: 392). Another article begins with this claim of a thirty-year ongoing lacuna of research on an issue of overwhelming importance: "This paper seeks to review and explore the relatively neglected notion of the adjustment of expatriate families to living abroad" (Haslberger and Brewster 2008: 324). Meanwhile, a third author (Lee 2007: 403) observes that "the most significant research conducted on expatriate failure by Tung (1982) was carried out over two decades ago," and yet the author comes to the same conclusion as all the others: "An inability on the part of the expatriate family to adjust to the foreign environment was the main determinant of expatriate failure" (Lee 2007: 403). All these articles produce similar results: that expatriates frequently fail because of family concerns, that companies poorly support expatriate families and that past researchers have done an inadequate job of understanding expatriate failure and families, except for their own article. The insularity of this field and limited scope of original research leads to a situation where broad claims are often based on the "conservative estimate" cited by Henry (1965) or statements such as "according to a number of recent studies," resulting in a game of "Chinese whispers" about failure rates and causes (Harzing 2002: 127–48). The myth of expatriate families and failure is perpetuated in the academic literature, and even more as that scholarship disseminates into the popular and applied business fields.

What Makes a Good Expatriate?

The inability of international business scholarship to agree on the additional expenses of employing overseas workers, the percentage who fail and why does not deter continued attempts to quantify these factors. Whereas later I analyze attempts to reduce posting costs (Chapter 3) and the importance of cultural preparation (Chapter 5), in this section I explore strategies for selecting the "right" expatriate and how families considering going abroad use the selection process to achieve their own goals. Also, while many in the field debate the accuracy of failure figures, I want to turn attention to the definition of a failed overseas worker. I suggest that the placement and selection process itself can configure expectations in such a way that workers and families are set up to fail.

If Alison and Jay were exemplars of the failed expatriate, Donald and Diane were an expatriate success story. In talking about attending an upcoming class reunion, they admitted that neither was a particularly good student when they met and fell in love in high school, although Donald showed some aptitude in auto mechanics. They believed that most of their classmates in Australia would have anticipated that they would end up in some outback town, Donald fixing cars and Diane taking care of their several children. Only the second part turned out to be correct, and they looked forward to sharing their success with former classmates. Donald turned from repairing cars to repairing heavy equipment during a period in the military and found that there was a great demand for his skills after he finished his tour. As they were young, broke and not yet encumbered by children or property, when Donald was offered a very lucrative position in Southeast Asia, the couple decided to take a chance, despite their families' objections. They had never traveled outside of Australia, even during Donald's time in the military, and came from families deeply rooted in suburban domestic life. Travel, apart from nearby beach vacations, was not a part of their previous lives, although Diane's family had considered going abroad for mission work but had decided not to at the last minute. "Look at us now, we have lived in six different countries in Asia—Bali was great—and here we are in Kathmandu," said Diane, anticipating the stories they had to tell their former classmates. The couple raised three children abroad, with Donald nearly constantly employed, even though he worked on a contract basis: "There were only six months I had without a job, and that worked out well because that was when we bought our house." Their home outside of Sydney was the base for the family; their daughters lived there after college as they looked for jobs, and everyone congregated there during holidays. Diane always talked about her new plan for the house—making curtains in Nepal that they would hang in Australia. "I'm just a homebody" she noted, and she did seem an unlikely expatriate. This couple, who had limited interest in "culture," had lived overseas for nearly forty years, and although they frequently talked about retirement and being closer to their children, they waited until Donald was turning seventy to finally stop their peripatetic life.

The employers Donald had worked for had invested a great deal, not just in him individually but in his family, including private schooling for all the children, annual trips for the family to Australia from their current posting and housing allowance and staff costs in various locations. The family was an expatriate success, as Donald had never left a posting prematurely (even when Diane had gone to Australia for nearly a year as a result of a difficult pregnancy), and their many postings abroad had been lucrative for them as well, Donald receiving a salary that, according to him, "no one without a degree" could have expected to receive. He suggested that it was likely that his path would not be possible today in light of the emphasis on credentialing and evaluation. "I just got lucky—I was at the right place when the jobs were there." Employers, using business research as well as consultants, are continually trying to predict who will be a Donald and who will be a Jay—or, more important—who will be a Diane and who an Alison.

Families often experience their first incorporation into the work of the primary employee before they even go overseas, in the selection process. The tests for personality and adaptability that are administered to workers are often given to family members as well, employers noting they are selecting a domestic unit, not just the right worker. Young children are asked questions about how they feel about new experiences and whether they like people who look different from them; couples are questioned about their relationship and ties with family. Through quantitative and qualitative examination, employers, or more often subcontracted experts, attempt to select the Donalds and Dianes, although little consensus exists on what makes a successful expatriate. One consultant suggested the following problem:

> If the ability to live in different places and speak other languages, an intellectual curiosity and an interest in different cultures aren't the principal factors for international success, what are? What, for example, enables a couple who have lived their entire lives in small-town Texas to move to northern England and do a terrific job . . . To predict how well individuals will adapt to a foreign environment, we have to look at the ways they think and act, what they tell us about their beliefs, and how they manage tasks, make choices and interact with other people. (Kozloff 1996: 2)

Organizations like Selection Research International—the company that the author of the above statement now works for—provide a way to operationalize the problem of high expatriate failure rates and the culpability of families. With both business professionals and psychologists on staff, these companies use popular personality-testing tools as well as their own experience to offer an evaluation of the likelihood that a family will succeed in living and working abroad.

Many development and diplomatic staff posted to Nepal recalled that their employers administered some form of personality testing early in their career, while those in the business community experienced these evaluations only when they were being considered for overseas positions and often in conjunction with a program produced by a subcontractor. Experiences varied as to when and whether these investigations involved family members, with one man in Nepal reporting that his new wife found herself "being grilled" just months after their marriage about their relationship, plans for the future, anticipation of kids, habits of her new husband and domestic tensions. Another family recalled how their kids had been placed in a one-way mirrored room to play games with a psychologist to evaluate their adaptability. Commonly, the adults in the family had been given some form of structured psychological testing such as the Minnesota Multiphasic Personality Inventory (MMPI) and the Myers-Briggs, or specialized instruments like the Overseas Assignment Inventory (OAI) and the Cross-Cultural Adaptability Inventory (CCAI).

These tests are best understood as cultural IQ tests, as they measure an absolute and inherent level of ability. Examinees are graded on a single scale as to how much cultural competence they possess. The CCAI is indicative of the nontechnical skills consultants seek to measure in order to determine how an individual will adapt to any cultural difference. "The culture-general approach assumes that individuals adapting to other cultures share common feelings, perceptions, and experiences. This occurs regardless of the cultural background of the person or the characteristics of the target culture" (Kelley and Meyers 1995: 1). The CCAI is arranged to measure four characteristics determined to be pivotal to success in foreign environments: emotional resilience (ER), flexibility/openness (FO), perceptual acuity (PAC) and personal autonomy (PA). Individuals given this test must respond to fifty statements and are given six options ranging from "Definitely True" to "Definitely Not True" to describe themselves in relation to the statements. The questions address each of the characteristics in random order and some are reverse scored, meaning the same characteristic is sometimes defined by the "Definitely True" response and sometimes by the "Definitely Not True" response. Questions include:

"I like to try new things." (ER)

"I don't enjoy trying new foods." (ER—reverse scored)

"I like being with all kinds of people." (FO)

"I am not good at understanding people when they are different from me." (FO—reverse scored)

"I have a realistic perception of how others see me." (PAC)

"When I am in a new or strange environment, I keep an open mind." (PAC)

"I believe that all people, of whatever race, are equally valuable." (PA)

"My personal value system is based on my own beliefs, not on conformity to other people's standards." (PA)

The completion of such a test allows organizations to generate a statistical profile of how successful administrators believe a potential expatriate or their spouse will be at surviving life abroad. The chief benefits of this type of testing from the perspective of the service providers are that the same test can be applied to any participant and that it generates numerical results, but there are limitations to conclusions that can be drawn from this type of "culture-general" testing.[3]

These personality tests often unintentionally provide a space for expressing unvoiced opposition to the planned move. Given the economic incentives to work abroad and threats of career stagnancy without overseas experience, many workers and their families find it difficult to explicitly express resistance to overseas work and instead mention the loss of family contact or diminished educational opportunities for children as reasons to decline an overseas posting. When asked about testing, several families discussed how they had used their testing experience to avoid working in a particular location or being posted abroad at an inopportune time for the family. Rather than showing outright opposition to the move, respondents might darken ovals corresponding to questions such as "I am not good at understanding people when they are different from me" to achieve their desired placement.[4] These covert forms of opposition may achieve the desired aims of the employer as well, giving notice of those who would rather not participate in the expatriate adventure before vast sums are expended on "failed" expatriates.

To prevent failure, one must also agree about what failure entails, and the most widely cited benchmark is the early return of an international worker from their overseas posting. Much of the cost of "producing" an expatriate lies in the initial selection, preparation and deployment of the worker and family, and thus an early return is a failure to fully capitalize on this investment. Workers return before the end of their assignment most often in their first placement abroad, although "failures" in subsequent postings also occur for diverse reasons. The opening story of Jay and Alison shows how careful attention is paid to some portion of the process, as the couple was thoroughly tested, but little thought is given to individuals, for example to the particular risks of sending a newlywed couple who had never left their homeland to Kathmandu. The high initial outlay means that experienced "successful" expatriates, those who have shown themselves able to remain in-country for the assigned duration, are often induced to continue to accept overseas positions.

The claim that families are the chief cause of failure has become an assumption of international human resources scholarship. In the everyday experiences of the expatriate family, this assumption makes its way into practice through attention paid by companies to the selection of workers based on their family dynamics, the care and preparation of families as well as the awareness of spouses and children of their potential as a liability to the company and the employed family member. As families are swept into the expatriate milieu, they learn of labels applied to them such as "trailing spouse" and "dependent," and monitor themselves to avoid becoming career hazards and being blamed for employee failure.

Structuring Expatriate Families

The very process of expatriation is seen to license employer intervention into domestic life, but the infiltration of work into home life is more than surveillance, it is regulation of family members' behavior and even of what constitutes a family. Through setting limits on who is sponsored by the expatriate package, the employer conveys a message about who is a part of the family and the role they will be expected to play in the labor of the employee. What results from the paradigm of expatriate employment is the structuration of affection,[5] a practice that transforms affective relationships but which must be overlaid with a rhetoric of emotion that confirms the choices made in everyday practices as not merely necessary but natural. Employers' intervention in the domestic world of workers is justified by their benevolent intent, a logic also seen in the interventions of development work, and thus made neutral and natural rather than economically motivated. Justified by forms of compensation for families, spouses are incorporated into the work of the paid employee (Callan and Ardener 1984), resulting in employers' access to labor that serves their business ends, described by one economist as "unpaid market labor" (Philipps 2008).

Families are incorporated actively into the work of the employer but also must serve as the support system to mitigate against failure—or be accused of causing the problem when it occurs. When the discourse on failure arrives at the home of expatriates, it takes on a different character from what international human resources professionals or the employer might intend. Suggestions become commands and mechanisms designed to reduce the stress on mobile families end up producing new concerns. These mechanisms create new responsibilities for the expatriate, exemplified by the "market basket" phenomenon discussed in subsequent chapters, but also seen in practices such as home leave and hardship allowances. The privilege of a biannual trip home can easily become a burden for a family when it becomes a command. In Nepal, several expatriates complained that they had not been able to explore either nearby countries or even Nepal itself because their vacation time was required to be taken as "home leave." Employer intervention in the domestic world of workers that is designed to help families not to fail can itself become a cause of discontent. Under scrutiny and burdened with the obligations of producing a "good" working environment, families are strained to the point where even a vacation becomes a requirement regulated by the employer.

The potential for failure arrives in the everyday lives of expatriate families in diverse forms. One project manager found his job threatened when his project was deemed to be "failing" by the home office when it did not meet deadlines for tasks during the nearly month-long Nepali holiday of Dashain. Another worker "failed" when his wife needed to return home to care for her ailing mother, while a third couple found their daughter's learning disability would not be effectively addressed by the local international school and left the post before the end of the contract. One long-time expatriate was found to have advanced-stage cancer and left Nepal and his job—a trauma that in internal documentation registered as a job failure. International human resources literature does not, and perhaps cannot, address these issues, but reducing them to a numerical quantifiable category of productivity and its absences results in significant losses in specificity and unacknowledged slippages between the descriptive and prescriptive agendas.

The discourse of failure is only one of many structuring elements that transform and mediate expatriate life (Bourdieu 1992: 72). What is often not appreciated about the influence of expatriate policies is the way in which global agendas such as outsourcing or just-in-time delivery systems are not merely ideas promoted by expatriates to third-world entrepreneurs but ones which affect their everyday lives as well. The discourse about expatriate success and failure thus moves between the rhetorical levels of corporate policies and everyday life. Questions about how project failure is assessed have occurred both in the work of expatriates, who are asked to define the numerical targets of an aid program, and in their everyday lives, as their own productivity is evaluated and causes of failure found in their domestic life. Those working on development programs in Nepal were aware of this conjuncture, as one project seeking to promote small business in Nepal was instructing local entrepreneurs on the value of outsourcing specialized tasks in the name of efficiency, while at the same time several of the project's expatriate staff were told that their contracts would not be renewed because the organization was turning to a subcontractor to provide business training for their program. Investigating the presumptions of and debates over expatriate failure uncovers the push to quantification and accountability impinging on international workers that is also a part of the policies middle managers are sent abroad to promote. When the calculus of efficiency and success invades their own homes, these promoters of strictly quantitative evaluation often come to see the drawbacks of such an agenda.

An Expatriate Family and Its Boundaries

In the case of the Nashes, moving between their home and postings abroad changed the boundaries of their family in ways that brought some members closer and threatened to exclude others. The Nashes in their early marriage had traveled throughout South America because of David's job as an advisor on road building projects, and when their first daughter was born, Denise gamely toted her through local markets, but when a second daughter arrived, she declared that although her interest in world travel continued, it would need to be suspended until the girls were older. David reluctantly concurred, despite the many incentives dangled by his employer, but promised that within a few years the family would again work abroad. At home in New Jersey, they settled into a new routine and David was given a stable position at the home office. Every Sunday the Nash clan would gather at their large suburban home, and a rotating cast of extended family and neighbors would round out the dinner table, with numbers reaching a dozen or more. The Sunday supper tradition continued even as the girls became adults, as their older daughter would drive in from the nearby college, often bringing a friend or two along, and their younger daughter introduced a few friends from church to the weekly ritual. Denise's mother often presided over some of the cooking, although standing over the stove was becoming more difficult. The family continued to be interested in the world, and both girls took Spanish in a nod to their early lives in South America. Denise remained in touch with many of her friends from their time as expatriates and sought to vacation overseas, even though she persisted in her opposition to an expatriate position before the girls were well along in their schooling. Each year, David pressed his family to consider going abroad again, but some aspect of the girls' school life or their parents' health intervened.

Fifteen years after their expatriate life ended, the opportunity to work abroad arose again and this time the family assented. David found himself trying to help the Nepali government design hillside roads that would withstand landslides and monsoon flooding. In Nepal, Sunday dinners continued, but now the table was much smaller—just the couple, their younger daughter and the occasional guest who they deemed in need of home cooking, such as myself, were invited to share Denise's traditional American after-church suppers. The Nashes struggled to maintain contact with Denise's elderly mother, who had difficulty communicating by phone or computer. They spoke regularly with her caregivers at the assisted living facility where she had moved a year before their posting. Ellen, the elder daughter, moved into her parents' house with her husband and young daughter while her parents were in Kathmandu. David and Denise's younger daughter, Katherine, accompanied them to Nepal. She had been a quiet, average student in New Jersey, focused on her volunteer activities and church social groups. Social outlets in Nepal were limited, and although mother and daughter became closer, Katherine was losing ground in school and her social life. She graduated from the local international school but found college too daunting a prospect; leaving her parents thousands of miles away for a new life was not something she felt ready for. Yet options were limited, as neither the company that employed David nor the government that hired his company had provisions for children over eighteen and not in school to live with their family. Katherine would need to obtain a visa to stay with her family, and the financial support that they were offered for her education would not fund Nepali language classes nor the walking tours that occupied both mother and daughter. David and Denise decided that these difficulties made extension of their tour in Kathmandu undesirable, and they left after only one three-year stint, having obtained the higher salary that would improve David's retirement income but without all of the cultural adventures that both had seen as potentially being a part of their second expatriate experience. David's posting was a failure: the investment even in this repeat expatriate could not be recouped in just one posting.

The problems faced by the Nash family are not unique. Families that are geographically separated as a result of work are not uncommon today. Yet the difficulties of elite transnational labor migration are not seen by employers as a result of separation itself, but instead are treated as character flaws that can be remedied either through better employee selection or new services and training programs. Ameliorating mechanisms can exacerbate the problems of life abroad, forcing families to respond to the expectations of the employer and follow a prescribed program that is supposed to "fix" them. Trying to describe the often-ineffective attempts to support families, one overseas worker in Nepal retold a story he had heard from his colleague in Japan, where a family had been sent to weekly meetings to resolve their problems with an overscheduled life. "Isn't that crazy . . . but they had to go because the company demanded it." The problems of elder care are often mentioned as difficulties encountered by expatriate families that are poorly addressed by centrally provided human resources tools. The Nashes found it difficult to find anyone to speak to about their concerns, as David's immediate superiors were unfamiliar with the world of international employment because David was one of only a dozen workers they had sent abroad. Difficult questions were referred to a general expatriate support office based in Europe, which did little more than provide the family with a list of eldercare support offices in the United States. The small size of Nepal's expatriate population made finding age-appropriate friends and activities for Katherine difficult, and she was ill-disposed to the many international travelers her age who were in Kathmandu. Again, David's employer was of little help because its solutions were drawn from the conditions of Americans living in Europe, the predominant audience of the secondary service provider.

Outsourcing expatriate selection and services is a technique pursued in recognition of the special skills and knowledge required as well as in the hope of saving money through making the process more efficient (see Sassen 1991). In the case of the Nashes it did the opposite, for while the external agency hired by David's employer had extensive experience in how to support families caring for elderly parents, they had no knowledge of or experience in Nepal, and limited capacity to intervene in the U.S. health care industry. The care work that is taken on by employers in posting workers abroad also implies expectations of similar work to be done by the family, creating links of caring that generate expectations of labor by other family and community members, often those with the fewest resources of time and money to provide such affective labor (cf. Hochschild 1989; Meerman 2001; Ehrenreich and Hochschild 2002; England 2005). The tools of expatriate support often take the form of demands, or requests that are received as demands, on the labor of a non-wage-laboring spouse. The employer's explicit and implicit expectations of the contribution of unpaid market labor of family members encounter resistance from women, who are the majority of the so-called "trailing spouses" (Philipps 2008). In addition to the frustration expressed over the lack of respect and money received for performing functions that are necessary for the success of the paid employee, women—still the predominant trailing spouses in Nepal in the 1990s—are also burdened with implementing the prescriptions of human relations professionals, with echoes of the family as source of employee failure still in their minds. The tasks of helpmate and homemaker are assigned to spouses, and their partner's success is seen to depend on their accomplishment of these responsibilities. Spouses are well aware of the rhetoric of "family failure" and thus they imbue their home labor as well as their own emotional practices with the pressure of generating success for their working husbands.

The process of removing expatriate selection from the purview of the employer to a secondary entity allows for a redistribution of responsibility and the obviation of employers' attention to the concerns of what were once friends and colleagues, who through this process become "resources" that may or may not be performing. Overseas employees often worry that being removed from the day-to-day conversations in the office places them at a disadvantage, especially in countries like Nepal where keeping in touch is challenging. The outsourcing of many aspects of expatriate management enacts a similar abstraction where the concerns of an employee shift from being those of a known colleague to issues of the failure of a human resource. Through specialized services and financial provisions, expatriate difficulties are presumed to have been "dealt with" by the service and thus employers are led to conclude that any lack on the part of the workers is a result of personal inadequacies. Although costs of expatriate failure are still in part borne by the employer, the risk has also been redistributed to the worker and the subcontractor. By producing a neat package of compensations that acknowledges the challenges of international employment through the generation of salubrious conditions and financial compensation, the employer can claim to have accounted for expatriate life and thus to have eliminated the problems of overseas employment. As one expatriate employment consultant said, "They have nothing to complain about—look at what they're making—wish I could get that." Yet it is not possible to eradicate many of the problems of expatriacy without eliminating geographical displacement itself—or discounting human connections. Most of the problems that families living abroad encounter are endemic to the expatriate condition, and yet the nature of work and distance are not able to enter into the accounting processes of IHRM. The result is a double-shift of labor for many women as they seek to ameliorate the difficulties of living in another country as well as the difficulties of living under a regime of accountability.

What Is an Expatriate Family?

Within the IHRM literature, failure is defined in relation to the job tasks of the employee, and although families are ascribed responsibility for that inability to perform, little attention is paid to defining the expatriate family. As in the examples where illness, a child's education, or a couple's happiness cause a departure from post, family success may necessitate expatriate failure. The stresses that cause many to leave Nepal before their contract is over are often inherent in the expatriate situation, and thus not epiphenomenal to working overseas. The endemic condition of living abroad cannot be meliorated by more testing, cultural awareness, or support hotlines. To understand the framing of "families that fail," it is first necessary to understand how the expatriate family is defined and transformed by life overseas.

The nature of the expatriate family is oftentimes taken to be self-evident, for it is the "norm" in contrast to the family patterns of the Other. Distinctive family structures are a subject addressed in cultural education classes where expatriates learn about polygamy and polyandry in Nepal, practices that differ from those of "normal" expatriate families. Even as companies are being required to make explicit policies that define the nature of a family, the expectation of a heterosexual nuclear family for expatriates is unquestioned, particularly in compensation and selection processes. The narrow demographic profile of expatriate families in Nepal is a result of constraints placed upon workers' family structure as well as those they place upon themselves.[6] Parents are discouraged from bringing their newborn children to Kathmandu because of health conditions and lack of what is perceived as appropriate medical care for Western babies. Conversely, many families are told that Nepal is an ideal place to have toddlers and preschool-aged children because household help is very inexpensive. One woman remarked that she had raised all of her children in "the third world" and could not imagine doing otherwise, while another mother remarked that after having struggled with finding and paying for day care in Japan, were she to have another child, she would do so in Nepal. The age at which many families are having young children also frequently correlates with a particular level in the career advancement of expatriate workers. Because Nepal is a small country and, to much of the world, of limited political importance, many in the diplomatic corps come to Kathmandu as their first overseas posting at a particular rank. Aid and business circles have similar practices in hierarchy and promotion, and young workers find themselves drawn into overseas careers partly by the additional salary that is part of work at a "hardship post," which sets a basis of income expectation that is difficult to replicate at the home office. As the story of Alison and Jay suggests, the narrow demographic of Expatria in Nepal can also have a self-fulfilling character. With many of the activities for spouses arranged around school events or volunteer and recreational clubs, Kathmandu can be a lonely place for expatriates with other interests and life positions.

Although families with children predominated in the early years of expatriate labor in Nepal, new family profiles appearing in the late 1990s and into the new millennium included empty nest couples, retired men "trailing" younger working women and men living apart from their families while in Nepal. Several expatriates were pursuing work in Kathmandu as a preretirement adventure or a postretirement second career. Diane, now in the preretirement stage of her expatriate trajectory, noted the advantages of living in Nepal with her husband: "I see my children more than I did in Australia. Everyone wants to visit Kathmandu." Her college-aged children did visit them, some as part of a vacation, while one used the opportunity to experiment with an interest in overseas work, staying with her parents for several months. One demographic group of expatriate workers grew rapidly after 2001 as a result of the increasing importance of subcontracting as well as safety concerns about Nepal—single men or men living as if single. These short-term workers often use a three-month period of lucrative labor to fund more free time at home as well as to enjoy liaisons in various postings. There was a distinct division in Kathmandu between these bachelor employees and the long-term posted families, both geographically and socially, and employers are still negotiating how to address this new constituency for which they currently lack housing, policy and statistical history.

Having identified "families" as the source of failure, expatriate employers seek to support them, but in doing so often redefine what constitutes a family. Katherine Nash found herself defined out of her family at age eighteen. James, a married man living in Kathmandu for over two years, found little support for the expenses associated with keeping in touch with his wife and many in the community openly criticized the couple's decision to live apart. One of Alison's complaints about life as an expatriate wife was her belief that if she had children, this would have brought her more acceptance and social opportunities rather than isolation and the eventual production of another expatriate failure caused by family issues. In the early part of the 2000s in Nepal, several governments and other employers were somewhat surprised that what they saw as merely a change in hiring practices to make their organizations more efficient had produced a demographic profile of workers very different from the one they had before; they had little experience or resources to support men like James, who were becoming more common in Kathmandu. Having lived for many years in one type of expatriate situation, the head of community and family services for one government was at a loss as to how to do her job: the single men and short-term workers whom she was now charged with supporting were unfamiliar to her and the tools provided by her superiors inadequate, still directed toward serving trailing spouses and children. At one point she sought my expertise as a social scientist, hoping I could explain why the population was changing: "These guys don't want movie nights . . . I can't even find enough kids to make an Easter Bunny work." One of her biggest problems was finding housing; the government had taken out long-term leases on houses in the Kathmandu Valley that were designed to accommodate families with children and associated servants. These homes held little appeal for James, who feared he would become lonely in such a large house far from the social life of the city. He pressed to be allowed to stay in the hotel suite that was supposed to be his temporary residence, and the government found it was less expensive than the staff, car and upkeep of a home, so it gave permission. She observed that the work that was being done by those with her government had not changed drastically, but the population of expatriate workers had, and she struggled to convey to her bosses that what they saw as minor policy changes was having a dramatic effect on her job and community.

Despite these changes, "normal" expatriate families are still the assumed demographic in Nepal, although with their numbers shrinking they are struggling to maintain long-standing social organizations and institutions. Concerns about whether there would be enough kids for the school swim team and the long-term viability of several sports clubs were frequent in the early 2000s. As membership declined in the international Christian church, the bridge club and other groups that had given expatriates an outlet for social networks lost through expatriation, many families turned inward, retreating to home movie nights, a practice seen as positive by some IHRM scholarship, which observes that expatriate parents and children often become closer while overseas. One consulting agency describes "the family bubble" this way: "An expatriate family is really the ultimate of nuclear families. . . . Father, mother, children, immediate members of the nuclear family, must look to one another for the support provided other families by their external community."[7] Often the displacement that defines the expatriate life requires families to use the family bubble not only as a source of sociality but to find jobs and develop skills.

The Morris family's bubble-like existence made expatriate life like a family business for them. It was Manuel's work that brought them to Kathmandu, but while there Cindy was able to use experience gained in other postings to secure a government position, assisting new arrivals and providing services to resident nationals. Her adult daughter had found an embassy position in their previous posting and she stayed on at that post when the rest of the family moved to Nepal. Their son graduated from an international school in Kathmandu and found a local position working with the government as well, although he was hoping to transfer to a job at their last posting, where he had fallen in love with a local woman who worked at the embassy with his father. A second daughter was hired as a consultant for an agency doing work in Kathmandu, although off the books, as her employment likely violated both her visa and diplomatic nepotism rules. Sharing diverse experiences as they had moved across the globe made the Morrises a very close family, but they found it difficult to integrate into the expatriate community in Nepal, in part because some people had objections to their practice of hiring family members and in part because they were described as "difficult." Other youth found the Morris kids unwilling to compromise on group activities and adults claimed the Morrises had few topics of interest on which they could find common ground. The husband's high position got them invited to many social events, but often not a second time. The Morrises were aware of their isolating tendencies, but were proud of how close they were as a family, and the children anticipated continuing their careers abroad, likely producing a new generation of bubble families.

Policy and compensation practices claim to respond to family configurations, but often produce families acceptable to existing policy instead, as expatriates find the decision to get (or stay) married or have children influenced by their employers' compensation practices. The relationship between employer support of families and the actual needs of families demonstrates its limits in a story told by Susanne, who had at least six postings to draw from. During a rambling discussion about the upcoming summer vacation period, women compared notes on the decision to keep the family in Kathmandu over the summer or to return home with the children, affording the opportunity for summer camps and reacquainting kids with friends and relatives at home. While many saw the break from life in Kathmandu as a valuable chance for children to experience the traditional joys of a summer vacation, there was anxiety about the men left behind. "At least it's not like Thailand," Susanne said, describing how her husband's company had offered to provide a colleague with a "summer wife" to take the place of his own absent spouse. She compared the company's procurement of staff for families with its willingness to procure sexual partners for employees, aghast at the hypocrisy of this practice alongside the corporate-sponsored "family nights," where the organization held a cocktail party in one room while kids were entertained nearby. The conversation then turned to the history of couples in the community, with particular criticism of men who had divorced their expatriate wives while overseas and subsequently married local women. The corporate provisioning of partners for employees indicates an instrumental understanding of the value of expatriate families as tools, not unlike colonial government practices in India mentioned in the last chapter. The attention paid to the happiness of wives and children is in the service of making productive workers, and if a summer liaison accomplishes this, some organizations are willing to supply that need.

I Want My *Own* Job

The work-leisure dichotomy and its association with a spatial division into public and private spheres has been a key framework for the post–Industrial Revolution examination of work lives (cf. Thompson 1967; Habermas 1995), although this division has often been questioned for its class and gendered assumptions (cf. Hochschild 1989; Fraser 1990, Calhoun 1992; Warner 2002). Expatriacy radically problematizes the divide between work and home, labor and leisure, and even the limits of defining what employment is—looking at times more like a pre–Industrial Revolution form of home-based labor that depends on a "primitive" definition of the working unit (Sahlins 1974;

Engels 1978; Pateman 1988). The division between a worker's career and a private family life, although often eroded in other situations, disintegrates in Expatria, exacerbated by the intervention of employers into domestic life (Tremayne 1984). The breadwinner's job is the reason families move abroad, intrinsically embedding family life within the paradigm of expatriate work. Compensation for expatriates is focused on the family unit, with salary supplements and hardship allowances determined by the number of "dependents" that the employee supports, making this form of labor exemplary of the "family wage" system, based, implicitly if no longer explicitly, on the assumption of a male breadwinner. Although the term is now resisted by many, the common referent for the partners of expatriate workers is *trailing spouse*—emphasizing the subsidiary and secondary nature of their participation in expatriacy. Through the mechanisms of support and transplantation, the family is incorporated into the male's job, which results not merely in financial incentives but also in expectations. While the employer takes responsibility for the education, food and housing of the employee and his family, it expects certain forms of labor in return.

Nancy, the wife of a high-ranking man in an organization with a large expatriate presence in Nepal, mounted her own campaign against these expectations, and although she achieved her personal goal, the gendered labor dynamics of the expatriate world were preserved. The organization held several events each week at her home, where she was expected to act as hostess. Although all the events were well-staffed and catered, it was nonetheless a significant demand on her time and necessitated being "on stage" for long evenings. In past postings, she had merely had to attend such events occasionally, but with her husband's promotion as a part of their move to Nepal, there were more demands for her presence as the boss's wife. Nancy had never enjoyed these employer-sponsored events, although she was a very social person and active in many clubs and volunteer activities in Nepal and past postings. Given her long experience living overseas combined with the new possibilities offered by the Internet, in the late 1990s Nancy decided she wanted to return to an old dream, to write a book, maybe a mystery novel, that utilized her knowledge of different parts of the world. She bought books on becoming a published author and set herself a writing schedule, one that made her regular attendance at receptions an even greater burden, and she discussed the possibility of skipping all but the most important events with her husband, which he fully supported. When he discussed this with the home office, the couple was called in to a phone conference where Nancy discussed her new interests and request.

The employer noted that all of the other attendees would be bringing their spouses and that her attendance was not only appreciated but also necessary. Nancy noted that she did not mind the use of her house, she was happy to retreat to her office during the events, but pressed her case, offering to attend some percentage of the events. The response from her husband's superior first called upon the potential impact on the employer's image and on the work of her husband, suggesting that her absence would negatively affect his ability to do his job, and ultimately threatening that some of the family's financial incentives might be taken away if she refused. "They said that the reason we were given this big house was so we could host events," Nancy recalled, wondering if they would really move them just because she would not attend every cocktail party. Several weeks passed and a compromise was found where she could skip some events as long as she could find another woman in the organization to act as hostess. Given Nancy's vast array of friends in the organization, she found many spouses or female employees willing to act in her stead on occasion. Among the expatriate community in Kathmandu, there were chuckles about who would be playing "Nancy" at a night's event.

Employers recognize the hardship of moving one member of a couple for career purposes and strive to employ spouses in their own organization when open-market local employment is impractical. Many women cultivate skills that they hope will help them secure positions as teachers, administrative staff and health care workers—the kinds of jobs they may be able to obtain while abroad. Although Nepal still has far fewer dual-career expatriate couples than the home countries from which families move, nonetheless, the changing gender dynamic of the work environment in their home countries is producing slow changes for many trailing spouses. Yet expatriate employment in Nepal is still largely led by male jobs. One husband, formerly an expatriate worker himself and now a "trailing spouse," remarked that the system just was not set up for him—"I have no interest in the coffee hours and sewing circles"—yet his wife's prominent position seemed to require his attendance. For example, since his wife was an ambassador, he was, by position, supposed to lead the national woman's organization in Nepal. In his complaint, one can see how the structures of the expatriate system (re)enforce gender and family norms in the elementary school teaching jobs reserved for spouses and the receptions for arriving spouses that focus on stereotypically feminine interests such as handicrafts and shopping.

Education allowances, subsidies for housing and moving costs and hardship pay are all assessed based on the family unit, which is supported with an eye to its positive influence on the primary employee. Many governments and companies are quite explicit about "hiring the family." The difficult working conditions in Nepal, including intermittent power outages, frequent local holidays and occasional shortages of various goods, often generate the need to call expatriate spouses into service to act as temporary secretaries for absent workers, feed last-minute guests or house displaced colleagues. While the idea of a "company wife" may hearken back to practices presumed dead (Callan and Ardener 1984), this may be a misrecognition, as even outside the expatriate context women continue to provide unpaid market labor or are asked to accede to demands for mobility and flexibility in moments of economic strain (Phillips 2008). Hidden behind claims of a company that is "like a family" or employers' programs of family support are time demands. Thus, expatriate wives find themselves exchanging their freedom for compensation proffered out of concern over the family's role in a worker's success. They are faced with a double-edged sword of paternalism, with the employer providing support for the family at significant cost to their independence.

The unalterable elements of expatriate lives have a great effect on success and happiness, yet cannot be considered potential sources of failure. The inability to have a second worker in the family often causes tension that cannot be addressed by expatriate service providers or employers. Many middle-aged women in Nepal were saddened by the inability to have a career, as most had strong educational backgrounds and had anticipated being part of a two-career couple when they married. Frequently, women noted that career concerns had been a part of their discussions with their spouses about an initial overseas posting and that often they had assented to going abroad as something that they would do for a few years, just for the adventure. Now, with an inquiring anthropologist listening, many were unable to pinpoint when "a few years" became the ten, twenty or more that they had lived abroad. One woman observed that the increases in her husband's salary made her own labor unnecessary for the family income and she found that she did not miss the career for which she had been trained. A very different perspective came from a woman who had trained as a computer programmer and continued to think of herself in this way. During our discussion she started to tear up, realizing that her training was now obsolete and she would be unemployable in the current European marketplace without going back to a university for a completely new degree, something she believed she was unlikely ever to undertake.

Women and the occasional male trailing spouse are inevitably and necessarily caught up in the work that has brought about the family's displacement.

These obligations of a secondary laborer have been observed in colonial practice, corporate expectations and the definition of the bourgeois family (Smith
1975). While many expatriate families in Kathmandu saw single-worker households as merely an echo of their own childhood with a single parent in the
paid workforce, other couples told of coming from two-career families and
noted that expatriate single-worker couples marked a change from their own
youth. Many expatriate women deeply felt the undervaluation of work within
the home, particularly in light of the widespread use of household help in
Nepal. The economic conditions in the country caused many women to redefine their value in terms of contributions to Nepal through volunteer work
with educational facilities, orphanages and health care, as they had lost their
self-identification as either professional women or homemakers. Yet labor is of
little value in Nepal, and many women found it difficult to find even volunteer
opportunities that were fulfilling. Devotion to the task of family security and
happiness was embraced by employers as well as some women who saw the
domestic sphere as a space to achieve the fulfillment that wage labor might have
provided outside of the expatriate context.

In Nepal, spouses are restricted by local visa laws from earning money in-
country, and many are banned by their husbands' companies from driving,
which becomes a necessity for those placed in isolated, detached homes across
the Valley; yet they are expected to have extensive social, familial and community responsibilities particular to expatriate life. The situation of expatriate families illustrates changes that are occurring elsewhere with respect to the
power employers have to dictate the structure of their employees' lives. The rise
of women in the market labor force was expected to precipitate a decline in
the exploitation of women's unpaid market labor, but there are still employer
expectations, in Expatria and elsewhere, of getting a two-for-one deal as well
as the potential for discrimination against those who are not able to bring additional labor-hours to the job in a situation of employment scarcity (Stroh
and Brett 1996: 198).

The "family wage" logic was used to justify disparities between male and
female compensation through the assumed need of men to support a family.
The assumption that the family is supported by male work persists within expatriate settings, as companies and governments are aware that couples lose the
opportunity to have a two-income family when working abroad, but they only
recognize this as a financial loss, not a loss of identity or self-worth. The expatriate contract itself is structured in ways that acknowledge the transformation
of the needs of the family as a result of overseas posting, providing additional

funds for children's private school education, travel expenses for holidays in the home country and a lump sum for buying household goods needed to set up a new abode. Although the expectation that spouses act as hostesses has long been a part of some corporate cultures, the financial compensation provided to families is seen to give greater justification to these demands. Given that the employer, be it corporate or government, is the only reason why the family is living abroad, it structures the lifestyle of the family in Nepal, viewing with paternal interest the activities of the family, or as one woman, complaining about attending her third cocktail party in a week noted, "They own us." In the end, one is left wondering whether expatriate failure is a function of families or family failure is a function of expatriacy.

Making Home in Expatria

Although Joan's shipment had only arrived days before my visit, she already seemed comfortably settled in. "It's not hard," she remarked, "I already know where everything goes." Joan's husband's employer had found a way to obviate some of the minor hassles of its employees' three-year rotations by building homes in the sites where they had offices that were largely identical. The couch that the couple had used in Hong Kong fit in the same niche in the Kathmandu house. The windows, Joan noted, were of a slightly different size in this house than in past ones, necessitating the creation of new curtains, but other than that, everything had already found its place from the recently unpacked crates. Making the family's domestic space the same across various postings eased the difficulty of moving for Joan and her husband. She remarked that she occasionally woke up not knowing which country she was in, but this was made less disconcerting because she could nonetheless find the bathroom in the dark. There were several designs for homes based on the number of dependents and the rank of the worker, but within a given classification of houses, everything was kept as alike as possible. Even when the family rotated home, they lived in identical corporate-provided housing. For Joan, the transnational Levittown created by this system was something she liked, as she found it enabled her to get started living in a new country more quickly than having to spend the first few weeks of a new posting acquiring furnishings and becoming accustomed to new layouts. Her husband had a military background, and she followed a military-like routine despite the many moves, keeping their meals consistent in both time and content. Just a week after arriving in Kathmandu, Joan already had the couple in their normal schedule. Not only had she organized the house but she had formed an exercise group like one in her last posting and found a volunteer position with a local library. There were local problems that she encountered, with finding cheese and running out of a favorite cleanser that was not available locally, but for this couple the ideal of Expatria seemed to be in effect. There was little disruption of their lives as they moved as long as they kept within the company framework. They could move effortlessly into an "E14" home, and Joan suspected the cat that had been with them through several postings did not even know that a move had occurred.

The physical space of the expatriate home is the site where many antifailure efforts are centered. Both families and employers presume that the creation of a domestic space that allows the worker to rest and recuperate is central to assuaging the difficulties of life abroad. The motives and means for generating this haven, though, are different. Having to move every few years is an obvious source of instability, but it also defines expatriate life. Thus employers try to smooth the transition through strategies like the identical houses in which Joan has lived. While it is impossible for spouses and children to erase the daily concerns of finances, report cards and everyday domestic conflict, many women strive to produce a calm space at home, which often entails making the house consistent across postings and relatively devoid of local context. Nepali influence appears in very limited contexts, such as the accessories and gifts collected by expatriates, and both spouses and employers work to eliminate reminders that they are in Nepal and strive to create a zone of "normalcy." Employers facilitate the provisioning of these displaced zones of familiarity, encouraging families to bring furniture, housewares and appliances with them in their moves. One woman went on a company-sponsored shopping spree for appliances before leaving the United States. These were shipped directly to Nepal, where she learned of the difference in electric current. A series of transformers had to be acquired, none of which could make her American dishwasher run. Furthermore, the washing machine that had been put in a covered porch area proved nearly impossible for her household help understand, and thus it remained unused most of the time. The familiar commodities provide only the framework for the household; they must be transformed into a home by the introduction of family labor.

Expatriate women go to great lengths to produce homes devoid of the problems of the local environment for their families. Although many expatriate families display art and artifacts from their various postings as part of household décor, the infrastructure of the home remains "decultured." The specificity of European, American and Australian homes is often glossed not as particular to their nationality but as normal, and women endeavor to make a "normal" home for their families. The language of war and battle is frequently used to describe the struggle to keep the local environment at bay. Even with the assistance of housekeepers and other staff, women struggle to keep dust and dirt out of the house to make the place "just like home."

The maintenance of a routine in Nepal is a trial, as spouses fight power outages, local holidays and frequent transportation strikes that threaten to undermine the attempt to ensure that the family eats dinner at a consistent hour, an obligation that is seen as a high-stakes demand by many. "I'm afraid [her son] won't do well in school," said one mother as she discussed with others the need to acquire posters of his favorite sports star to overcome his unhappiness with the family's latest move to Nepal. Another woman fretted over her inability to personally, or with the help of her staff, keep things clean enough to suit her fastidious husband, and worried that the disruption of how he liked the house kept would harm his work performance—bad housekeeping could eventually lead to his being fired. The job of homemaking—producing (in Nepal with the aid of local servants) a familiar and comfortable house—is a task seen as vital to the capacity of the family to be successful abroad. The creation of children's space is addressed both in terms of protection from the local and of generating a "normal" experience. Guilt over taking kids away from the childhood they might have otherwise experienced is a common concern, and by generating bedrooms filled with the latest electronic toys and posters of popular musicians from their home countries, women hope to mitigate the effect of a choice that their children did not make for themselves, to live abroad.

Holidays have often brought out the most vigorous attempts to produce a familiar routine in Nepal. Over a pre-Christmas dinner in Kathmandu with the Connellys, I remarked on the profusion of holiday decorations, including an elaborate wooden manger scene and a tall brass carousel made to revolve by the candles burning below it. The dinner table was set with red flowers and a complete set of dishes with Christmas trees at the center. "I had to give up a lot for these dishes," the hostess remarked, noting that she brought these as part of her limited shipment rather than other more frequently used items because she felt that having a feeling of home around Christmastime was very important. The menu for dinner had remained the same over the family's five different postings. The couple described how various dishes came from the Midwestern American background they both shared. The Connellys enjoyed sharing their family traditions with nostalgic fellow Americans as well as introducing expatriates of other nationalities to their special holiday treats, including the divinity fudge made with a recipe passed down for many generations. Comparing the challenges of Christmas overseas became a central topic of dinner conversation as Mrs. Connelly described how she had convinced their children that Santa would find them in various locations and that the absence of a chimney in one of their houses would not deter him from bringing gifts. Although their children were now in the United States, they maintained many of the same rituals, explaining that with all the moving they had done over the years, the familiarity of the decorations they had carried across at least three continents continued to bring them comfort.

It is in the labor of creating normalcy that women see themselves as obviating failure in the expatriate experience, yet this is a labor that is often undertaken above and beyond the other work that spouses do to prevent the "failure" feared by expatriate management professionals. The creation of a familiar domestic space and family routines, many expatriate spouses believe, is their best hope to help their families while abroad. Employers facilitate this through income supplements and goods, but rarely pay attention to the labor expended by women in this goal. Only fellow expatriates recognize the expenditure of effort in this pursuit and provide a venue for empathetic discussions of the struggle to maintain routine. In this environment, a woman at the end of her tour in

The Snack Bar at Phora Durbar, the American Recreational Club. Author photo, December 1999.

Kathmandu anticipated the family's return to the United States, and what she most looked forward to was the lack of surveillance by the employer, when she would no longer have to fake being happy all the time for the good of her husband's job. "Just like Disney," she explained, her husband's employer expected her to be smiling at every moment. Complaints about the lack of recognition of women's carework in general, and about the requirement to produce expatriate normalcy in particular, were often the beginning of more vociferous complaints about an employer's exploitation.

Conclusion

The resistance of expatriates to what they see as employer intrusion into their private lives is a product of the life changes that occur as a part of expatriation. The same employer that at home exhibited a benign neglect of workers and their families, when abroad becomes deeply invested in the minutiae of family life, especially given the costs of failure. It is the mere fact of taking a family unit, moving them because of one member's career thousands of miles across the globe, and putting them down in a necessarily incomplete cocoon of "normalcy" that generates many of the problems of expatriate life. The divide between work life and home life that families have come to expect is eroded as they receive "advice" about shopping, decoration, health and education from their employer. The family also takes on new importance as a source of anxiety rather than support. The affective work of the domestic unit has been incompletely replaced by the employer, and the family becomes a threat and is threatened. The accusatory finger of blame points at the wife and children, suggesting that something might be wrong with them that could impact the worker's on-the-job success.

The intrusion of the company into the life of the expatriate family cannot be merely addressed as an intervention of the public world of work into the private world of the family, for that barrier is crossed in the mere act of expatriation. In removing families from the embrace of a familiar set of social and economic supports, the employer takes on responsibility for replacing those services, but how this task is implemented has its basis in quite contemporary practices of neoliberal business. In outsourcing both the philosophy and practice of expatriate support to secondary, specialized agencies, employers redistribute blame and labor onto families. Companies purchase their absolution, enabling them to presume that a well-vetted secondary contractor will do the right thing and hoping, through careful measurement, that the services they procure will reduce the chance of worker failure. Yet each participant seems blinded to many of the motivations of the others, presuming that the agenda of the company is equivalent to that of the worker, that the pursuits of the human resources professional align with those of the employer and ultimately, that passing money along the system will purchase the employee's success.

Once, outsourcing and offshoring appeared as a blue-collar problem, discussed in the business pages as an economizing strategy that affected only "menial" factory work. NAFTA's advocates suggested the mobility of labor would ultimately help American workers through better utilization of their superior job skills as well as economizing within U.S. corporations. Over time, Europe and the United States have seen new anxiety about outsourcing as awareness is increased about the potential mobility of nearly all jobs. With this comes a greater fragility of white-collar jobs and a diminishing ability to resist new corporate structuration. In this environment, executives find themselves advocating for greater market control, privatization and efficiencies for their company, as they (or their coworkers) are downsized, deskilled and made redundant. Expatriate workers exist at the pinnacle of the global labor market, seemingly in command of transnational flows of capital and projects. Yet, as the discourse on failure suggests, even these power brokers find themselves subject to the negative repercussions of disintegration and outsourcing.

The field of international human resources management demands its own form of deskilling, a process whereby the specificities of any job or career are transformed into generalizable units that can be subject to processes of accountability (Strathern 2000a). The work of eliminating leprosy, negotiating peace treaties or importing carpets must be made comparable through translation to a generalizable labor unit—an equivalency process familiar to Marxists, but with a novel twist in the outsourced economy. Understanding workers as resources makes their output an element in the quest for efficiency and maximization that translates Taylorist processes to non-assembly-line, "highly-skilled" tasks. In the quest for expatriate success, the mechanisms of productivity are ever further outsourced, deskilled and subcontracted, creating a never-ending linage of processes of measurement, documentation and self-sustaining reports of accomplishment. On the ground, the challenges of this system, long known to those already impinged upon by these neoliberal processes, are appearing in the lives of expatriates. This has particular irony in Nepal, where the necessity and limits of quantification and measurement have long been a part of the critique of development, but now the same questions are raised in the lives of the developers themselves (cf. Escobar 1995).

The evaluation of expatriate practices is constrained by the preconditions of evaluation and the mechanisms that are permitted to apply. Given the networks and types of agents participating in expatriate assessment, the attribution of failure to families is inevitable. The testing tools of psychology are enrolled to produce acceptable conclusions, ones that attribute the problems of international employment to individual character flaws rather than structural dysfunction. Families provide the ideal site for placing blame, as it externalizes the obstacle, making the family, and especially the spouse, a scapegoat for the worker, who could continue to be promoted as a good choice for overseas employment if only those problematic domestic affiliations did not exist.

The betwixt-and-between position of the elite expatriate worker is crafted by the different lenses through which mediation is viewed. To the human resources scholar, the expatriate is a laborer, and the deskilling of his labor, either in practice or in theory, facilitates a more transportable and translatable analysis. By homogenizing the work of the expatriate, the expatriate family and the home and host countries, those who provide expatriate services can attain greater economies of scale and thus greater efficiency. From the perspective of the local targets of expatriate work in Nepal, the expatriate professional is himself the homogenizer. His job is often to simplify and translate local culture, problems and practices into the transnationally understood language of business and governance, a language with its own presumptive universality. What is often neglected is the culture of Expatria itself, which disrupts the duality of a global-local view of the world. The career path of the expatriate, as he passes between various locations and job titles, persists as the continuity-granting narrative that makes expatriate life tenable for many, and yet this culture and life course is largely invisible given the presumptions about who "has culture" in this world.

The desire to avoid "having culture" is bound up with a linear progress narrative (Fabian 1983) wherein distinction is something possessed only by "Others." Mechanisms provided by the employer are designed to shore up the family against the intrusion of difference from the surrounding territory, as if, like the premonsoon dust, culture is, for expatriates, matter out of place (Douglas 1966). The goal is a clean, culturally pure home which is seen to be the ideal setting for cultivating successful expatriates. Women, by and large, are tasked with these two missions of purification, of removing dirt and removing difference. Yet what is left is not a void. The expatriate home is deeply enmeshed in understandings of the "right" way to live, which is not acknowledged as particular and instead is claimed to be universal, or just the normal way things are done. This normalcy requires a great deal of work that is acknowledged only monetarily by employers. Therefore, while the development professionals wonder why their carefully designed project, although quantitatively successful, has not generated local acclaim, human resources professionals wonder why the development workers, who tested well on the cross-cultural exams and received generous financial support, come home early. There is only one answer—it must be the family's fault.

3 Market Basket Economics
The Practice of Paperwork and Shopping like an Expatriate

COMMODITY AND BRAND AWARENESS begin early in life and, even at seven, expatriate children in Nepal are aware of the distinctions that rule their parents' consumption choices and able to influence what goes in the family shopping basket. Shakti Flakes just were not the same as real Kellogg's Corn Flakes according to Justin, and he refused to eat them. But his mother hadn't had a chance to go shopping at the commissary recently and the Indian-made brand was all that was in the house. When she realized they were out of cereal, she had sent a member of her household staff to the neighborhood store, where Shakti Flakes were the only brand on sale. This morning Sarah was trying to convince her son there was no difference between this cereal and the one they ate every morning for breakfast. Without the rooster on the front of the box, her son was not going to be persuaded even if it tasted the same. After some bribery and a literal sweetening of the deal, she was able to get Justin to eat and out the door, only a few minutes late for school. Her son's temper tantrum had made her late for Bible study and her profuse apologies were greeted with sympathy by the other young mothers in the group who had similar stories to tell. All of them had experienced problems with children unwilling to accept the substitutes that were available in Nepal for favorite foods or toys. One mother offered a tip—she had held on to the containers for the commissary-purchased snacks her son loved but occasionally refilled them with local products when the commissary was out of stock. "I can't believe you would do that," remarked one member of the Bible group. "Just wait until you have kids," was the response, and conversation continued about what each woman had endured in order to accommodate children's demands.

Cornflakes at Bhat Bhateni Supermarket. Author photo, April 2012.

The Bible study group digressed into discussing a difficulty that was on the mind of many expatriate parents of daughters in late 1999—how to acquire American Girl dolls. Heidi had just begun her posting in Nepal in the fall, moving with her two daughters and husband from near Chicago, where the family had been posted at the home office for three years. Heidi's daughters had visited the newly opened American Girl Palace in Chicago over the summer before leaving for Kathmandu and had brought with them several dolls that spurred the interest of other girls in collecting. These personalized and collectable dolls were difficult to acquire in the U.S. in 1999, and unheard of in Nepal. The popularity of these toys among the girls in Heidi's daughters' classes was extensive, and many mothers found themselves besieged with requests for American Girl dolls for Christmas, if not sooner. Expatriate parents contacted friends and relatives in the United States to try to acquire particular dolls and some were able to use diplomatic mailing privileges to get them sent to Kathmandu. Such quests for foreign goods, especially those important to children or associated with family traditions, were frequent for expatriate families in Nepal, and stories of skillful utilization of networks were mined for strategies by newcomers and produced a sense of accomplishment in those able to procure elusive goods. Although the American Girl doll phenomenon proved particularly challenging given the quick rise in popularity of the dolls and their scarcity in the United States, nonetheless, I saw many of these dolls clutched by young expatriate girls after Christmas.

In expatriate Nepal, quests after particular goods for the family are generated not only from fears of children revolting but also by an expatriate compensation system that expects particular types of purchasing, which are dictated as much by the labels attached to particular piles of money as the labels expatriate children demand. The system of compensation in many ways defines who is and is not an expatriate. Salary supplements and hardship allowances announce to all that a worker is employed in a career transcending the posting in Nepal and that working in Kathmandu is a sacrifice worthy of additional recompense. This divide is particularly important in Nepal, where there is a large population of resident foreigners who are not, by this compensation-driven definition, expatriates. The tension that existed between long-term resident foreigners and package expatriates was often explained to me as a divide between those whose work brings them to Nepal (expatriates) and those who will do any work to stay in Nepal (resident foreigners). The compensation packages that are a part of expatriate employment orient families towards a relationship with Nepal and their home country through salary scales, consumption expectations and career demands. This chapter explores expatriate consumer practices in Nepal and how they are shaped, initially by employer regulations and dispensations, and subsequently by interactions within the expatriate community in Kathmandu. The structure of overseas employment compensation generates a prescription of what goods are appropriate for foreign families. The "balance sheet" approach to compensation, which includes practices such as "market basket" supplements, incorporates assumptions about the expatriate family, including a call for the use of "decultured" or "acultural" consumer products. Through financial dispensations, employers seek to bring the expatriate family the opportunity to acquire a set of "normal" goods, ones that would not disrupt their way of life merely because of their overseas posting. The assumption is that expatriates want to eat meals just like the meals at home, and that they will be able to find the appropriate ingredients to do so. In this chapter, the oft-proclaimed global marketplace finds its limits with the struggle, and sometimes failure, to get real Kellogg's Corn Flakes and American Girl dolls in Kathmandu.

The complex bureaucracy that expatriate compensation entails is produced in service of several employer goals, such as standardization of career experience across postings and making the conditions in different locations equivalent through financial incentives, all the while minimizing expenses. Through the diverse forms of expatriate compensation, experts seek to generate a precise and globally equitable calculation of the financial costs of a worker's geographic displacement. In practice, these procedures do little to negate displacement and often generate work for those responsible for gathering the prescribed goods. Furthermore, spouses, who are seen in other contexts as a source of potential failure, are assigned a new duty of procuring the decultured goods and generating data about consumption in Nepal by which their families, as well as their neighbors, will have their compensation determined. Still, the social nature of shopping undertaken by expatriates and the frequent need to learn new consumption rules in a setting of constant mobility also produce an opportunity to develop a sense of belonging. Thus even though this system of market basket and balance sheet compensation is treated with great cynicism by many recipients, the shared struggle to work within and around these bureaucratic structures defines, through everyday consumer practices, who is a part of Expatria.

This system of compensation for displacement is based on the claim that all difference can be overcome if only the correct metric can be produced. Yet it also generates an unintended outcome, a sense of expatriate culture produced by the shared negotiation of these practices. The ability to numerically account for difference affirms the validity of the processes of cultural translation that are central to the expatriate task. Thus, while women are engaged in trying to translate their favorite recipe into locally available ingredients, male workers are seeking to translate the new project on gender equality from the head office into something that will work in Nepal. The need for such translations is central to the valuation of expatriate labor itself, justifying employees' physical presence in Kathmandu and their skills as cultural mediators. The quantification of difference denies the most radical assumptions of one approach to globalization: it must not be the case that "the world is flat" (Friedman 2005). The compensation framework for overseas labor acts as an illustration of the heterogeneity of the world and thus the need for expatriates.[1]

In describing a system that exerts its power through bureaucratic minutiae, one risks replicating the "baffle them with bullshit" aspect of administrative excess (cf. Gupta 2012). In an attempt to minimize, if not eliminate, the tedium of regulatory detail, I focus on one example of expatriate compensation, the U.S. government's calculus of a foreign retail price schedule commonly known as the market basket. This is one of several tools used to analyze what salary supplements will be necessary to allow overseas employees to live and consume abroad as if they were living in their home country. The market basket presents itself as a neutral tool for analyzing the costs of overseas living, yet it also generates implications about what type of life expatriates will wish to make for themselves abroad. In examining the calculation of expatriate compensation, I want to pay particular attention to how those to whom these regulations are applied are imbricated as authors of the bureaucracy and how they read and utilize these regulations. Some read the precision of the market basket as a requirement, an expectation of certain behaviors. In other cases, the accumulated surveys and regulations sit ignored, as in one particular case where they served as convenient shims for imbalanced table legs in an embassy's offices. Meanwhile, in the everyday lives of expatriates in Kathmandu, the market basket takes on a problematic role as the source of an expectation of nationalistic consumption. Looking beyond the bureaucracy and its documentary practices, one comes to observe a set of anxieties about the appropriate type of life for an expatriate. The second part of the chapter looks at the work done, mainly by women, to implement an ideal expatriate life and acquire the goods that are enumerated in the regulations. The character of expatriate consumption is in part determined by forces such as the market basket, but also by the community expectations and social practices of Expatria.

Comparing Recompense

Although talk about the exact amount of money one makes is largely taboo among expatriates in Nepal, conversations about the vagaries of compensation policy and different employer bonus practices is commonplace. Over cocktails at a dinner party, an Australian couple mentioned that during a recent contract negotiation they were able to get their company to pay for memberships for both of them at a golf club in Kathmandu, which set off a flurry of competition and comparison. The group at the party consisted of long-term expatriates—couples who had been posted to at least three different countries. Men talked about how golf outings had been a regular part of workplace sociality in other places and that they had received memberships when posted in East Asia, but had never thought of asking for this in Kathmandu "because the course is so awful," remarked one golfer, contemptuous of what at the time was called the Royal Nepal Golf Course, located under the airport flight path. A better-maintained course lay several miles outside the city, largely utilized by Indian businessmen. "It's not the same as Korea," remarked another golfer, noting that golf club membership there was easily justified by its importance as a business outing, something far less common in Nepal. Other participants in the discussion began to speculate on what they might be able to claim as a comparable need from their own employer, such as packages of yoga lessons, membership to the American Club or seasonal entrance to a hotel pool.

The experience of frequent moves that is shared by all expatriates means that there is ample material to draw from in discussing how to navigate the system of job and location changes, with disaster tales of the incompetence of corporately hired movers[2] and fish stories of the amazing package that some apocryphal worker was able to extract from their employer acting as shared contexts by even those new to Nepal. In discussions of expatriate compensation packages, the topic was not always who was able to acquire the most but sometimes how someone had been harmed by not fully understanding the system. A story of compensation struggles that generated a great deal of sympathy was told by a mother who learned that because of a downturn in the value of the currency in which they were paid relative to the British pound, the education allowance they were receiving would no longer be sufficient to keep sending their two children to the British Primary School, which sets its prices in pounds. Those assembled urged her to fight with her husband's employer, and the family was eventually able to lobby successfully for a supplementary allowance from the company to allow their kids to stay in the same school.

The supplements, allowances and bonuses that are given to workers and their families are part of the process of avoiding employee failure. They are generated by the desire to retain those workers who have proven their abilities to navigate expatriate life, especially those who have survived in a hardship post like Nepal. Compensation comes under particular categories and with the employer's stated expectations for use: recreation incentives, education supplements, hardship allowances, and so on.[3] The minutiae of how sums of money are allocated are mired in bureaucracy. Most expatriates describe feeling conflicted about these bonuses, on the one hand expressing contempt for the process and the demands placed on them by the complexity of the system while on the other hand voicing the desire to get "what everyone else does," or their "fair share" of such allotments.

One of the most complex systems of allowances and compensation is the one used by the U.S. government for Foreign Service personnel.[4] The structure generated and utilized by the State Department holds the advantage of being publicly available, unlike those of the many for-profit agencies that offer to calculate overseas compensation for private employers but are careful not to disclose either their proprietary data or compensation formulae. In addition, the U.S. government data are also widely used by other international governments and some multinational companies that often start with U.S. numbers to generate their own employees' compensation packages with slight transformations for domestic standards and expectations.[5] The iconic character of the State Department system is an outcome of the size of the labor pool managed, the detailed number of compensation scenarios addressed and a long history of available data. In addition, its role as a benchmark for a variety of expatriate employers was known among expatriates and thus they paid particular attention to changing U.S. practices. In describing the State Department system, I am able to illustrate three elements of the influence of compensation on Expatria. First, it demonstrates how a single system that attempts to detail all possible situations often ends up generating a litany of impractical documents rather than achieving the comprehensiveness and efficiency desired, producing paperweights of regulation.[6] Second, the frameworks provided by the State Department system become a part of expatriate daily life through deployments of the funds provided to consume as the categories demand, thus influencing how families think about themselves and their shopping practices. For example, the availability of an allowance for holiday cards suggests to some that this is a duty expected of them. Finally, the structure of the compensation system of expatriate employment acts as a definition of who is truly a part of the system— particularly in Nepal, where so many other foreigners are present. Expatriate compensation systems not only define what overseas workers get paid, but also demarcate the very boundaries of Expatria.

The U.S. State Department's Grocery Cart

Understanding how the U.S. State Department views the compensation of expatriates begins with the Office of Allowances. Reporting to the Bureau of Administration within the Office of the Under Secretary of Management, this organization is responsible for generating policy for all direct employees posted overseas. Grouped with other entities that address the operation of U.S. activities abroad, such as Consular Affairs and Diplomatic Security, yet under the Bureau of Administration, the work of this division is in the generation of structural and regulatory frameworks. There are thousands of pages in the three central documents that govern overseas employees produced by this office: the *Foreign*

Affairs Manual (FAM), the *Foreign Affairs Handbook* (FAH), and the *Department of State Standardized Regulations* (DSSR). This collection of documents dictates policy, determines promotion and allocates funds to offices and individuals; the structure and categories enumerated in these texts influence how people think about themselves and the work they do.

The *Foreign Affairs Manual* is a document designed to offer a one-stop source for policy and philosophy to be used in U.S. Missions abroad, laying out the levels of responsibility and delineating mundane aspects of U.S. government ideology, such as the history of the Foreign Service (2 FAM 012) and policies on displaying the U.S. flag (2 FAM 150). Sections of the FAM appear designed for use as a reference text, providing definitions and technical information, for example 2 FAM 152.3 part 6:

> *Notorial wafer.* A notorial wafer is a round, red, blank paper wafer used in notorial acts when the instrument or document to which the notorial act relates consists of more than one sheet or when the certificate will be attached and not written on the document itself. The impression seal of the post is impressed on the wafer.[7]

Such banal information is unnecessary for most day-to-day responsibilities, but the *Foreign Affairs Manual* is utilized by protocol officers to provide the final answer to infrequently arising questions of procedure and official record.

The Foreign Affairs Handbook offers different material from the historical and structural information of the FAM, instead focusing on everyday practices required in overseas jobs, including information on hiring and firing of local staff, how correspondence should be addressed and proper accounting procedures. The document initially appears intended for daily use, but like the information about domestic life offered to international workers before departure, the need for generality and abstraction produces a list-like character that offers little in the way of actual practical advice. Instead, boundaries are generated that demand a local interpretation and context and offer only threats for not following procedure, insisting that workers stay within a set of limits or face recrimination. For example, in a section on information technology (5 FAH-5), employees are given information on the regulations regarding office computing systems and the necessity of preparing a "Benefit-Cost Analysis" (BCA) for any information technology initiative. The sixty-nine pages on the BCA process seek to cover a wide range of topics, but given the diversity of situations to which they might apply and the quickly changing nature of technology, the text can only offer generalities. In discuss-

ing computing systems for Mission offices, the document offers the following
in 5 FAH-5–621.2–2, "System Capabilities":

> System capabilities are the resources required for providing peak demand
> customer service. Some examples of system capabilities are:
> (1) 100 megabytes of disk storage space;
> (2) Help Desk personnel to support 50 users; and
> (3) On-line access to 100 users.[8]

These definitional statements cannot and do not address local problems or demands, for example language issues, the impossibility of obtaining local equipment repair and unreliable power, which are the daily hazards of computer
users in Nepal. Instead, they demand that employees should be attendant to the
local demands for "system capabilities" and ask them to determine what that
might entail at their posting.

I learned of these regulations on computer equipment when talking to a
member of the American Embassy staff frustrated with the Internet connection available in the U.S. Mission offices. Local electrical and telephone outages
in Kathmandu combined with various hardware and software security measures meant that the system in place at the office was broken more often than it
worked, and as a result, few utilized email for interoffice communication even
in 1999. "I wasn't hired to be a computer tech," he cried in a moment of pique,
as he sought to bring several modems to life again. The FAH was of little relevance to him as he tried to keep the U.S. hardware communicating with Nepali
infrastructure. Instead, he relied on a twenty-year-old employee of a local tech
company who would ride his scooter to the Mission offices with a collection of
wires, mysterious boxes and switches that could usually be cobbled together to
get things working again—but as there was a general strike on this day, it was
unlikely he would get any help in fixing the current outage. The FAH had nothing to say on the matter and with no technical help on staff, the Mission would
be without an Internet connection for yet another day.

Apart from the FAM and the FAH, a third set of documents regulates life for
overseas personnel, the *Department of State Standardized Regulations* (DSSR).
The DSSR addresses the allowances and benefits granted to U.S. government
direct employees abroad. This text provides the framework for government
employees' residential and work requirements, and pay regulations, although
the particularities of how this document is applied in a given country are outsourced to other government agencies, private subcontractors, or overseas
workers themselves. There are dozens of categories and frameworks under

which workers might be eligible for compensation, such as foreign travel per diem allowances, cost-of-living allowances, recruitment and retention incentives, living quarters allowances and a catch-all of "other allowances."[9] The last category includes the particular expenses incurred by workers as part of their official representation of the U.S. government as well as a wide variety of compensations accorded to workers for extraordinary circumstances, such as mandatory evacuation. While few expatriates can rattle off the details included in these handbooks, many conversations are conducted about how much one can receive for private school education (DSSR 270), holiday trips home (3 FAM 3430), learning local languages (3 FAH-1 H3914.4), storage of goods in a home country (3 FAM 3195.2–1) and, importantly in Nepal, compensation for the hardship of life abroad (DSSR 500). Thus, although the documents and technical language may be unfamiliar to expatriates, the results of these regulations are a part of daily life.

Several direct U.S. government employees I spoke with in Nepal about official government regulations had consulted these three sources at some time, often when they were considering a new post offer, to figure out what supplements they might be entitled to at a given location. Some had consulted the State Department FAQs on compensation or talked to friends posted at different locations who could offer more practical insight into expatriate life in another place and what strategies they might use to gain a better deal. Perhaps in acknowledgement of the deeply pedantic and generalized nature of the DSSR, the State Department provides supplemental discussions and online consultations that attempt to answer the everyday questions that employees may have about how these regulations apply to them. For example, under the category "Cost-of-Living Allowances" (DSSR 200), section "Educational Allowance" (270), a subsection titled "Supplementary Instruction" (276.9) seeks to address unusual events that might by be encountered by employees: "Supplementary instruction may be reimbursed up to the maximum shown in Section 274.12a in addition to the 'school at post' education allowance. . . ."[10] The few details that follow offer little guidance to parents seeking to utilize this allowance. Parents might instead consult a less-formal section of the Department of State website that further elucidates the allowance by describing sample situations such as the following: "Help! The base school requires that a child have completed Algebra I to enter the 9th grade. My son has only completed Pre-Algebra courses. Can I use supplementary instruction to get him caught up in math?" and "My daughter has not taken chemistry and is entering the 10th grade. Students in the school at post's honors program take chemistry in the 9th grade, while others take it in the 10th grade. Without chemistry, my daughter will not be allowed in the honors program. Can I pay for it using the supplementary instruction allowance?"[11] These are questions closer to the daily worries of expatriates, concerns that often slip between the regulatory cracks of even the ostensibly comprehensive DSSR.

Comparing notes with other expatriates was often seen as a more fruitful way of gaining information than either handbooks or websites. As an example, one mother sought advice from her friends over lunch about her son, who was headed to college next year. He had done well at one of the local international schools, despite having significant learning problems, success which she attributed to the small class sizes and several conscientious teachers who were trained in working with special needs students. Yet he had not had been formally tested for learning disabilities and his college was requiring documentation in order to grant him accommodations. She was panicked—considering taking a special trip home with him to have him tested. A fellow mom was able to reassure her. "My daughter has the same problem," she interjected and explained that the college had tested her on arrival. Although this did not fully assuage the mother's concern, she dropped questions about funding a special trip and the conversation changed to the high costs of a college education.[12] Documents like the DSSR are unable to address such parental worries, although at times they appear to attempt such a feat. More often, they generate fear, producing new concerns and introducing regulations intended merely to set limits.

Hardships and Market Baskets

There are two elements of expatriate compensation that are most frequently discussed in Nepal: one adds to the income of most people living in Kathmandu, while the other demands their labor. In Nepal, the post differential, commonly know as the hardship allowance, provides a substantial boost to any direct U.S. government employee's salary, and nearly all employers offer some form of financial incentive to live and work in settings deemed difficult or dangerous, such as Nepal. Through this element of the compensation system, workers receive an additional 25 percent of their base income as recompense for the difficulties of living in Kathmandu. Many central African countries also rate a 25 percent supplement, while a few such as Afghanistan, Iraq and Tajikistan are assessed the government's highest rating of 35 percent. Most of Europe generates no supplement. The ranking of various countries enters everyday conversation among expatriates when it comes time to consider new postings. The U.S. Foreign Service has a complex system whereby its employees rank their preferred locations for future postings.[13] Similar systems are in place at many large expatriate employers that seek to match the desires of expatriate families to work in certain locations and the needed skills at a given posting. Workers and their families try to get as much information about the salary supplements they would receive and whether the conditions in a country are as difficult as supplements would suggest.

Sitting outside next to the tennis courts at a local expatriate club, several women sought to pool their knowledge about hardship supplements in various locations before making the decision as to where they would seek placement. "Bamako isn't worth it," remarked a woman formerly posted to Mali, "you can't get anything there." She went on to describe the daily hassles of finding food, especially fresh meat, and isolation she felt while living there. "But it's 25 percent," replied another woman who was encouraging her husband to seek a position there, "just like Kathmandu." A discussion ensued about how the "hardship" of Mali was much greater than Nepal's and that no amount of money could make up for conditions in Bamako. The club itself became a topic of conversation, as comparisons were made between the various social and recreational opportunities in Kathmandu and in Bamako. No conclusions were reached, although the former resident of Bamako conceded that the situation may have changed since she was posted there and the woman seeking to go there seemed chastened about her expectation that since it received the same hardship ranking as Nepal that she would enjoy similar amenities. Several women questioned how exactly hardship allowances were determined, since they concurred that similarly ranked countries did not always mean similar experiences, and no one was aware of exactly how this determination was reached by employers.

The market basket supplement is discussed less as a financial incentive in Nepal, as it provides little or no additional money in Kathmandu, and is more frequently mentioned because of the hassle it entails. In Japan and other posts with a high cost of living, cost-of-living allowances (COLA) were frequent topics of conversation, with employees granted a supplement of 60 percent of their spendable income for living in Tokyo.[14] Most expatriate employers grant no cost-of-living supplement for living in Kathmandu, although at some times and by some employers Nepal has merited a small supplement.[15] Most overseas employers utilize some form of consumer practice calculation, which compares the cost to maintain a family in the employee's home nation versus what similar conditions would cost in a given posting. Expatriates are aware of how the cost-of-living allowance is generated as a result of the frequent surveys they must fill out, and often the very process of enumerating the household's expenses makes them more attuned to the various expenditures necessary to live in Kathmandu. Family arguments often occurred in the midst of completing such surveys, as discussions about spending that happened as a result of the need to fill out an annual COLA form uncovered the amount spent by a household on clothing or restaurant meals. In other cases, the tension was not about what one family member had spent on clothing but about exceptional expenses incurred at a particular location, like Nepal, where a school trip might involve international travel. Often such costs were not addressed by the supplements workers received. There was an abundance of finger pointing when compensation was not seen to correlate with expenses: direct U.S. government employees blamed Mission personnel responsible for collecting and correlating posting-wide data, while employees of other governments and private companies blamed the United States (and, at times, their American friends), as many employers utilize U.S. government numbers when calculating their compensation statistics for a small posting such as Nepal.

The nature of how the COLA numbers are determined is more familiar to expatriates than the hidden procedures that determine the hardship allowance, because workers and their families are responsible for providing the data that generates COLA. Most expatriate families (whether government workers or private-sector employees) are required by their employer to submit annual reports about their expenses, shopping habits, and consumption needs. These forms are utilized by employers to determine compensation not only in a given location but also as a means to compare employment conditions across different locations and industries. In addition, some employers sell this data to third-party subcontractors engaged in generating expatriate compensation systems for sale to employers. Apart from family surveys, there are also locationwide assessments of the expenses attendant to expatriate life that compare the costs of living as an expatriate in a given country to some external benchmark. As expatriates themselves are intimately involved in generating COLA information but are often unclear about exactly how this data is used, there is a good deal of resentment about the work entailed in completing surveys and speculation about how this data is used.

The details of these documents tell an important story about employer expectations of expatriates and the demands of bureaucracy for standardization. Rather than offer a reading of the hundreds of pages enumerating information about the types of bread surveyed and the number of movies it is anticipated that the average expatriate will attend, I study these documents less as artifacts and more as part of an ethnography of documentary processes (Riles 2006b).

I argue that the social procedure of completing, and even more important, complaining about completing these documents affects the consumer behavior of expatriates (Reed 2006). The process of comparing one's own buying habits to the survey has the potential to turn the metaphoric market basket into a shopping list and to reify and accentuate cultural differences between home and host countries. Observing the influence of the documentary process on the choices expatriates in Nepal make about consumption reveals that the precision of the calculation has the capacity to lend authority to both their work as cultural mediators and the surveys as their production. Expatriates in this system play the role of both the generators of the regulations and the regulatees.

Fill Out This Survey

Two key surveys completed by expatriates around the globe determine how the U.S. government cost-of-living allowance is calculated: the Living Pattern Questionnaire (LPQ) and the Retail Price Schedule (RPS). The LPQ is filled out by every direct U.S. government employee regarding his or her family's buying habits and consumer needs. Posts are required to receive responses from at least two-thirds of direct employees and are encouraged to attempt to get all to respond, with threatened audits for low response rates. Each family is asked a primary and secondary location where they purchase a list of several dozen household goods and services. The RPS is a more-extensive document prepared by a member of Mission staff for the entire post that consists of four parts: an enumeration of the types of shops expatriates use in-country, a summary of the individual LPQ survey data, and a study of local prices of goods and services more extensive than the LPQ and data regarding any official U.S. government sales outlets such as a commissary. For groceries, the RPS asks for the costs of items at two stores determined to be the most commonly used to purchase these particular goods, as well as the costs at the government commissary, if appropriate. The stores are determined separately for each product and subcategory; thus one must list the most common two locations to purchase beef steak, two for beef roast, and two for beef hamburger—an example which might be particularly challenging to determine in largely Hindu, and thus beef averse, Nepal. Several versions of the survey must be done to account for the costs in various cities within a country and the different economics of shopping at local stores versus government-run businesses, in part as a concession to the use of the resulting figures by other employers. Beyond food items, everything from toasters to DVD players to a dental cleaning must undergo similar accounting. The official responsible for completing the RPS also quantifies the importance of various categories of goods in the particular location. Thus, even as one might state that snow shovels are of zero percent importance in Kathmandu, it still would be necessary to report their costs at two outlets. The RPS, in a thirty-seven-page section titled "Retail Prices," asks for a list of locally-preferred brands of everything from tea bags to maids, ranks the percentage of fresh, frozen and canned beans used by the community and assesses what percentage of clothing people buy locally, buy from the commissary, bring with them at the beginning of a posting, have mailed from third-party outlets or bring back with them from home leave. In addition to the LPQ summary and the RPS survey, there are other accounting documents demanded by the RPS including The Outlet Report, Relative Use of Commodities and Services, accounts of local taxes paid and the costs of meals at frequently visited restaurants, all of which must be completed every three to four years, or more frequently if economic conditions change dramatically. In the end, for expatriates in Nepal, all these statistics add up to nothing—no financial adjustment is generally prescribed for the costs of market basket goods in Kathmandu—yet the surveys must still be completed and entail a great deal of work.[16] The work of documenting consumption may not transform the expatriate paycheck, but it does frequently transform social relations and consumer choices through the bureaucratic labor of completing forms and the contemplation produced by the documentary process. The practice of paperwork in this case leads not only to completed forms but also to a sense of community brought about by the shared experience of bureaucratic frustration (cf. Hull 2012).

Several mothers were chatting as their kids played in the pool about release of the year's salary supplement figures from various employers. Many women noted that they had anticipated this year to have a COLA adjustment, given a recent decline in the value of the Nepali rupee that had inflated local costs for imported goods on the open market. They placed the blame for this on a new U.S. Embassy hire, a single man, who was responsible for filling out the posting-wide survey: "He doesn't understand. He doesn't have children." This launched several conversations recalling how the family situations or time-in-country of the people responsible for COLA locationwide surveys had influenced the compensation of all expatriates in Nepal. One woman recalled that the man in her husband's company responsible for collecting local shopping data had relied on his locally born wife, who, she noted, did not shop the same way as those in the group did. Many supported her complaint, "especially in Nepal, where there is one price for foreigners and one price for locals." This concern also appears within official U.S. government instructions on the LPQ and RPS that forbid the completion of the survey by certain potential respondents, stating, "[A] LES member or foreign-born spouse may not be familiar with the spending and buying patterns of the American family. This means that, in all likelihood, the survey results will seriously disadvantage the vast majority of post personnel."[17] Employees assigned to fill out information about their family's consumption patterns, as well as the officials completing post-wide reports, are encouraged to consult with their family, with the assumption that their family is one deemed "typical"—although the typical can often be anomalous within the community.[18] The division between who is commonly purchasing goods for the family and those charged with completing the forms also causes problems. In Nepal, many families enlist household help to shop at local venues and thus are often unfamiliar with the cost of some staples in situations where their staff purchases them.[19] Yet the punitive repercussions of insufficient response or incomplete data mean that workers attempt to answer the questions put to them, even if it requires some creative fiction or hidden outsourcing.

The delineation of a special category of items as part of the expatriate market basket can also perpetuate a distinction between local consumption practices and those of foreigners. For example, two women in a local supermarket frequented by foreigners were discussing what to do about the lack of rice at a foreigner-oriented store. The shelves, which had been filled in the past with boxes of Uncle Ben's and Minute Rice, were conspicuously empty. They discussed how to change a planned dinner party menu as a result as well as other stores they might visit, never considering the dozens of small shops with barrels of rice sold by the kilo that they would pass on their way to the next destination, and where their housekeeper purchased rice for the staff meals. The ubiquity of rice in Nepal contrasts with how it appears in the LPQ, where respondents are asked for the cost of "Rice, Regular," which is assumed to be a 16-ounce box rather than what a local merchant would dole out as regular rice.

The data from expatriate workers is generated in the hope of attaining accurate and widely applicable information about the expenses of international employees. It is expected that this information reflects the patterns of some "typical American family," but this assumption is then ignored in the use of this same data by many non-U.S. governments as well as multinational private companies. While the explicit goal of these surveys is to generate data for compensating personnel, the documentary process speaks back to those under scrutiny, acting as a legislative tool as much as reportage and making the survey not objective but objectifying (Latour 2005: 58, 230). The LPQ and RPS are, by their administrators' own accounts, inexact tools for attempting to reach some fair and generalizable standard, but the multiple levels of analysis that remove such accounting from everyday life experiences introduces an unintended homogenizing effect. Whether or not expatriates wish to consume as if they were residing in their home country, they are compensated as if they did.

Shopping for the Market Basket

This survey-driven system cannot account for a major input to the generation of an expatriate market basket: the labor of consumption. I turn here from the financial compensation provided to allow people to consume as if they were not abroad to what it takes to turn that money into goods and services. The allowances calculated by surveys do not make the actual goods magically appear and the questionnaires themselves have the potential to produce previously unfelt needs, transforming the permitted or suggested consumption patterns of expatriates into demands or prescriptions of appropriate buying practices. Consider the previously described injunction against "foreign-born" wives completing consumption surveys—a command that is easily read as a condemnation of certain consumer choices and even certain families. The nationalistic consumption patterns described in the LPQ rarely accord with what expatriates themselves would want to purchase. Although few seek to fully take on local cuisine or fashion, the homogenization of market basket lists often means no one is actually buying exactly what the LPQ prescribes. The work of producing a "normal" life through consumption falls particularly on accompanying spouses.[20] Through compensation structures, input from the expatriate community and the local consumption expectations these generate, those who shop for the family are drafted to produce a comfortable life through goods, outside of the "cultural chaos" of Nepal. In what follows, I explore how expatriate women in Nepal are engaged in two processes: learning how to consume like an expatriate and engaging in the everyday labor of purchasing the family's own unique market basket, influenced as much by the community as by employer-generated lists. The cost-of-living and hardship allowances received by workers are merely money. Employers are often blind to the labor necessary to transform money into a particular set of goods and acknowledge the work that goes into consumption only when the process fails.

In transforming a list of goods into food for the family, the dissonance between the expectations of the survey and the everyday lives of expatriates comes to the fore. The U.S. State Department LPQ includes a category for peanut butter but no role for America's favorite condiment, salsa—an item frequently mentioned in the culinary fantasies of expatriates in Nepal. The surveys often fail to account for what families living abroad actually do eat or wish to consume. Instructions dictate the minutiae of translating products across the world, demanding, for instance, that respondents "[r]eport smooth peanut butter . . . exclude brands with nuts (crunchy-style)."[21] But the forms do not address the diversity of expatriates or their preferences. Even as they demand cosmopolitanism, these surveys imply an expectation that expatriates consume in hypernormative ways that rarely accord with their own desires, which are often influenced by their many overseas postings. What these documents provide is financial support for expatriates to realize their own understandings of a "normal" life abroad. Expatriate families reject the normalcy suggested by the LPQ, instead pursuing a market basket reflecting the remembered foodstuffs of their various homes. In addition, the way in which shopping activities often are intertwined with other social events contributes to a socially produced understanding of consuming like a foreigner in Nepal. Focusing on the financial compensation granted to expatriates for the greater expense, say, of buying pasta in Kathmandu as opposed to Washington, D.C., can obscure the importance of face-to-face discussions of how to shop in Nepal and the extensive labor endured by women to try to procure a pantry of goods that creates the illusion of "normal" life—in its diverse forms—in Expatria.

The conversation at gatherings of expatriate women in Kathmandu is frequently about children or shopping, and often the relationship between the two. Whether it is after an Active Women of Nepal board meeting or one of the casual get-togethers that regularly occur at clubs and schools, there is always some new discovery to share or horror story to tell about the quest to get "normal" products in Nepal for the family, and especially the children. The weekly crafts group that met at the house of a foreign-government official generated numerous discussions about what products could be trusted and where a stash of a particular treat could currently be found. As women knitted, sewed and pieced together quilts, the conversation turned one day to a genre of food craved in Nepal by expatriate adults and children alike: Mexican, or more accurately, American-style Tex-Mex. The tourist district of Kathmandu, Thamel, provides what backpack travelers see as a paradise of food options. Hundreds of small restaurants provide every imaginable cuisine at prices ranging from very cheap to inexpensive, at least for expatriate budgets (Liechty 2005b). Many of these establishments make some gesture to Mexican cuisine—along with every other possible culinary desire of a foreign audience—yet the beans and tomato sauce offered to backpack travelers did not satisfy the expatriate patrons, given that they are ensconced abroad for years rather than weeks. One of the oldest restaurants in Kathmandu, long popular with foreigners, provides what was seen as credible huevos rancheros and burritos to an eager audience of expatriate families. Mike's Breakfast (pictured on the cover of this book) is a popular site to alleviate Tex-Mex longings, and Sunday mornings often found the garden of Mike's filled with expatriate families catching up on the week's events while enjoying breakfast burritos. Yet even Mike's Breakfast was unable to replicate tortilla chips and salsa in a way that lessened the cravings of slightly embarrassed parents, let alone teenagers, familiar with Tex-Mex food from home.

It was this longing and a lack of satisfaction with local options that began the stories of quests for "real" Mexican food at the crafts table. One woman described her attempt to make salsa from local ingredients with limited success, another noted that a Nepali man had started producing salsa and selling it at the organic market, but it did not pass the test of her teenaged son. A knitter contributed that she had bought what she "thought was salsa at Bluebird, but it was thin tomato sauce. Tasted like Ragu." Tortilla chips provided an even greater challenge, being difficult to import. Local restaurateurs had tried their luck at creating tortillas—all the components were available—but many were basing their attempts on the advice of tourists. Having never tasted the food themselves, the restaurateurs achieved results that were often more like fried corn *chapattis*. One local entrepreneur who had experience manufacturing foreign-style snack foods for trekkers produced a version that was eagerly awaited, as many expatriates knew he had lived in New York for two years, but the resulting contents of his small bags often became crumbs before they reached their consumers. "The Commissary has Pace, I can pick you up some," noted an American knitter. The U.S. Commissary was the site of last resort, as well as guaranteed success, in the quest for the authentic taste.[22] The RPS offers no category for salsa and even if it did, such a document would be unable to account for the labor and social knowledge required to transform money into salsa. The surveys generated by the State Department are designed to reflect a normal American diet, but the practices of expatriates suggest that such attempts at normalcy obscure the particular cravings of a close and yet transient community that drive expatriate desires.

Other foreign nationals had their own unique quests for goods typical of their home country. Marmite, Branston Pickle, Skippy Peanut Butter and cans of San Marzano tomatoes were always being smuggled, exchanged and discussed among expatriates. At the British Club's weekly bridge game, while relaxing over a pint of Guinness pulled from one of the club's taps, one table discussed a crisis. Judith exclaimed, "It is three months until my next home leave and I've run out of Branston Pickle." Most of those in audible range understood the gravity of this matter. The condiment was difficult to find in Nepal, despite its origins as an alteration of the chutneys and pickles that the British acquired a taste for during Indian colonialism. After several minutes of discussing the inadequacy of local substitutes and an extended nostalgic story of a favorite pub's chutney and cheese sandwich in the Cotswolds, a savior was found, a single man who had an extra unopened jar he did not anticipate needing. After brief jokes about a bidding war, the low price of a pint of beer was agreed on as well as a promise to replenish his supply during Judith's next home-leave. Turning to the actual expatriate consumption behaviors of families in Kathmandu refocuses attention on how one learns, and must frequently relearn, how to be an expatriate consumer. Education about how to shop in a new posting and teaching others about local commodities is mainly the provenance of female trailing spouses, and their work to generate community through shared consumer practices presents different challenges from those produced by the cost-of-living surveys and compensation negotiations.

Making Expatriates Through Shopping

Welcome to Kathmandu! We hope you will be able to settle in quickly to Nepal, and thoroughly enjoy your stay. Nepal is indeed an interesting place.

You are now faced with the immediate task of finding a house and transforming it into a home for you and your family. We hope that this guide will be of use in helping you find your way about the city.

A shopping expedition in Kathmandu can be both an exciting and frustrating experience. Shopping can sometimes take a lot of stamina for you to achieve your objectives, however we hope that the suggestions on the following pages will help make it easier.

(UNWO 1998: 1, 13)

Notwithstanding the success of Maoist parties in recent Nepali political history, when expatriates refer to the "little red book" they usually mean the *Newcomers Guide to Kathmandu*, quoted above. This short booklet is given as a benefit of membership in either of the two largest expatriate women's organizations in Nepal: the United Nations Women's Organization (UNWO) or the Active Women of Nepal (AWON). The advice given in this booklet, supplemented by the guidance of those in these groups, is vital to learning how to consume like an expatriate in Nepal, and its prescriptions are a part of the daily life of expatriates to a greater degree than those of the LPQ or the RPS. Often when a worker leaves his position, the house his family lived in, his household staff and a copy of the *Newcomers Guide* are bequeathed to his replacement. The book, updated every four or five years, is something many expatriates in Kathmandu carry on their person daily, at least for the first months of their stay. In contrast to the surveys they must fill out to determine compensation, this locally produced text focuses exclusively on the practicalities of being a foreigner in Nepal. Most of the book is devoted to such concerns as how and where to get particular items, service providers that have been used by other expatriates and social organizations that cater to different interest groups. It includes contact phone numbers and practical information necessary for the unusual demands of foreigners living in Kathmandu, such as where parking is available and what non-Nepali-language street signs can be used as guideposts to reaching a destination. "Nepalese culture" is given only three pages, which discuss bargaining and tipping practices as well as social situations foreign workers might actually encounter, such as an invitation to a child's first rice feeding and conditions allowing admission to a Hindu temple. The esteem for this pamphlet is largely because it provides valued practical information, yet it also acts as a boundary-making text for Expatria in Nepal.

Although the *Newcomers Guide* is officially available only through membership in AWON or UNWO, the guide has a wider circulation and the practices it describes define who is part of the expatriate community.[23] Other foreigners may reside in Kathmandu for long or short periods of time, but following the dictates and information in this book separates the tourists and resident foreigners from the professional package expatriates, for its contents reveal the particular needs of its expatriate audience. Through this text, particular shops come to be known as ones that accommodate expatriate preferences. Although one craft store may appear indistinguishable from its neighbors, a teenager with good English skills or the availability of a space to park one's car in the back can make the "Pottery shop next to Kumari Baskets, Kupondole Road, Patan. Second set of blue doors (see Yum Yum Noodle sign overhead). Best selection in town. No phone" (UNWO 1998: 40) the favorite of expatriates. The *Newcomers Guide* serves as the manual of an epistemic community of expatriates in Nepal (Knorr Cetina 1999: 8). Such a text, when combined with other social practices, creates a continuity of knowledge about consumption, even in a community disrupted by frequent mobility. Through everyday shopping practices and social exchanges with other expatriates, newcomers learn what it is to be an expatriate in Nepal, and those who do not buy according to this paradigm are not considered part of the community. Other resident foreigners in Nepal remark on the provincialism of expatriates, how "they pretend they aren't really in Nepal" by buying foreign goods, and they chide them for not "getting to know the country they are living in." Yet the *Newcomers Guide* is not a manual on shopping in Nepal but a guide to consuming like an expatriate who is in Nepal for his or her latest posting. What gives continuity to Expatria is knowing that each new posting will have such a guide, and yet each new location will require new textual and social education in how to provision the family home.

Expatriates often have little time in their early days in Kathmandu for getting to know the city. Instead, they must rush to enroll children in school, discover the peccadilloes of their household staff and reinstitute patterns of consumption that have served them well in various locations. The question of *if* one should buy mayonnaise in Nepal is less of a question than where and how to buy it in this new location. Although formal mechanisms exist for larger employers and countries to provide an introduction to a new location through systems of mentorship and classes, in Nepal expatriates must rely on informal connections. A newcomer's first social event in Kathmandu usually leads to ad-

Vendors at the Gazebo at the Summit Hotel during the Wednesday Farmers Market. Author photo, August 2010.

vice and information about other meetings, as the constant turnover of popu-lation means that all expatriates are sympathetic to being new to town: it is often said that a year in-country makes one an expert, two makes one a veteran. As a result, women often sweep unfamiliar faces into their social circles and educate them on the ways of life in Kathmandu and the perils and pleasures of its consumer opportunities.

On any given Wednesday morning, nearly two dozen expatriate women can be found drinking coffee and sharing cinnamon rolls in the garden of the Sum-mit Hotel. Wednesday is the day of the organic market, to which local farmers and shopkeepers bring produce and baked goods desired by foreigners and array their wares on small wooden tables. A day's wares may include local honey, sea-sonal vegetables and occasionally a delicacy like fresh strawberries. The Summit is located in an area off the main tourist path and in the midst of a popular area for expatriates to rent homes. Many women stop by the market after escorting their children to the British School nearby. Those who come after the 9:30 A.M rush are likely to miss out on the focaccia bread and mini-pizzas that are the most popular items. Most women buy very little from the vendor stalls set up in the garden gazebo. Instead, the major activity is catching up with friends and enjoying the attractive garden where children play within the safety of the hotel grounds. The jam or beets women may buy at the Wednesday market make up only a small part of the family's diet; instead the greater part of the morning is often taken up discussing past events and planning future opportunities for sociality and shopping. Over coffee, women exchange stories about where they have found particular goods, what local restaurant they ate at that made their family sick and food they long for from home. In sight of the tables of the or-ganic market, women discuss where they shop and their everyday struggles to obtain food for their family.

A large percentage of the food consumed in an expatriate home comes through pathways unseen by expatriates themselves, a convenient ignorance. For staples, it is often the cook or housekeeper who will appear daily with bags of rice, vegetables and eggs bought at small markets scattered across the city. It is a common practice to give a member of the household staff a weekly bud-get to procure items from local sources. When I talked to the housekeepers (*didis*) who made food appear in expatriate homes, they reported that they often shopped at markets near their homes on the outskirts of Kathmandu, bringing bags with them on board the small white Tempos that provide trans-port along standard routes, or visiting nearby stalls in the city if they lived with the expatriate family. The rice, lentils and vegetables that were the majority of these purchases often went to the preparation of a staff meal, but also made an appearance in the expatriate diet. The nominal amount given to a staff member each week was a small fraction of the overall household food budget of an expatriate family. Occasionally, conflicts arose as expatriates complained that their *didi* was taking a profit from this allowance or not providing good products. Yet the ability to remain blind to some elements of Kathmandu shopping was for many a valuable and necessary expenditure in and of itself.

The desire to engage in some willful ignorance is prompted in part by the everyday experiences of market life, particularly the meat shops that line the streets expatriates travel. Near the embassies in the area of Kathmandu where many expatriates live, there are a number of small stores where live chickens and goats are tethered to tables laden with fish and eggs. Although many expatriates shop for meat themselves, buying frozen imported packages, the display of freshly killed meat and its accompanying smells is a part of daily street life in the city, and it prompts some to want to know less about the sources of their diet. Expatriate women are occasional visitors to "cold stores," neighborhood shops carrying a few vegetables for forgetful shoppers and chocolate bars and snacks for schoolchildren. Few expatriates have seen the wholesale vegetable

Cold Store in the Lazimpat Area. Author photo, April 2010.

markets dotted around the city that are the mainstay for the exchange of Kathmandu's agricultural bounty, and those who have seen the markets are hesitant to use them as shopping venues, less because of hygiene concerns than because of the crowds, narrow lanes and aggressive negotiations that are common. An average expatriate family in Nepal may source its food from as many as ten different vendors, visiting a weekly market like the one at the Summit for some things and the commissary for others, bringing some from their home country, buying goods from the large supermarkets oriented to foreigners, having household staff purchase some goods, visiting a variety of specialty stores for cheese and bread and patronizing other concerns run by foreigners for locally produced boutique products like honey or coffee. In Kathmandu's difficult traffic, food provisioning for some women constituted a twenty-hour–per-week job, but most of those who did devote such time to grocery shopping saw this outlay of time as part of their social life as well as a domestic obligation.

Although willed ignorance is one element of expatriate consumption strategy, the acquisition of knowledge is also important. Indeed, shared knowledge and strategic shopping wisdom formed an important currency for generating connections as well as controversy among expatriate consumers. Often the desires of children provided the beginning point for conversations about the difficulty of shopping in Nepal, or sometimes children were used as a conceit for the preferences of other family members. "I just can't stand it," began one conversation, as Jane consulted with a group of fellow expatriates about how to negotiate the purchase of milk in Kathmandu. In this case, she was noting that she shared her children's abhorrence of the ultra-high-temperature (UHT) milk, which was the preference of many European expatriates in Nepal. The shelf-stability of UHT milk meant that imported brands were available at many of the local supermarkets. Like many Americans, Jane had not experienced boxes of milk that could be kept at room temperature until opened, and she found the UHT milk unpalatable. Some American expatriates had their staff buy locally packaged milk, available at many cold stores in bags, and then heat it for twenty minutes. But there was debate among the group whether this was sufficient to kill all bacteria as well as whether local milk was any better than powdered milk, which some suggested was the underlying source of "bag milk." Jane had been frustrated by both bagged milk and UHT and was continually on the lookout for better alternatives. During a group visit to one of the largest supermarkets in the city, three women talked to Jane about the merits of various UHT milks and ways that they had found to make the contents more acceptable to them and their kids. An American woman shopping nearby overheard the conversation and contributed information about a shop she bought her bagged milk from that she and many other expatriates trusted. A companion pulled a small notepad out of her purse to allow the interjecting woman to draw a map for Jane. As soon as the American was out of earshot, the group reiterated their concern over local milk, regardless of how many other expatriates had vetted the source. Jane never did solve her milk problem, and eventually decided to shift her family to soy milk after hearing a report on its health benefits relative to cow's milk.

The social guidance provided by the community on how to shop is seen as a necessary part of survival as an expatriate. When life must be reinvented in a new location every few years, expatriate social organizations and the attendant relationships that emerge from them are a shortcut to everyday social networks. Everyone faces the need to find goods and service providers upon moving—finding a new plumber, a new favorite restaurant, a new hair stylist—but expatriates must reformulate these networks every few years. Moreover, the most basic elements of where one can buy household goods have difficult answers in new countries. Finding the grocery store or local "big box" outlet resolves many recently moved families' needs in Europe or the United States but such multipurpose shops are less common in Nepal and there are logics to which stores carry what items that many expatriates find baffling. One woman searched nearly a month for a store that carried brooms, while a father sought help finding shops carrying the soccer balls that are ubiquitous in Kathmandu but to him seemed unavailable at local outlets. "They must get them somewhere," he remarked. There is neither uniformity in the opinions of the expatriate consumer body nor a blind adherence to the advice of others; recommendations are always provided and usually gratefully received. The combination of sociality and advice that is central to Expatria is generated by sympathy for the situation of mobility that is the shared life of expatriates. This combined with the social nature of much expatriate shopping contributes to a small orbit of sites visited, with a point-to-point pathway created through many trips. Discovering how to shop in each posting often requires knowledge that does not transfer to other foreign postings; instead it is knowledge of where to acquire such information that creates continuity between postings. Furthermore, the education of new arrivals is not the only learning process that occurs, for shopkeepers in Nepal also learn how to attract expatriate consumers.

The narrow alleys of Kathmandu provide a challenge to foreign shoppers in large chauffeur-driven cars, and one can search half the city before discovering that most of the sporting goods stores are found in the area just north of the Bagmati River or that brooms are not found in hardware stores with other cleaning supplies but in special broom and straw shops. Even after the right shops are found, there is still a communication gap that worries many expatriate consumers. The Indra Chowk area of Kathmandu is home to dozens of fabric shops, each displaying bolts of fabric draped to protect them from the dusty city streets. Some specialize in cloth for men's suits and shirts, others in silks or saris, but it is at the Linen Club where the expatriates can be found. The Linen Club, which until recently had no visible sign to indicate its name, can be found by taking "the road on immediate right of the temple with shawls and following it to first major courtyard on the left hand side. Inside the courtyard, it is about 3rd shop to your right" (UNWO 1998: 26). Although lacking the requisite parking that attracts many expatriates to shops—in fact it is on a road that the white Jeeps used by many foreigners cannot navigate—the Linen Club has a devoted following. On either side are fabric shops with similar wares, yet these rarely receive expatriate customers. Over time, the Linen Club has gained a reputation that has been exploited by the owners, who now employ only workers with some English-language skills. As they became the expatriate fabric store of choice, they expanded their franchise with a branch on the high-end shopping street of Durbar Marg. When I inquired why expatriates visited The Linen Club, women mentioned the owners' understanding of the needs of foreigners, ability to speak English, fair prices (which meant set or posted) and an inventory of fabric attractive and familiar to foreigners. It had been vetted by others who had first explored the stall and was therefore less threatening. "I'm always afraid they're not going to speak English," said one woman, discussing how she rarely ventured from the stores recommended by other expatriates.

Expatriate consumption entails a geography and an epistemology that has elements of continuity and difference across time and space. In the last twenty years, the stores utilized by expatriates for grocery shopping in Kathmandu have expanded extensively in both number and type. The few large Western-style markets that existed in the early 1990s have since opened up multiple branches, seeking to service the two zones where foreigners most frequently live: Lazimpath in the north and Sanepa in the south. In addition, small cold stores in these areas have grown to resemble supermarkets, with refrigerators for cold goods and open shelving eliminating the need to ask for items from a shopkeeper. I experienced my own encoding as a naïve newcomer unfamiliar with these changes upon returning to Nepal in 1999. With the few expatriates who remained from my visit in 1997 I discussed what I saw as a dramatic shift in the landscape of the city: the worsening traffic, the fluctuating tourist population and the growth in supermarkets. These changes, and my lack of knowledge of new consumer preferences, were sufficient impetus for an educational trip around the city to see new stores and sites. "You've been to Bhat Bhatini, haven't you?" questioned one woman as we were nearing the end of the tour. When I said that I had not heard of this place, there was great surprise, followed by the planning of an expedition to visit the following day after a lunch meeting. Although a bit off the regular routes of most expatriates, Bhat Bhatini had become a favorite destination. The store provides ample parking, air conditioning, several floors of goods, both groceries and housewares, and an English-speaking staff. The same organic farmers who supply the market at the Summit Hotel were also paying visits to a stand just outside the main store. Much had changed over just a few years, including what health scares motivated the concerns of foreigners. The blue-green algae that was a terror in 1997 had declined as a concern, while new concerns about air pollution had ascended. Kwality Ice Cream, formerly the trusted brand of choice, had been blacklisted due to concerns over sanitation practices. The Living Pattern Questionnaire could not keep up with these issues, nor could the *Newcomers Guide*. But owners of stores like Bhat Bhatini with a stake in the expatriate market and the weekly conversations at the Summit were always on top of the changing maps of expatriate consumption.

What is continually produced and reproduced by these everyday social interactions is a consumer mapping of Kathmandu that floats over the city itself.[24] Scholars focusing on the new geographies of globalization have observed a decline in the importance of proximity as part of understandings of connection and belonging. Time-space compression has changed the way people, goods and money move through the world, not only increasing speed and volume but also the ability of aspects of modernity to "hop over (rather than flowing through)" contiguous spaces (Ferguson 2006: 14), thus permitting some to be left out of the global equation. Similar technologies have enabled the rise of global cities and connections between global cities that bypass their proximate nation-states (Sassen 1991). Expatriate topographies of their temporary homes participate in two different scales of selective contact, or point-to-point movement. The first is a mapping of the familiar expatriate sites in Nepal that overlays the broader map of the city. Within the ubiquitous white Pajero Jeeps and with the assistance of local drivers, expatriates develop a vision of the city with dense nodes of expertise in some sites and chasms of unfamiliarity elsewhere, a phenomenon that is shared to some degree by all who do not walk everywhere. Expatriate employment and life participates in a different form of point-to-point linking. Herein, expatriates are deeply tied to one another and to known posting cities, generating the discontinuous place I refer to as Expatria. It is the ability to translate what worked in Karachi to Kathmandu that defines a global expatriate geography that, rather like a network of global cities, defines an alternative spatiality linking non-proximate sites. Expatriate families work daily to bring the goods of the market basket to the table. The transient nature of expatriate life means that many elements of these everyday tasks must be learned and relearned in each new setting. Yet the overarching structure of expatriate life is premised on such exchanges and frequently it is these sorts of discussions that both bound the community and allow continuity across various postings.

What Are We Compensating For?

The structures of compensation are what defines the expatriate labor contract, and practices such as hardship allowances are how expatriates themselves define who is part of their world and who is a resident foreigner. The salary supplements that expatriates receive are earmarked to distinct categories that prescribe how they should be used and thus what an expatriate life should look like. The precision with which equivalencies in compensation are calculated[25] and the involvement of workers in determining what constitutes an equivalency is not exclusively a process of bureaucratic enumeration. It is also a means of gaining workers' assent that through these payments hardships and costs have been fully and accurately accounted. Resident foreigners in Nepal expressed their frustration with this system. As one Australian living in Nepal for many years stated, "They have nothing to whine about—with what they get paid." While the expenses of expatriate employment are undoubtedly high (to repeat the statistics commonly cited in international human resources literature, "three to five times" the cost of the same worker employed in a home country), expatriates were resistant to the idea that this bought their silence or fully compensated for their hardships. "Nothing can make up for missing my mother's funeral," said one woman about the assumption that financial compensation made up for the challenges of expatriate life.

The salary supplements and support structures provided by employers to overseas workers generate productive and constrictive frictions in modes of expatriate consumption (Tsing 2004). Hardship post differentials tell expatriates that there are hardships to be endured, while allowances for security and household staff inform families that these are expectations of international living. The market basket supplement is premised on providing support for those living abroad to buy a familiar selection of goods for their family and a globally equitable and stable consumer experience for workers, but it also dictates what that consumer experience should be. The injunction against "foreign-born" spouses completing consumer surveys is an instructive example of how the process of generating statistics and the demand for generalizability also present messages to expatriates about the definition of normal consumer behavior and normal families.

The market basket supplement, hardship allowance and other incentives for living abroad received by expatriate families posted to Nepal are part of their "compensation package"—a now-commonplace phrase that for a moment I want to unpack. Within the business world, compensation is often synonymous with pay, as a more-inclusive and less-direct way to talk about salaries and benefits, the "extrinsic monetary rewards that employees receive in exchange for their work" (Lee 2001: 295). What is considered in determining compensation includes the worth of a worker, equity among workers within an industry and employing best practices of transparency and efficiency. Yet within the expatriate situation, employers consider far more than what work an employee does, incorporating a different idea of compensation as recompense. The expatriate condition—career-compelled displacement from a home place—is framed as a situation worthy of financial reward above and beyond just that given for the labor of the expatriate worker. Expatriates are compensated via mechanisms that are correlated with particular aspects of the experience of overseas living. Employers are eager to take care of their workers, for the high costs of not doing so have been vociferously argued by the literature on families as a cause of failure. Carework, particularly when outsourced, is "increasingly audited for procedural efficiency, for cost cutting, and for service delivery rather than for the difference actually made" (Townsend, Porter, and Mawdsley 2002: 835; cf. Latour 2005; Foucault 2008). In seeking to compensate expatriates in this mode of monetized carework, employers also are deploying an economic or labor-based understanding of compensation, as well as ideas that seem more familiar to legal or psychoanalytic concepts of compensation, in so far as they include ideas of loss and trauma.

Within the fields of psychology and psychoanalysis, compensation indexes attempts to make up for some lack or deficiency, often in inappropriate or excessive ways. Legal scholars work with an understanding of compensation as a financial calculation of equivalence, not for work, but for loss or damages. Amidst the muddle of these semitechnical uses of compensation lies part of the difficulty in understanding expatriate compensation, as it participates in all of these understandings and it is particularly difficult to unpack because many social scientists slide between these understandings within their own work (Fischer 1999; Pugh 2002). Allison Pugh's work on how parents "compensate" for their absence from their children's lives and their lack of time through consumption comes closest to encompassing the several understandings of compensation at work in the lives of expatriates (2002; 2009; 2011). These different concepts of compensation also emerge in discussions of financial remunerations awarded by courts in cases of intimate relationship (see Zelizer 2007) or for victims of disasters (see Lascher and Powers 2004). These diverse uses of compensation highlight the necessity of seeking to understand what expatriates are being compensated for and whether compensation accords with the losses they describe feeling while abroad (Tornikoski 2011).

In the normative consumption engendered by instruments such as the market basket survey more is at stake than merely encouraging expatriates to buy "as if" they were at home. One of the mechanisms of globalization, both as thing-in-the-world and as a mode of research,[26] is the creation of an unquestioned and unquestionable category of the unmarked. The category of the normal is co-determinative of the category of the particular or cultural, not unlike the relationship between the self and "the Other."[27] The unmarked in a global context is a position of power, one particularly felt in the capacity to define both the form of alterity and the conditions of contact (Trouillot 2003: 73).[28] The force of the illusion of unmarkedness is also seen in the production of a perception of globalization as a universal and unstoppable force, which allows "the bankers, the developers, the corporate CEOs and the web masters" to claim to "have become the universal and unmarked subjects of history" (Gregory 1998: 63). What I contended is that this powerful unmarked position must be created, not merely through a lifetime of privilege, but through structures that define what is "normal" and instruct global actors how to perform unmarkedness. In the enumeration of the "right" list of things for an expatriate to buy abroad, employees learn what normalcy means in this new setting, developing an international market basket that travels with them.

The bureaucratic complexity of expatriate compensation parallels the diplomatic and development worlds that are the career of many expatriates in Nepal. The act of calculating compensation as a means of obviating damage is made through bureaucratic tools into a seemingly objective and technical act.[29] In development and diplomacy, compensation, in its many meanings, is increasingly discussed as a means to address the cooptation of land for development projects (Roy 1999; Cernea 2003; Maldonado 2009), the utilization of indigenous knowledge in medicine (Posey 1990; Reddy 2007) and as recompense for past wrongs of colonialism (Yang 1997; Hein 2003; Dudden 2006). Expatriates are often called on to participate in such enumerations of culpability and responsibility, and yet are themselves also subject to a regime of compensability. For expatriate employers, the allotment of compensation for housing and hardship, combined with the expatriates' everyday invisibility from their coworkers and superiors at the home office, can imply that all problems have been dealt with through compensation. Through the physical distance of the workers combined with the bureaucratic rigor accorded to compensation calculus, employers can claim due diligence in responding to the needs of workers, albeit it is an abstract worker they address rather than a friend and colleague.

Above all else, the market basket compensation structure works because it says it does. More energy is devoted to the systematic, regular and extensive evaluation of the elements of the LPQ and RPS than to questioning if this process actually "compensates" expatriates. The work of review is displaced back on to expatriates, who must now evaluate themselves and their consumption in order to generate a financial system that is then reapplied to them, in part forcing them to dig their own grave. The audit regime, as exemplified by the market basket system, when it forces "all activities through the language of such accountability inevitably feels as if it is variously missing, traducing, or misrepresenting much of the infrastructure of everyday working life" (McDonald 2000: 127). Those who have investigated the workings of audit cultures in practice (e.g., Harper 2000; Strathern 2000a; McDonald 2000) observe that these are zones "where trust has to precede verification" as the collecting of data is comingled with the assent that this data is representative (Strathern 2000b: 7). Creating agreed-upon systems of review and regulation requires the production of a veneer of systematicity in order to act as a shell protecting extremely tenuous polities and presumptions (Gill 2008). Through processes of compensation that are grounded in the different living conditions present for expatriates worldwide, difference itself is "bulletproofed," both in making quantitative the abstract struggles of working overseas but also in affirming the need for mediators whose job it is to transit between here and there (Strathern 2006: 190). At a moment when the very practice of expatriate employment itself is in question as a result of claims about a globalizing workforce, compensation practices establish that there is real difference at stake. If it requires a fifty-page document to enumerate differences between shopping in the United States and in Nepal, the work of translating between the two countries must also be a difficult one.

Conclusion

Most employers see the separation from home as one of the key elements of expatriate life that must be compensated. Replicating life at home is presumed to be a means of facilitating expatriate success, although this is changing, as will be discussed in subsequent chapters. The cost-of-living allowance is a "home compensation" system, attempting to replicate the employees' class status in a new location, giving workers additional salary if obtaining the commodities of a parallel family in their home nation would cost more than they do in the new location. Hardship allowances participate in a similar logic, but in this case the goal is to compensate for lost comfort, security and the difficulty of life in a new location. In addition, various income adjustments seek to remunerate workers for the frequent moves that are a part of their job and the additional expenses of schooling and health care outside of a state infrastructure. All of these forms of financial compensation by the employer attempt to make up for loss, to recompense workers and their families for absences. The traditional economic analysis of compensation asks what it would cost to reproduce the labor of a given worker. In contrast, the market basket element of expatriate compensation asks what it would cost to reproduce the shopping list of a given family. Home leaves, social club memberships and other kinds of financial supplements participate in what is closer to a legal analysis: what has the expatriate worker (and his family) lost in going abroad? Like lawsuits regarding domestic labor of an intimate partner or negligence in the death of a family member, hardship allowances and some household incentives are designed to replace what is irreplaceable while abroad, including a spousal career, a grandparent's daily attention or a neighborhood best friend. The psychological element of compensation can be seen not in employer financial practices but in the concerns and behaviors of parents. As the Connellys worked to have a complete set of Christmas dishes, or the parents who had not had slumber parties themselves, yet hosted their children's friends for such events in Nepal, many expatriates seek to (over-) compensate for the displacement of overseas life by producing idealized lives that may not represent the practices they would have enjoyed outside of Expatria.

The market basket and its assumptions about what expatriates will be buying encourages families to consume as if they were at home. The cost-of-living survey can become not a reflection of a normative shopping process but a means of producing a shared commodity field, as families see the list of goods they are expected to price as a prescription. The dissonance between the expectations of the market basket list and expatriate consumer desires is seen in situations like the quest for Mexican food, where the nationalism of the U.S. State Department survey implies that there is something less than American in purchasing salsa. Representing the nation is often a part of the expatriate lexicon, but, as will be discussed in the next chapter, the compensation systems that mandate normal homes and diets take no account of the mobile lives that most expatriates have lived. The most important thing one Australian expatriate brought back in his luggage was candlenuts, a necessary ingredient in the food the family had learned to love while posted in Indonesia and which he had taught his Nepali cook to make. The desire to represent a home country exemplified in some practices of Expatria is crosscut with the global life experiences shared by all who follow this path.

The familiarity with a life that entails moving every three years encourages expatriates to help in the acclimatization of new arrivals to a country, as the struggle to understand Kathmandu's shopping culture is fresh in the minds of every member of the community. Social outings that move from lunchtime lectures on Nepali culture to group trips to the delicatessen encourage newcomers to follow the ways of more experienced expatriates. Thus, although where to get soccer balls may be different in each posting, the knowledge that there is a monthly coffee for new arrivals in nearly every location of Expatria enables new arrivals to quickly find experts in local consumption practices. Chatting about favorite new shops or anxiety about a new health scare promotes homogeneity in consumer choices through the desire to be part of Expatria and the social nature of consumption. Yet the impetus to engage in normative consumer choices did not stem from the anxieties of Expatria alone; these fears are in part learned from the commands of the compensation and employment system.

In his essay on "The New Business Class," Pico Iyer describes the life of the frequent business traveler, for whom the displacements of travel are eased by a consistency of experience, where everyone is in transit and similar facilities can be found in whatever airport, hotel or shopping mall one visits (1998; Kaplan 1997). Expatriates spend longer on the ground but rely on a similar set of continuities, familiar routines, houses and even dinners. Some scholars and expatriate employers presume such continuities, in the age of globalization, can produce a homogeneous experience, bringing to life the idea of a "McWorld" that would enable the moves of expatriates to be obviated by the availability of Starbucks everywhere in the world. Nepal, without either a McDonalds or a Starbucks, illuminates the limits of this presumption, which is not to say it escapes homogenizing or Westernizing influences in its consumer marketplace (cf. Liechty 2003). Kathmandu is not O'Hare airport, nor is it the Singaporean island of business, and with three or more years to spend in-country, expatriates quickly find its commodity lacunae. Breakfast cereal reappears as an example in the statement of one expatriate spouse who returned from a visit to the United States. She recalled being overwhelmed by a visit to a grocery store in Chicago: "They have whole aisles of cereal. I had forgotten that." While stores like the U.S. Commissary and Bhat Bhatini may offer a variety of corn flakes brands, the myriad options common in large supermarkets in the United States and Europe are not yet available in Nepal.

Thus, compensation packages affirm global distinction. The very idea that Nepal entails hardship and that expatriates need extra money to consume a market basket of goods not common in Kathmandu affirms the diversity of the world and the labor of translation that expatriates are living abroad in order to accomplish. The social nature of expatriate consumption produces Expatria, an operation that is of value to employers but not necessary for them to pay for. The structure of compensation enacts a claim that business practices are universal while cultures, at the very least in their commodity forms, are distinctive. These two processes are far more necessary to the ongoing validity of expatriate labor than the claims to fairness and equitability that are the explicit logic behind the market basket. Total recompense is never complete and an entirely different set of labors must be undertaken to compensate for life abroad—the work of refilling cereal boxes and trafficking in American Girl dolls.

4 The Protean Expatriate
Flexibility and the Modern Worker

OVER BEER AT AN OUTDOOR CAFÉ IN KATHMANDU, I was being regaled by stories of the horrors of trying to get construction work done in Nepal. The four expatriate men were complaining about the difficulty of getting supplies delivered on time and the poor quality of what eventually arrived. It was the end of a long week, and the waiter kept bringing cold San Miguel beer—although Alan had to insist that he bring the really cold stuff, from the bottom of the ice chest. I regretted teaching him his only word of Nepali, *chiso* for cold. As the lights turned on in the garden, the group decided that it was time for dinner. This was the routine for most of the expatriate workers on this job: a shuttle to the hotel—their temporary home—from the job site, a quick check of email in their rooms, then beer and dinner in the hotel's garden café. I met the Antigone Hotel crew by accident, but quickly became a regular. "Without you, it's a sausage fest," said one, noting that their embassy liaison was the only other woman (by implication foreign woman) they usually saw in a day.

The stories of how the Happy Hour gang at the Antigone had come to Nepal had commonalities and differences. Most had previous military experience and it was their security clearance gained while in the service that had made them particularly valuable on this job. Their work on this construction job was several levels removed from the initial Turkish contractor, who had successfully bid to build this new complex of buildings; most of them received their paychecks from the U.S. or Canadian-based companies that directly employed them but got daily orders from the Turkish managers. They ranged in age from late twenties to late fifties, but nearly all were well-traveled and had worked together on various jobs across the globe. Most were on short-term contracts varying from three months to twelve, depending on how long their specialization was needed, but those dates had limited meaning: "Everyone gets extended," they noted. Jobs, especially in places like Nepal, always take longer than the employers anticipate and they had experienced many delays due to strikes, lack of supplies and personnel gaps. Their indefinite posting to Kathmandu provoked different reactions: some celebrated the high wages they received while abroad, whereas others worried about children and wives left behind. Nearly half of those staying at the Antigone were contract-dependent employees, ultimately self-employed, their primary employer calling them in for service when the company was successful in bidding for a contract that required their particular skills. For these men, delays were welcome: "The job market at home sucks," noted an electrician from the southern United States. He was able to work odd jobs in his hometown when he was not overseas, but the dramatic difference between what he was paid to string electrical wire in Nepal and the casual labor he could pick up at home made the latter alternative unappealing. Most of the independent contractors were able to pick up enough lucrative overseas work that they did not work at all for the three to nine months a year they were without a contract.

Our group for dinner this evening had an easy camaraderie, sharing frustrations with past and present job sites, a conversation topic that often turned competitive as each tried to one-up the previous speaker with tales of horrible bosses, terrible food or incompetent coworkers. Nepal seemed to fall in the middle range, thanks to the variety of food available in Kathmandu and the relative infrequence of illness experienced by the group, but it lacked the attractions of other job sites. Complaints focused on the lack of activities, social events and recreational destinations, so much so that several of the men had taken to working for part of the weekend rather than face two days of boredom. Although not expected to work on Sunday, most joined the Nepalis on the project for at least part of the day to have something to do. Several of the men worked on wiring and computer networking, and they criticized the telephone and Internet capacity of the country, both from a personal and professional point of view. While in other places they had been able to video chat with family at home and watch favorite television programs online, this was often impossible in Kathmandu due to a combination of power outages, slow Internet connections and the significant time difference from home. Criticism aside, nearly all hoped to continue for many years what several described as a second bachelorhood. Three months of work with only the minor privations of a slow Internet allowed them to support families at home and have more leisure time when they were not abroad.

Difference That Makes the Difference

The Antigone residents, although doing some of the same jobs formerly done by career expatriates, were living a very different life from the families stationed in Kathmandu for multiple years of service. This chapter examines how the structures of overseas employment—for example the separation of workers from the initial bidder by as many as five different companies, as was the case of one Antigone regular—change the relationship of expatriate workers with their employers, as well as with Nepal. I explore how expatriate employment itself is changing and how those changes are transforming the population of foreigners in Kathmandu and around the world. Lifetime expatriates, like Donald and Dianne discussed in Chapter 2, are becoming less common, while short-term contracts and highly compensated consultants are replacing the earlier model of careers of mobility with families raised abroad, which characterized the expatriate profile in Nepal throughout the late twentieth century. In recent years, employers have sought to reduce the high rates of failure and additional expenses associated with career expatriates by generating new forms of flexible employment, relying less on employees within their organization and more on subcontracted workers. This process is evident throughout global business in the hollowing out of many companies that divest themselves of the expenses associated with permanent staff (Hindman 2011). But this approach is not merely the purview of business: it is also seen in the practices of development agencies and governments, such as when the U.S. military seeks to reduce its numbers through utilizing contract workers (e.g., Pelton 2007; Singer 2008). New theories of employment draw from the widely discussed practices of outsourcing associated with globalization, yet these interact in novel ways with ideas of diversity and culture that are salient for those working abroad. International employment experts have sought to develop new categories of work and new accounts of how employees are (or are not) connected to home and family in order to transform the compensation and treatment of overseas workers. While many of these approaches have found proponents within the business sector due to their promised cost savings, their implementation has been less successful than theorists anticipated. Few expatriates have embraced these new forms of flexible labor, and the demographic and economic differences between these new contract employees and past forms of expatriacy have created divides in the community in Nepal, and likely in other places across the globe. Such forms of precarity have become commonplace, but have a different character in Expatria (Neilson and Rossiter 2008; Stewart 2012).

Within the paradigm of "balance sheet" or "market basket" employment of expatriates, whereby workers were expected to live as if at home and to be deployed in many settings, training workers and their families in approaches to specific cultural differences and generalized issues of diversity was an important part of the preparation of expatriates. In the mid-1980s and early 1990s, new considerations arose as more companies became involved in international business and the sending organizations had employees with some connection to destination countries. "Internationalization" was occurring in both the workforce of Western employers and in the diversity of entities—government, business and aid organizations—sending workers abroad.

The rise of Japan as a business and aid force in the world startled many in the West and promoted new considerations of what a globalized workforce might look like. The attempts to emulate Japanese business models as well as anxiety about the potential success of new countries promoting themselves as being already "global," in combination with antiregulatory movements in the United States and parts of Europe, precipitated new employment procedures for overseas workers. This chapter explores how these moments of change in the "best practices" of expatriate employment interweave with the changing systems designed to provide workers with the tools to live and work overseas. Emplotting globalization onto employees such that they could be considered coming from a "non-place" (Augé 1995) would enable expatriacy to disappear: there would be no displacement and thus no need for compensation. In my own ethnography in Nepal, such unembedded people are rare, and few embrace the demand of permanent itinerancy that such a structure would demand.

For the expatriate who is tasked with global mediation—translating home office policy into local practices—the "problem" of difference comes from two directions, professional and personal, and structures of outsourcing mean little connection is made between the two. Difference and diversity must be addressed in the expatriate employee's interactions with the other in the workplace, and it is the demand for cultural awareness and sensitivity that is cited as key to the need for a mediator to bridge the divide between home policy and local process. Meanwhile, in their private lives expatriates are asked to defend against the culture of the Other at home, or deculture themselves in pursuit of being non-place persons. These two very different roles for the "culture problem" mean that culture is at times supposed to be celebrated and at other moments obviated, a process that can create or enforce stereotypes and produce new fears of difference in what is supposed to be a process of cultural connection.

Approaches to preparing expatriates to work abroad have changed over the last several decades and the changes have intersected with changing employment practices. As with previous research on the high rate of family failure, employers are now continually seeking new ways to minimize the expense of sending workers abroad in conjunction with new ideas on what facilitates successful expatriates. Two concerns meet in this uncomfortable conjuncture: what an overseas worker should look like and what the best way is to do business in a transnational setting. Since the 1970s there has been a substantial shift in employer expectations of the employee, especially a change from the idea of the employee as a "company man" to advocacy for a more flexible and independent worker who might go through several careers and employers in a lifetime. In addition, the techniques for providing transnational professionals with "global" skills, and the proliferation of services providing such training, have shifted in light of new populations experiencing the world outside their national borders. The conjuncture of these two changes has produced a decreased expectation of long-term knowledge of a given location as workers are asked to be acultural, unattached to either their home or host locations. In limited ways, employers have been able to implement changes to the structure of expatriate employment that follow this "non-place" approach, but the result has been workers unattached to Nepal or their employers while they become more, rather than less, attached to their home countries.[1]

Flexpatriates, International Citizens and the Cosmopolitan Ideal

To understand the way in which the problem of sending workers overseas is construed, one must first consider how a worker is thought to belong to a place and thus the implications of separation. If one were able to produce a worker without an identity or home attachment then the problems of culture shock or displacement would disappear. The description of this perfect attachment-free expatriate worker sounds remarkably like Karl Marx's description of the alienated worker in *The Economic and Philosophic Manuscripts of 1844*, where he observes that the capitalist reduces the worker to the lowest and most general standard, denuding him of all needs and social connections in the service of maximizing labor (Marx 1964: 149). Some business scholarship has attempted to theorize such a worker, estranged from his society, his nation, his culture, his family, his career and ultimately himself. Another pathway to rethinking the problem of overseas labor is to reconfigure whose responsibility it is to address concerns of where work is to be done. In the era of the virtual office, the physical locale of labor is, for some, ever less important (cf. Sassen 1991). This refiguring of location and the divisibility of the laboring body from other aspects of life was seen in a novel 2009 proposal from IBM entitled "Project Match," wherein fired U.S.-based workers were offered the opportunity to apply for jobs at IBM offices in India and Nigeria, where their positions were being relocated (McDougall 2009). A different strategy of rethinking the relationship of the worker to the job allows the employer to deny responsibility for the international worker by making the job into an avocation: the job becomes a fun opportunity for overseas travel, a combination of tourism and work (Butcher and Smith 2010; Grewal 2011). In either case, the worker is cast as a flexible, free agent without attachment to either company or society. Another approach takes the "flat world" or "McWorld" theorization beyond the commodity realm to the human product, anticipating a culture-free worker who would be equally at home anywhere. The unconnected, decultured worker proves a useful fiction to deploy in research on expatriate life, but often its as-if character is forgotten as ideas move between arenas of scholarship and business, and eventually the model trickles down to the worker as a demand for certain behaviors. In the quest for maximizing the labor of international elite workers, several theoretical models of idealized, unconnected employees have emerged, including the "international citizen," the "boundaryless career worker," and the "flexpatriate," which seem to offer up a solution to the problems incurred by sending workers and families abroad, but these models must often ignore the lives and actuality of expatriates.

International Citizens:
At Home Everywhere and Nowhere

One construction of the future of expatriate labor is found in the "international citizen" model. Beginning with the claim that globalization was making the world more homogeneous, scholars analyzed how such a fully globalized world might negate the necessity of an expatriate employee. A 1995 article in the journal *The International Executive* seemed to offer a solution to many of the problems and expenses of expatriate employment. "An Alternative Approach to Expatriate Allowances: An 'International Citizen'" proposed that current policies for compensating workers sent abroad were out of touch with the realities of a globalized world (Freeman and Kane 1995). The authors suggested that compensating workers posted abroad based on a divergence in living conditions between their home and host postings resulted in a compensation structure that did not accord with the vision of a global business environment. The claim was that excessive allowances granted under such a paradigm threatened to undermine corporate competitiveness in a global economy and neglect talent in non-Western countries. In contrast to the balance sheet approach that offers financial recompense for various aspects of international displacement, Freeman and Kane proposed a new category of employee, the international citizen, who would not be subject to this compensation system. Under the international citizen (IC) approach workers would not receive additional compensation or support for work abroad, but instead a properly selected IC employee would integrate into the local economy effectively. Such a worker would more fully instantiate the idea of a global company than the traditional balance sheet employee who continued to maintain loyalty to a home country. Their proposal was part of a discussion of expatriate management research that had been going on for some time seeking to capitalize on a newly imagined cosmopolitan workforce, and to turn the projects of celebrating workplace diversity in domestic office environments pursued in the 1970s into assets in the 2000s globalization era (cf. Gordon 1995).

The origins of this new way of thinking about employees came from an earlier sea-change in business research. In the late 1980s, the major business journals were filled with anxiety as well as applause for the Japanese mode of employment management. Even those authors not directly addressing the "Japanese model" were influenced by a wider set of concerns that it was seen to encapsulate, including the previously presumed superiority of Euro-American multinational corporations and the unquestioned universality of Western corporate models of employment.[2] In this period, global trade and a globalized economy went from something done *by* the West to something that might be done *to* it—if there were not significant changes in the Western ways of doing business. This wake-up call to the business world had a particular significance for those looking at expatriate employees, as these were the people on the front line of internationalization, those who somehow should have seen this coming. The shift from "multinational" to "global" corporations was under way, a shift associated with a new approach that moved beyond a variety of locally targeted strategies to a universal strategy to "operate with resolute constancy—at low relative cost—as if the entire world (or major regions of it) were a single entity" (Levitt 1983: 92). If a single global economy was emerging, all the money spent on sending workers abroad suddenly seemed irrelevant. Even more concerning for those in the West, Japan was seen to be doing a better job of targeting this monolith of the global.

The dramatic discussions of the Japanese business model and the perception of a single-market system raised interest in different ideologies of employee compensation. Those investigating expatriate employment seemed shocked (again) by the high costs of expatriate employees. In the late 1980s and early 1990s, several authors sought a solution to this dilemma in the form of eliminating home country expatriates in favor of local managers.[3] In a 1988 issue of *Human Resources Management* devoted to "Setting the Global Human Resources Management Agenda for the 1990s" (Tichy 1988), the editors attempted to find a way for Western multinational companies to thrive in what was perceived as a less-advantageous era for the forms of management that had previously prevailed. The journal devoted over half the issue to new Japanese management techniques and the need to change the way in which Western companies did business abroad. Only one article by Stephen Kobrin offered a dissenting voice against the rush to changing past forms of expatriate management, arguing that the reduction in the employment of expatriates by American companies had been ill-advised and the scale of expatriate pull-back had been much greater in the West than in Japan, adding that further reductions would put not just American companies but American workers at a disadvantage (Kobrin 1988). In his examination of these reductions, he found cost-cutting measures, deskilling and an unsubstantiated perception of expatriate failure the leading motivators for the shift in employment. While he lauded the rhetoric used to justify this transformation by American companies, which claimed the goal of this new employment style was a more diverse workforce, in his research he had found programs driven by a desperate attempt to trim employee costs with little attention to workers themselves or any real desire for diversity, and the end result, he suggested, would be not a workforce more competitive with the Japanese but one less familiar with the rest of the world and therefore at a disadvantage (see also Gordon 1995: 3).

Freeman and Kane's international citizen model was an early alternative to the employment of expatriates under the balance sheet model. While other authors had proposed expanding the employment of local nationals or more extensive training of Western expatriates, Freeman and Kane sought to rewrite the ideology of international employment in a way that would meet the objectives not of global competitiveness, but of international compensation specialists and their newly claimed expertise in assessing cost effectiveness, fairness, retention, constancy and motivation (Freeman and Kane 1995: 249; cf. Dowling and Schuler 1990: 117). The authors focused on how elements of the compensation package could be recalculated to reflect a different set of employee buying practices. This would require companies to demand that all workers serve abroad at some point, and thus international deployment would no longer be seen as an anomaly.

The international citizen paradigm assumes a new form of overseas life and work that "largely depends on the ability of the organization's expatriates to become assimilated into the large community of their host countries . . . because a real home base may cease to exist" (Freeman and Kane 1995: 253). Freeman and Kane noted that in addition to the financial benefits to an employer, an IC approach would also promote greater cross-cultural understanding and a more globally adaptable workforce, precisely the opposite of what Kobrin found (1988: 74). Freeman and Kane also observed, in a section titled "IC Approach in Practice," that many companies found that their employees rejected this new ideology and that several organizations that attempted to instantiate the IC approach returned to more traditional forms of compensation rather than lose their experienced workers. Since the initial publication of the Freeman and Kane article, many new theories have been put forth on how to cut expatriate costs, from minor recalculations to the elimination of the category of expatriate itself, but the IC model is one of the earliest and most extreme examples of the attempt to invent a worker to fit desired models of employment regardless of the actually existing workforce.

The Boundaryless Career of the Flexpatriate

This idea of the atomized and unattached worker reappears in a more utilized attempt to transform international employment, not by hypothesizing a new definition of the disembedded employee, but by redefining his or her motivation to work and relationship to the employer. The starting point for this new relationship between worker and employer is a rejection of "traditional" patterns of career employment and company loyalty, instead proposing for the worker a "boundaryless career," a paradigm that can be read as an opportunity for worker freedom or a denial of employer responsibility, depending on one's point of view. In the United States, the stereotype of 1950s employment seemed to offer new affluence, with both the rise of unionized factory jobs and the long careers of white-collar workers celebrated with retirement watches. Social scientists observed that workers of the period exhibited a strong identification with their career and considered their company a part of their personal identity. In the extremely influential *The Organization Man* (1956), William Whyte described a post–World War II style of suburban and corporate life wherein the worker closely allied himself with the company in the hope of profiting in tandem with the patron company and experienced a

sense of belonging in the homogeneous suburbs he shared with his coworkers. For Whyte, this was a Faustian bargain, one that negated the value of
individual achievement and ingenuity. Yet Whyte also discussed the reasons
behind the domination of the organization man system in the 1950s, which
he attributed to the rise of scientific management models and the quantification of human life. Whyte's disdain of the 1950s corporate worker model
emphasized the loss of creativity and the rise of bureaucracy and compliance.
In his critique of the conformity required of the employee, he proffered an
alternative in the form of a system that might allow for a more creative and
independent worker. Despite this cautionary tale, the company man has been
central to the image of how white collar work is done and continues to exist
in the imagination of some as the perfect job, perhaps particularly in America
(Coontz 1992; Engelhardt 1995; Conley 2009).[4] The icon of the retirement
party for the career employee still resists erasure as an ideal, and while it may
or may not have ever been the dominant paradigm, it is a powerful image of
the white-collar workplace.

This close employer-employee relationship was claimed to be outdated
within business scholarship as well, as seen in the work of Douglas Hall, who
in 1976 coined a term for its opposite, the "protean career." In *Careers in Organizations*, Hall put forth his idea of a new work practice in response to what he
saw as a changing paradigm of employment: a structure that would put workers in charge of their own career management and advancement. For Hall, this
was a hopeful development, one that escaped the stultification of *The Organization Man*, this time in favor of a more "countercultural" idea of freedom
and choice that Hall saw as a fulfillment of Whyte's concern. Borrowing from
psychologist Robert Lifton's article entitled "Protean Man" (1968) and a new
agentive idea of career paths exemplified by *What Color Is Your Parachute?*
(Bolles 1989), Hall described a class of workers who are driven by internal
ideas of success and satisfaction rather than the rungs on a career ladder and
who, as a result, will be flexible in their job location and tasks as well as more
personally satisfied with their work (Hall 1976: 201; 2004: 4). Hall's interest in this new idea of career seems born of the idealism of the era and his
discussions of the protean career are embedded within a rhetoric of personal
choice, individual ethics and self-satisfaction. But this concept has since traveled widely and many within the business and human resources community
celebrate the protean career from a different point of view—for the flexibility
it allows employers rather than employees. If the individual worker is a free
agent, responsible for his or her own success and satisfaction, the employer

might be forgiven for abjuring many obligations for reproducing and supporting a workforce. Flexibility is "increasingly seen as intrinsically valuable" (Martin 1994: 149) but it is this unquestioned value that makes the occlusion of who exactly is attaining flexibility possible (143–49).

The protean career idea contained within it several concepts incorporated by theorists of expatriate employment, including the idea of mobility as an inherent value, the shifting of career path responsibility onto the worker and the presumption of the worker as a free and independent actor. This concept was translated into a new language that found favor among human resources scholars and practitioners in the idea of the "boundaryless career." With the release of a book of the same title (Arthur and Rousseau 1996), international employment professionals gained their own phrase to describe a shift in the treatment of international employment—reveling in the potential to overcome job boundaries and national boundaries. Contributors to the volume contrasted this new form of work to the old organizational career and focused their research not only on the emotional opportunities this new approach offered the worker but also on the changing nature of work. This work, the editors observed in their introduction, has strayed from the vertically integrated corporate models that they believed still operated as the underlying assumption of much labor research (Arthur and Rousseau 1996: 4). Interestingly, the Arthur and Rousseau volume has little direct discussion of expatriates or international mobility, but their phrase has proven resonant within the literature on expatriate employment and enables authors to capture a new way of conceptualizing the globally mobile worker.

By the early 2000s, many of the major authors on expatriate employment were promoting the idea of boundaryless careers as a solution to the problems of high costs and family failure that continue to be debated in the literature. Moshe Banai and Wes Harry's "Boundaryless Global Careers" begins with an examination of various theories of careers and creates a new category, the "international itinerant," who is defined by having worked for at least two organizations in at least two countries (Banai and Harry 2004: 100). In positing an expatriate with a different orientation towards personal and professional goals, the authors suggest that this new category of workers offers many advantages to employers, including lower compensation costs, the potential to pay expatriate employees based on local living standards and a diminished level of corporate responsibility. They observe that given the high costs of traditional package expatriate postings, the expatriate return on investment (ROI) will likely be better with this new form of employment, regardless of the job performance of the expatriate worker. Thus, even if, as their research suggests, the international itinerant is less competent than his balance sheet-compensated counterpart, if the focus is only on the return on investment, the company might still come out ahead—a poorly paid, bad employee is calculated as more profitable than a well-compensated good one (McNulty and Tharenou 2004). This conclusion seems to lay bare the financial bottom line—that employment compensation is the most important quantifiable. Ethnographic evidence as well as data collected within the business literature on actual expatriate workers suggests that international itinerants do not meet the same performance standards as the company-bound expatriates, and furthermore, employers have difficulty finding qualified people willing to be employed as boundaryless workers. In studies of actual boundaryless workers, researchers find they are often former organization men who came to this new career orientation after having "failed" as expatriates or "gone native," rather than in an idealistic quest for career flexibility (Banai and Harry 2004: 101). Despite this, their qualifications for international work are proposed to be self-evident from their multiple postings abroad, even if these were a result of firing. Their transience in relation to jobs and employers is taken to mean that they "almost by definition have the knowledge, awareness, and skills necessary" to engage in "successful globalization" (101).

Flexible Life for Precarious Workers

The flexibility that spurred interest in the protean career continues to compel scholars and managers, but the lives of workers (expatriates or not) demonstrate that flexibility is ultimately held by the employer rather than the employee. Many balance sheet expatriates are reluctant to transform themselves into boundaryless expatriates, as they are aware of the personal and financial repercussions of such a redefinition. Employers benefit under the boundaryless approach by dispensing with the problem of families by eliminating them completely: "[t]here is rarely support for the international itinerants and their spouses and families . . . [they] are not concerned too much with the adjustment of the employee's spouse and have little responsibility for the employee's family" (Banai and Harry 2004: 107). Furthermore, international itinerants' "pay rates could reflect cheaper local conditions, and the itinerant would normally be responsible for their own career and family needs whilst working in an expatriate capacity" (McCarthy 2007: 94) while the "employer could, apparently, avoid equal opportunity and antidiscrimination legislation" (95). The implications of this new employer-employee relation reach far wider than the literature on expatriate management. Throughout business scholarship, employers are reanalyzing the dispersal of risk and responsibility within the employment relationship. Subcontracting and vertical disintegration provide similar examples whereby companies are able to divest themselves of employees. Through these practices, employers cut costs by avoiding paying a living wage or benefits, escaping having a permanent staff in a variable-need situation and thus "hollowing out" their offices. They are also able to distance their organizations from responsibility for wrongdoing and, furthermore, are able to market this change as something done for the benefit of employees, rather than as a result of financial motivations. The protean career reflects a form of hypersubcontracting[5] that creates organizations with extreme levels of flexibility that enable them to nimbly shift and move as the market demands. These new levels of instability have, by and large, come to be accepted in the contemporary workplace; what is novel is the capacity to sell this paradigm as a benefit to the worker. As several studies note,[6] the self-employed are paid less than direct employees for the same task and this disparity is addressed via a claim that most people, particularly Americans, appreciate the independence of a subcontracting situation and value being their own boss more than money. Thus, the protean man is not a victim in this understanding but a victor, able to escape the bounds of corporate life for freedom, in this case on a global scale.

Flexibility, as David Harvey notes (1990: 147), is a method in the service of the mobility and circulation of capital but it also serves double duty, being a phrase of artifice that is attractive to all—who wouldn't want to be more flexible?[7] In the global setting, the boundaryless career approach allows the employer to refigure mobility itself as a value, turning displacement and relocation from something necessary to compensate a worker for into compensation in and of itself. The idea of an international boundaryless career suggests the blurring of both national and career boundaries, as this new independent style of work demands a worker motivated not by loyalty or salary but by "internal" goals. Thus, living without running water is transformed from a hardship into an opportunity and what workers are being given in an international job is the chance to fulfill their own dreams. In the rise of "flexibility," Emily Martin sees a rhetoric that erupts in a wide range of fields, including human resources management (Martin 1994: 144, 208), often as a celebratory formulation, but which threatens the worker who must "glance uneasily over a terrifying edge into an abyss, inhabited by the unemployed, underemployed, temporarily employed, and destitute, fearing extinction from neglect and disease" (224).

These paradigms, which transform displacement from a source of concern to a job benefit, presume a freely choosing actor who is completely autonomous. Much research on mobility as compensation in and of itself is generated with cost-cutting in mind, while studies of actually existing expatriates suggest a different experience of these paradigms. In one of the studies of expatriates' career expectations and motivation to work abroad, Gunter Stahl, Edwin Miller and Rosalie Tung surveyed nearly five hundred German expatriates[8] and found that most cited the potential for advancement as their key motivator for overseas employment, although their interviewees also mentioned that they had not actually attained any promotions as a result of their expatriate positions (Stahl, Miller, and Tung 2002: 218, 220). For Stahl, Miller and Tung, this suggests they must also be driven by "intrinsic motivation," thus confirming the logic of self-directed, boundaryless careers. Yet they also note that this new focus on personal fulfillment may be because "most German companies have reduced the sizes of compensation packages for expatriates in recent years" (220). "Culture" and exposure to a cosmopolitan life appear to be secondary justifications given that "61% believed that rejection of the [international] job offer would have limited their subsequent career opportunities within the company" (220). It seems that most expatriates feel that they have limited choice when offered the opportunity to pursue overseas employment under a flexible compensation system and thus "the powerless employee flexibly complies" (Martin 1994: 145).[9]

One of the advantages initially claimed for workers in boundaryless careers—greater opportunities for "work-life balance" and gender equity—when rigorously investigated, appears to produce the opposite effect, particularly in the expatriate context. The rhetoric of flexibility and orientation to personal goals was initially cited by many human resources researchers as a family-friendly policy, one that might encourage the promotion of women in business (Fletcher and Bailyn 1996; Fondas 1996; Caligiuri and Cascio 1998). Yet, as even advocates of the boundaryless pathway note, this new orientation of careers and employment often further disempowers those already struggling in their desired career, making minorities ever more marginal and job security more tenuous (Arthur, Inkson, and Pringle 1999: 11). Often these compunctions are set aside as topics for future investigation, as those promoting boundaryless careers have noted that extant research has neglected these populations, and has "tended to construct women, ethnic minorities, blue-collar workers, the poor and uneducated as 'the other,' as deviations from a dominant pattern" (Pringle and Mallon 2003: 842). One of the few articles that actually investigates the issue of gender in boundaryless careers finds a problem, a split whereby women are pursuing boundaryless careers and men traditional ones, such that "the boundaryless career could continue to reinforce gender inequities in earning rather than advancing the cause of women's career success" (Valcour and Tolbert 2003: 783). On the one hand, the boundaryless career is touted as an opportunity for those desiring to follow "nontraditional" career paths, for example by taking time off from wage-labor for carework, to find a space in the employment circuit. Yet, it also presumes a free actor without history, community, family or even identity—a career actor without attachment—a pure individual. Thus, what was claimed to be a mode of activity that would allow more humanity in business, when transferred to a global setting, encourages only those without family responsibilities, community involvement or social markings of any kind to participate in the workforce (Baker and Aldrich 1996: 145–46).

Nepal and the Flexpatriate

The tension between the ideal of a flexible career and its manifestations in the everyday life of an expatriate family is evident in the changes occurring in the makeup of Nepal's expatriate community. In the late 1990s and early 2000s there was a greater receptivity to employing female expatriates, and although they were still the vast minority in Kathmandu, there was frequent talk of the emergence of new populations of expatriate workers, including the need to respond to the needs of dual-career couples, single women pursuing international careers and male trailing spouses. By 2007, this conversation had died down significantly. One justification for what appeared to be a rise in single or unaccompanied male expatriates in Kathmandu was the political tension in the capital, as seen in the ongoing street demonstrations and strikes occurring as part of the change of political regimes. Yet the way in which people were employed had also changed. More and more workers were in-country on short-term contracts of less than a year and many were discouraged from bringing family with them, either by a lack of compensation or through the promotion of Nepal as an unsafe place for families. The resulting new group of unattached male expatriates from North America and Europe were exemplars of the population able to pursue the boundaryless career options, and many thrived in the boom-bust cycle that was generated by short periods of high-paying work overseas followed by periods of unemployment. One technician who, at the point I met him, had lived in Nepal for six months on what was originally supposed to be a three-month contract, spoke of his enjoyment of this life, of a difficult relationship with his wife and children and the freedom allowed by his job. "It's like being a bachelor again!" he remarked, exchanging stories with fellow workers about their time in the military and about this job as a reprise of those halcyon days, although with more money and less physical risk. He was not particularly fond of Nepal, it ranked poorly in the list of places he had worked in the past few years, but through saving money on overseas jobs he was able to pursue his interest in motorcycle touring across the United States for the six-to-eight months a year when he was not under contract. Although he would have never used the term "boundary-less career" to describe his life, he was pleased to be fulfilling personal goals rather than striving to climb the corporate ladder.

The change in demographics of the expatriate population was less of a cause for celebration in the account of Janice. She was an unusual figure in the world of expatriate Nepal, having come to Kathmandu first in the mid-1990s as part of her work in development, and although her husband eventually found a job there, she was clearly the lead worker and he the trailing spouse. At that time, our conversations, often involving beer and rather apart from the rest of the expatriate scene, were a result of her eagerness to tell her story to a fellow female professional. She felt a great deal of pride in being a woman in a largely male industry, although she believed that neither the trailing spouses nor the foreign residents in the community found value in her careerism and success. Janice was a never-ending repository of stories about how she dealt with her unusual situation of foreign female superior working abroad, including her circumvention of laws against driving and unaccompanied women in some Middle East countries in which she had worked and the clever responses she had developed over the years to the assumptions of the largely male world—"No, she was not going to get tea, but if they were getting some, she'd like coffee—black." In the mid-1990s, she was hopeful, even boastful, of the new potentials for women in expatriate positions, not only in development but in business and diplomacy as well. She had actively mentored several women she had met in her initial years of overseas work and found that new policy statements from employers left space for a rise in the number of female professional expatriates. The assumption that every expatriate would have the uncompensated labor of a female spouse was, although still the norm, being questioned more and more, she noted, by wives as well as by companies. She saw herself as a trailblazer and proudly spoke of how the male expatriates might not be able to protect their lucrative jobs from the enthusiastic young career women with whom she had worked. In 1999, she speculated that in a few years, there might be equal numbers of male and female expatriates in not only "helping" and "cultural" positions but in business as well.

We spoke again when Janice found herself in another posting to Kathmandu in 2007, and our conversations about careers, gender and overseas work took a different tone. She was on what she suspected would be her last tour abroad—her mentees had left the expatriate track and she doubted there would be many more. She said, "Things had really been looking up in the 1990s: more and more women . . . now, that is all gone." She searched for a reason why the next generation of female expatriate professionals she had believed she was cultivating had not appeared in Nepal by 2007, and we speculated for nearly an hour, raising a variety of possible explanations: changing attitudes towards raising children, the rise of Maoist violence in Kathmandu and general cutbacks in the money devoted to aid projects. In the end, she seemed unsatisfied with any of our conclusions—she decided it was not discrimination, it was not fear or politics, "it was only business." Most of the career expatriate workers had been replaced by subcontractors and overseas work was now more often based upon three-month rather than three-year contracts. Flexibility and networking were the name of the game—and willingness to move and eagerness to make connections were the keys to success. Overseas work was no longer skill-based but connection-based, and many subcontractors spent most of their time looking for the next job—if they wanted it.

Although Janice and I did not talk about this at the time, I later found out another reason why women were rarer in diplomatic circles and some businesses. Nepal was increasingly seen as a security site—and more tasks were requiring security clearance. Military subcontractors were taking over many of the career expatriate jobs—utilizing wartime connections and the ease of their employment—especially given one report of a two-year delay in obtaining U.S. security clearances for nongovernment employees working on government contracts (Hindman 2010; 2011). By 2007, women were being kept out of overseas work—often not because they resisted the flexible regimes being imposed and the protean career path but because it was assumed that they would. "Mothers won't be willing to take these short-term contracts," said one employer. "They are thinking about the school year and their kids."

The situation in Nepal presents particular challenges to the desire to employ the international itinerant. The large number of Western tourists in Kathmandu and a substantial population of resident foreigners provoke traditional package expatriates to defend their unique situation and their distinction from this mass of transients—identified by leisure and a lack of professionalism.

Valuing the desire to experience other cultures and lead a self-directed life to many in expatriate Kathmandu sounds like the motivations of other groups of foreigners in the country—the seekers and resident foreigners (Moran 2004). It is necessary for expatriates to make clear to several different audiences that it is the career that brings them to Nepal rather than a spiritual quest, a hippy adventure or a passion for mountaineering. The city is filled with eager foreign volunteers picking up work for a few months or trying to stay on for several years, and these potential protean career pursuers could be seen to present a threat to the livelihood of lifetime expatriates. But the different styles of movement adopted by the two populations make distinguishing who is pursuing which type of overseas employment clear, and the demographic pull of the two paths is very different. One career expatriate I spoke with noted the importance of the distinction in the context of stories about other postings. He remarked, "for me, it has always been about the job. In Thailand, there were all these guys who were just there to find a nice Oriental girl." As he explained it, many of those he had worked with in Southeast Asia were struggling to find ways to stay in the region, either because they were seeking a relationship with a local woman or because they had succeeded in finding a local partner and were now reluctant to leave. Many such would-be hangers on in Nepal find local life desirable because of its low cost of living, outdoor adventure opportunities and spiritual communities—yet the plethora of available foreigners and low wages in Nepal makes acquiring appealing jobs from within the country difficult. Contempt for these resident foreigners is shared by both organization man and protean career expatriates.

Most of these theories of a worker disconnected from company, family and nation are grounded in transparent cost-cutting motivations, and when these economically driven practices are introduced, employer values expressed elsewhere about cultural competency and local knowledge are cast aside. The financial advantages of this deferral of risk and costs onto workers have, in large part, obfuscated earlier concerns about failure, families and cross-cultural skills. These new disposable international workers find themselves engaged in promoting a global "race to the bottom" as a part of their official duties, and yet in the theories of international human resources management the same policies of flexible labor are applied to them. In a study of flexpatriate issues, the authors conclude that "flexpatriate assignments are financially less complex to administer in that there are no relocation costs or repatriation costs and no complicated international compensation packages . . . Many stresses arising from relocation that result in work, family, and personal difficulties, which have been well documented in the expatriate experience, are not obviously present for flexpatriates" (Mayerhofer, Hartmann, and Herbert 2004: 652). Workers who are not accompanied by their families and who are expected to live at some level of remove from the local culture, albeit on a local salary, are not seen to have family tensions or cultural problems—they are assumed not to have families or culture. In the initial propositions of international compensation experts, these new paradigms of employment are presented as hypothetical solutions to the problem of expatriate costs, yet their hypothetical character is often lost in the enthusiasm for economization. Like the reductio ad absurdum often generated within neoclassical economics, the notion of an international citizen presumes a maximizing actor disconnected from any social relations, and yet this creature does not exist in the world. On account of the exigencies of the contemporary workplace, some are strategically willing to appear unattached so as not to face unemployment; thus they fulfill the fantasy of theorists of the international citizen.

The claim that this new paradigm of flexibility would generate a more diverse group of international workers who are more closely integrated into the local economy was having the opposite effect in Nepal. Short-term contracts meant that most workers were housed in hotels, eliminating the need for day-to-day errands, and for contact with Nepali staff and neighbors. Shuttled by a company-supplied van from hotel to worksite, these contract workers saw very little of Kathmandu. Alan from the Antigone and his coworkers were typical in this respect: when I met them several months into their time in Kathmandu, they had not seen any part of the city other than their workplace, the hotel, the local international clubs and the tourist district of Thamel. Trips by those who ventured out to see "the monkey temple" or "the Buddhist eyes thing" were poorly reviewed, as the entire endeavor was deemed "not that big a deal, and it's really hot and dirty." Alan, who had a greater desire than many of his colleagues to see the city, arranged for a guided tour with a driver and English-speaking guide. Although one participant was pleased that he had actually gotten out and seen the sights, the consensus was that it had not been worth the heat, expense and risk of illness. "From now on, I'm just going to stay here at the Antigone," one man remarked, noting that he had eaten at the hotel for the last three weeks without getting sick and in one trip out he was ill, even though he had only had a package of potato chips and a soda while waiting for the driver to pick his group up at a temple. As in other places he had visited, after this tour Alan had checked off the major tourist sites, collected some trinkets and was now waiting out the time before his job would be done and he could collect his paycheck. Contract workers felt little motivation to familiarize themselves with Nepal because at any time they could be off to a new location—a situation that produced not eagerness to see their temporary home but a belief that it was not worth the trouble (see also Hindman 2011). Furthermore, most remained connected to another life at home that included children, wives and parents with whom they conversed on a daily basis through Internet chats, Skype or phone calls. One member of this group frequently left our dinners at exactly 6:30 P.M, so he could wake up his son in North Carolina for school. If these subcontracted workers were any indication, the international citizen worker was more connected to his home nation than his balance sheet contemporaries, as more of their lives were left behind while posted abroad.

The international expatriates whom these maximizing policies are applied to play dual roles as both managers and managed; they are between the metropolitan policy and the local instantiation. They are charged with facilitating and implementing policies of the organizations that employ them, but often they are also the potential victims of the negative repercussions of the very policies they are propagating. Strategies like the international citizen, boundaryless careers and flexpatriate appeal from the position of executive privilege as well as from a grassroots vision of a cosmopolitan utopia, but implementation often proves untenable and it is the middlemen of globalization who are on the front line of the dissonance. The tension between the roles culture is expected to play in the work versus the home lives of expatriates is often unreadable in a subcontracted setting, wherein workers are estranged from both social relations and the process of policy production through the restructuring of international employment. While the abstract idea of a worker equally at home in different locations might make sense sitting in Geneva with considerations of travel to Sidney or even Hong Kong, one would not mistake Kathmandu for a European capital, and the presumption that all displacements will be experienced in a similar way seems to suggest that those who theorize international itinerates have a more circumscribed network with New York, Tokyo and London in mind rather than Kathmandu, Kuala Lumpur and Bamako. One expatriate working in Nepal described having received a briefing from his home office about the importance of respecting local religions and traditions on the same day he was chided for the decreased productivity of his sector that had occurred during the long fall holiday of Dashain celebrated in Nepal. How, he wondered, should he both "respect local culture" and meet his quota? All the while subcontracting and outsourcing of global processes reach further levels of efficiency and remove, the negative effects of these phenomena on the ground become more visible, and it is the engineers who do far more than neutrally turn policy into practice. They have a front row seat for what is transformed in translation.

5 Saving Business from Culture
Cross-Cultural Training and Multicultural Performances

TO UNDERSTAND THE AMBIVALENT ROLE that culture and difference plays in the world of overseas employees living in Kathmandu, I want to return to the Antigone Hotel and look at one of Alan's coworkers who had a different experience of being in Nepal than any of his compatriots. John was one of the quietest members of the group; he did not share their military experience nor their tenures abroad, but was valued as a member of the group for his local knowledge. It was not his telecommunication expertise that was central to their conversation but his perceived comprehension of Nepal—of Kathmandu's horrible traffic, the strange outfits and customs seen on the drives across town. On this particular night, John was responsible for deciding what was for dinner. He was asked to interpret the menu, as several members of the group had grown tired of the limited choices on the first page, which was mainly Western food. It was hoped that John could guide them through the other options and suggest what to order. The impression of his expertise on all things local was something he tried to reject, but it was foisted on him again and again because he was Indian-American.

It was only after everyone else had left that John began telling his story of a difficult three months in Kathmandu and his frustration with being posted to Nepal. John had been born in South India but had left at a young age to move to Canada with his family. After school and a few years at university in Toronto, John was offered a job with a technology company that required a move to the United States. His wife was reluctant, but John was eager for both the adventure and substantial salary. John had worked for the company for nearly ten years when they asked him to make this trip to Nepal. His company was rarely involved in international work, but had been asked by another company to provide workers of an uncommon expertise for a project for which sufficient staff of his specialization was unavailable. The job was already circuited through several different subcontracted companies: the organization seeking to build a new headquarters, an international design agency, a third-country engineering firm, a general contractor, a subcontractor for internal systems and a specialist in technological systems. John's employer was the end of this outsourcing series. Although many people in his company possessed the necessary skills for the job, John was their first choice for the job because he was "Indian."

In his small company in the United States, he was one of a very small number of non-white employees, and the same was true in the city where he lived and where his children went to school. Previous to this posting, John claimed that, despite his slight accent and the occasional curiosity of friends, his birth in India had rarely been a subject of workplace conversation. Now, in Nepal, he was being called upon as the representative of all things "local." Without language skills or any experience in the country, John found himself no more prepared for life in Kathmandu than his colleagues and perhaps less, as most of them were veterans of the same overseas labor circuit. The other three men present at the dinner had been posted together numerous times, including in sub-Saharan Africa, the Middle East and other locations in South Asia. Most of the pressure on John to represent the local situation was good natured, and his vegetarianism eventually became a source of greater fascination than his "Indianness."

Our conversation about his discomfort at being seen as the source of local knowledge began with his thanking me for, in part, taking over the role of local expert. Recent Maoist roadblocks on the street outside the Antigone and on their route to work had brought forth conversations about politics in Nepal, and my willingness to discuss this had turned attention from him. Overall, John was quick to absolve his coworkers of their assumptions about his familiarity with Nepal; it was his company and to a lesser extent his extended family that frustrated him. "I warned them this wouldn't work out," he noted, as he explained how his employer had selected him for this assignment despite his lack of previous overseas work experience. John felt he received less respect from the third-country nationals in charge of the contract, as well as from Nepali workers on the project, than his white colleagues. Furthermore, he was trepidatious about what might happen after a recent phone call from distant relatives now living in New Delhi announced they were coming to Kathmandu for a visit.

His company had selected him because they anticipated his ability to perform well in South Asia, a characteristic they had determined by his skin color rather than any cross-cultural testing. Such unscientific methods might be attributed to the employer's inexperience in international employment, but that the selection proceeded against John's protest seems to suggest that in this case of international employment some types of difference mattered more than others. John had objected to the posting and also tried to point out to his employer that his ethnicity would likely be a disadvantage in Nepal[1] and that he had no local skills, ability to "pass" as Nepali or experience living abroad (unless Canada counted). Yet John, compelled by pressure and financial incentive, assented to the position and was hired. Assumptions about his "natural" fit in Nepal meant that his company bypassed any predeparture training, and given that his contract was only expected to last three months, the employer had little concern about separating John from his family or the home office. As his time in Nepal was already extending beyond the short trip he anticipated and his coworkers told him that three months often became a year or more, many of his worst fears about this position were coming to pass.

John's unwilling emplotment as a "local," or at least as "culturally competent" to work in Nepal, tells only part of the story of how overseas employers are seeking to deal with "culture." Culture plays a role in Expatria as a barrier but also in a celebratory form, one shared by many in the international community—a common grammar for exchange that establishes the limits within which difference is permitted as well as defining who is a part of Expatria. This chapter brings together three sets of concerns about culture: the preparation of overseas workers to respond to life abroad, "internationalism" as a social and professional structure and finally, the demand that "culture" be addressed as part of globalization. The last element, the expectation that products and practices be adapted to local conditions, is one familiar within the literature on globalization and consumption (cf. Burke 1996; Howes 1996; Watson 1997; Dávila 2001; Foster 2008). I focus here less on how products are adapted for a local market than on expatriate mediators as those responsible for the work of adaptation. Importantly, I found in the experience of expatriates a conflict between the expectation of cultural specificity for products and projects and an understanding of the universality of business practices.

While the status of expatriates and their work is being refigured by labor and business scholars, a different set of experts are in the process of creating a new epistemology of alterity that efficiently intersects with the demands of global business and employment. The management of culture must be addressed in the deployment of workers abroad as well as in the work that they do. The first section of this chapter investigates the messages that expatriates receive about difference, particularly how they are prepared to deal with working in a new cultural environment. Through a rubric of "cultural types" and participation in games of cultural understanding, cross-cultural experts seek to generate workers who will be able to join the global workplace with a minimum of conflict and corporate expense. These techniques of codifying difference are deployed not only in expatriate preparation and workplace practices, but also in the transformation of goods and services into new settings. The infamous, if likely apocryphal, "Nova" problem said to have been encountered by Chevrolet in Spanish-speaking countries has made businesses aware that projects cannot always be exported without any transformation, yet the impulse is to keep such changes to a minimum. Development professionals must figure out how to translate the current project on women's home-based enterprises to Nepal, businessmen work to figure out what might expand the market for life insurance in Kathmandu and diplomats struggle to understand the motivations and historical tensions that underlie resistance to their entreaties.

It has become incumbent upon organizations to proclaim awareness of difference and a transnational orientation, although not necessarily to enact it at any deep level (Ho 2005: 88). These performances of global reach and local knowledge can be expensive, as organizations attempt to place their footprint in many sites across the world and understand how to make their project or product attractive. Those who do this successfully are able to create "global presence" through only minor and standardized transformations at every target site, implementing the bare minimum necessary to convey the image of local awareness to their audience (85). Development proposals slot a "local context" section into all of their projects, but seek to retain as much of the overarching agenda as possible. Expatriate workers and their employers face similar questions inside and outside of their formal businesses: How can you understand and control cultural knowledge? How does an organization efficiently engage with local culture without investing too much time and money? How is it possible to inexpensively convey the image of diversity?

Solutions to these dilemmas lie in the regularization of difference, systematizing culture contact into typologies; through this process of codification, culture itself and the response to difference can be addressed through the same mechanisms worldwide. Although one product may not fit all, if one can figure out that many places are of a type, one can reduce the number of variations: one system for "developing Asia," one for the BRIC countries, and so on. The address to "culture shock," which has become the popular term of art for the results of contact with difference, is a good example, as in this pathologization of the experience of cultural disorientation employers have a concept that turns the experience of difference into a set of treatable symptoms that exist independent of the forms of contact or the location of placement. This general response to the problem of displacement is supplemented by classificatory modes of cultural analysis that address cultural specificity by reducing difference to a set of variables. The system of international business and employment embraces culture as a signifier as long as its conceptualization does not intrude into actually meaningful domains, such as the operation of global capitalisms (Gordon 1995: 4). These codifications of culture exclude discussions of power, history and belief—transformations that demand a more complex shape for difference. Thus, distinctions in clothing, art and cuisine are acceptable, but distinctions in values and beliefs are unacceptable. In this asymmetric approach to difference, other cultures are reviewed and critiqued, but the "culture" of business and the practices of a neoliberal global regime are excluded from the examination. These paradigms turn culture into an ahistorical list of traits, some in a dyadic construction such as individual versus collective cultures, others delineating a grid of national character types or a list of cultural categories to consider, including values, truth-telling and family orientation. In Geert Hofstede's "dimensions of national culture," Richard Lewis's "culture active tool," Fons Trompenaars's "cultural dimensions" or Clotaire Rapaille's "culture code," the complexities of global human interaction are transformed into a set of categories that are intended to give guidance on how to communicate with "the Other." This creates additional problems for those going to Nepal, a site too small to merit attention in these systems, and thus specific guidance for people about to live in Kathmandu is limited. Even though cultural instruction is acknowledged as an important part of expatriate preparation leading to knowledge necessary for work, one family headed to Kathmandu found their cultural instruction consisted of a printout of a Wikipedia article on Nepal and copies of relevant pages from *Kiss, Bow or Shake Hands: How to Do Business in Sixty Countries* (Morrison, Conaway, and Borden 1994).[2]

Is Your Culture Masculine Future or Feminine Past?

The profile of what makes someone successful living in a new cultural environment would be difficult to discern by looking at the population of those resident in Kathmandu at any given time.[3] At an expatriate social gathering, one might find a former missionary or military child who grew up moving from country to country, a German who spent a gap year traveling Europe but with little other international experience and an American whose family has lived in the same small town in the Midwest for generations. The lack of either ethnographic or statistical evidence as to who will thrive in a country different from their homeland bedevils international business researchers. Although occasionally the question is framed as one of nationality—do Japanese succeed in Europe relative to Americans?—it is more often addressed through assessments of some generalized cultural skills (cf. N. Ferguson 2004: 204). Cultural competency, with little agreement as to what that constitutes, is frequently mentioned as key to determining who will be successful, both in their work of cultural translation and in the experience of living abroad.

My own ethnographic research and studies by a few contrarian scholars suggest that despite the extensive discussions of scientific modalities of testing for cultural competency, in practice many of the decisions about expatriate selection reside in the informal mechanisms of ascertaining who is willing to go and discussions around the water cooler. Yet most contemporary expatriate employers have their workers undergo cross-cultural testing and training, often outsourced to secondary service providers, as one aspect of their expatriate selection process, because it affords two benefits over less-formal means of selection. First, it provides employers with some infrastructure to support decisions they may have already made (Harris and Brewster 1999)—a form of generating trust and defending ambiguous processes that can be redeployed in the case of either failure or success. In placing trust in the test or an outside agency administering predeparture training, they create a structure of culpability that absolves the employer, and to a lesser degree the employee, from failed postings (Power 1997). After one unsuccessful worker posting to Nepal, a senior officer justified the hiring, noting that the worker had "been off the charts" of the Overseas Assignment Inventory (OAI), the cultural adaptability test their subcontractor had used. In addition, testing and associated forms of cultural classification generate data about difference that can be deployed in the work of expatriates, who through this process are not only examined for their ability to respond to difference but also learn what difference to expect and how to transform their work in response.

The first element of cultural competency assessment are the "cultural IQ tests" discussed in Chapter 2, that attempt to ascertain international competencies associated with the ability to work and succeed in a multicultural environment under categories such as openness, emotional resilience, flexibility and the like. These tests, administered to the worker and often to his family as well, seek to get at inherent personality traits that will assist them in living abroad for an extended period of time. Psychologists and human resources scholars suggest to employers that the intercultural skills they measure should be privileged over technical abilities, as the latter can be taught while the former are innate (cf. E. Miller 1973). In one case in Kathmandu, this testing process resulted in workplace tension as a cohort of expatriate workers eagerly anticipated the arrival of an electrical specialist so their work could proceed. On his arrival, they discovered that, although deemed culturally competent, the worker dispatched by headquarters lacked the necessary skills for the job. By introducing cultural competency as a single, innate and universally applicable personal characteristic, these tests affect as well as categorize the employee, excusing him or her from responsibility for any lack of internationalism.

Given that many in the industry insist that "the people with the best technical skills are not necessarily those with the best cross-cultural adjustment skills" (Black, Gregersen, and Mendenhall 1992: 56), how can employers get qualified personnel overseas and avoid the project delays that occurred in Kathmandu when the electrical specialist turned out to have no skills in the field? Although the perspective on cultural competency put forth by many in the cultural-competency testing field suggests that it is a characteristic that individuals possess in a fixed quantity, other scholarship is seeking to redress problems of "cultural incompetency" through cross-cultural training. This compensatory training relies on understandings of cross-cultural conflict as generated by the personality differences of different cultures. Not unlike the workplace seminars based on Myers-Briggs testing, cross-cultural training is designed to help workers coming from one national personality type cope with the approach of another, suggesting that the problem is not a ranking of cultural competency but a claim that there are inherent tensions that occur between people from "masculine" versus "feminine" cultures that can be remedied through understanding this distinction. In the widest framing, such preparation for culture contact can include everything from lectures on the history of a specific nation to role-playing games. While much of the initial research on cross-cultural training was designed around the needs of foreign students and expatriates, such training is now discussed as a fruitful experience for everyone, justified by the multicultural nature of the contemporary workforce and the need for people in many careers to travel and engage diverse populations. At job sites across the world, one can find employees engaged in exercises designed to help them "deal with" diversity in the workplace.[4]

Those seeking to define cross-cultural training generally cite two topics and two methods as being key divides in the field: culture-general training versus culture-specific training and intellectual versus experiential approaches. Intellectual approaches are derided in most contemporary scholarship as ineffective, with claims that they are too abstract, lack an "emotional" character or are anticipated to be difficult for participants to apply (Puck, Kittler, and Wright 2008: 2186; Peace Corps 1999: 137). The "university model," or the intellectual approach, had some adherents among early cross-cultural trainers, but it is now seen as an inferior means of conveying information, although this approach must be used in some settings because the culture under consideration is too "obscure," in which case videos or university lectures are seen as an acceptable alternative to more "emotional" forms of cultural education (Harrison and Hopkins 1967; Bhawuk and Brislin 2000). Experiential learning is widely preferred, as this technique is seen to help "develop 'the emotional muscle' which is needed in intercultural interactions" (Bhawuk and Brislin 2000: 168). Whether in experiential form or university style, culture-specific training is lauded as necessary and preferable for the cross-cultural training of expatriates, but it is rarely on the list of services provided by intercultural services agencies, as culture-specific approaches require expertise in the many different nations and regions that might be in demand among companies. Most studies of cross-cultural training denounce the lack of attention to specific cultural areas and call for more attention to training targeting the particular destination of the trainee, but they acknowledge that this is rarely possible given the practical difficulties of employees headed to many different locations. Thus, of these four quadrants of cross-cultural training, most programs focus only on one, culture-general training provided in an experiential format. As a result, expatriates rarely receive the information they regard as most important—information about their specific destination and everyday life as an expatriate there. One woman in Nepal, reflecting on her experiences with cultural training and preparation, stated that she really wanted to know only one thing from her predeparture training and no one could answer her question—should she bring her own washing machine or buy one there? In the days and weeks before departure, such practical concerns are on the minds of most expatriates, thus many resent what one woman described as "playing games" and "group therapy" rather than help with packing and enrolling children in local schools.

Nearly all nongovernmental agencies, and many governments, have moved to utilizing outside companies to lead cross-cultural training for their expatriate workers. Companies such as Advanced Global Connections, Aperian Global and Leadership Crossroads provide one- to two-day workshops as well as specialized programs on doing business in Asia, leadership in a diverse workplace and global negotiation techniques. It can be difficult for expatriates to discern which organization is actually providing their training, as employers often outsource the process of expatriate selection, compensation calculation and training to a large "expatriate services" provider that may further outsource some or part of the training to another entity. In the chaos of departure, expatriate families meet many different service providers, including movers, psychologists, communications professionals and compensation managers. Amidst this flurry of forms and information comes cross-cultural training, and it was often highlighted by those I spoke to in Nepal as the least useful form of help, and discussed with some hostility as workers complained that it took time way from more important concerns such as health insurance and packing-weight allowances.

Many soon-to-be overseas workers participate in cross-cultural training seminars run by human resources professionals, psychologists or past expatriates. Companies pay the tuition for their employees to attend seminars, which can cost $5,000 or more depending on the type of workshop, length and number of participants, or hire specialists to provide quarterly "cross-cultural seminars" for both expatriates and home-office-based employees. There are some organizations offering inexpensive seminars for employers of a small number of expatriates, where large lectures or videotaped discussions with online participatory elements are the more common mode of instruction. As in the case of cultural competence testing, there is little conclusion as to whether these methods work, but the high costs of expatriate failure are used to justify the expenditure as companies use these procedures to create an external infrastructure on which to hang the risk of expatriate failure.[5]

Many of those offering expatriate cross-cultural training services jealously guard their proprietary techniques, but most follow a similar format that combines discussions of culture shock and examination of different cultural types, with small-group activities teaching people appropriate reactions to different cultural behaviors and beliefs. These experiential techniques, particularly for those going to Nepal—a place with limited preprepared information on culture contact—are supplemented by books and movies available on the public market. Several organizations seek to give participants a hands-on approach to novelty and discomfort through outings to domestic cultural sites such as Chinatowns or in "home stay" programs with immigrant families.

The professionalization of predeparture cross-cultural training has dramatically changed the nature of preparation that expatriates receive to go abroad. In the past, predeparture "training" was a network of informal connections within the company, mimeographed lists of items to bring and newsletters like the *Spouse's Underground Newsletter* or the *Outpost Network* of Shell employees and families. Connections were often on a one-to-one basis, with departing expatriates being tasked with the job of preparing their replacements not only for the job but also for life in a new country. I saw one example of this more intimate form of predeparture preparation in the mosquito net one family used as a decoration in their Kathmandu home. The wife explained to me that this had been given to her by a woman whose husband had worked in the same company as her husband and had lived in East Africa, where they were first posted. Nearly twenty years ago, they had shared several dinners before the couple's first overseas position and she had carried this elaborate bed net with her through several countries as a symbol of the friendship this family had shown them and the value of the knowledge they had passed on. This sort of informal contact has been to a large degree supplanted by professional services and proprietary information, as well as the availability of online information. The professionalization of cross-cultural training has turned attention to techniques of cross-cultural communication, cultural types and preparation for culture shock, with little time remaining for such one-on-one relationships.

How Should You Deal with Your Collectivist Colleagues?

One of the most-utilized tools for refining the complexity of global diversity into a smaller set of rules and applicable character traits stems from the "culture and personality" school of anthropology. This approach, popular from the 1930s through the 1950s, combined ethnographic research with psychological approaches to produce national character studies. Franz Boas emphasized a holistic approach to culture, brought to prominence in part by the wartime context in which many of his students did their research. This approach combined with the rising popularity of Gestalt and Freudian psychology in the period. Culture and personality approaches proved popular with a public audience as well as governments (Stocking 1986). Edward T. Hall arrived at this school of thought as its popularity was waning, but his affiliation with U.S. government agencies made its continuance as an approach to the understanding of culture appropriate despite the changing trends. Drawing from the culture and personality school, which understood the nation as the primary unit, and a psychological approach to research, Hall added his own focus on linguistics, formulating a new means of understanding language that demanded an attention to language beyond words, developing ideas such as low- and high-context language-cultures and monochronic and polychronic approaches to time (E. T. Hall 1977; 1992; Rogers, Hart, and Miike 2002). Although initially focused on language and linguistics, Hall's theories found an audience among foreign service and business professionals, although limited respect within the anthropological academy. From this beginning, intercultural or cross-cultural communication came into being, and shifted from the domain of ethnography and linguistics to psychology and business.

Hall's 1959 book *The Silent Language* preceded by only a few years the research of Geert Hofstede, who was hired at IBM as a corporate psychologist to understand both the corporate culture of IBM and how to manage its international operations. Leaving the official employ of IBM for several years in the early 1970s, Hofstede had more opportunity to review the extensive survey data he had collected there and found that analyzing the data on a national level showed more correlation than any other factor. From this, he was able to develop a set of national characteristics that he found correlated well with other data he was collecting on expatriate managers. At the time, according to Hofstede, IBM and other companies were uninterested in his conclusions about cultural types (Magazine Intercultures n.d.); Hofstede and Hoppe 2004). By the time of the release of *Culture's Consequences* in 1980, Hofstede's division of national cultures into four characteristics—power distance, individualism, uncertainty avoidance and masculinity—had found a larger audience, and his framework spawned imitators as well as defining the approach of cross-cultural communication as a field. From its difficult beginnings, the "Hofstedian grip" has come to exert its control over business understandings of culture, as can be seen in the availability of a "CultureGPS" application for the iPhone, which utilizes his cultural dimensions approach (Bjerregaard, Lauring, and Klitmøller 2009: 211, citing Søderberg and Holden 2002; Sackmann and Phillips 2004). Similar paradigms purporting to typologize culture—in which the nation-state is often the presumed unit—are produced by scholars such as Clotaire Rapaille (2006), Richard Lewis (1996) and Fons Trompenaars (1998). Although these researchers produce distinctive conclusions and use different methods for data collection, their output takes similar forms, generating rankings and lists of characteristics similar to those produced by the Myers-Briggs, assigning nations, rather than individuals, personalities. Marketing professionals see value in this approach, as it allows them to perform minor transformations that will make their products desirable in a masculine culture or a linear-active nation or one that associates their automobile with their identity—frameworks of Hofstede, Lewis and Rapaille respectively. These archetypes-cum-stereotypes are often acknowledged as limited, but tolerated within the business world as easily applicable and supported by sustained research. Several scholars in the field of cross-cultural communication have criticized these decontextualized approaches to national culture, often citing anthropologists as a valuable counter to the cultural types model. As one article observes, the typologies often presume absolute divisions of culture incompatible with the globalization they are pursuing in their marketing, and put forth ideas that are problematic given that the functionalist use of culture "tends to become a static and decontextualized concept of little use in analyzing actual intercultural encounters" (Bjerregaard, Lauring, and Klitmøller 2009: 208).

The cultural types approach to difference makes it to the expatriate world of Nepal, albeit in marginal ways. One of the values of this literature is that it is self-service—requiring no hands-on training and available at airport bookshops around the world. Nearly all the expatriates I spoke with had at some time picked up *Kiss, Bow, or Shake Hands* (Morrison, Conaway, and Borden 1994), *World Wise* (Denslow 2006) or *Do's and Taboos Around the World* (Axtell 1993), although few had thought these texts worthy of bringing with them to Nepal. In their estimation, these books were more suited to short-duration business travelers or marketers. Expatriates in Nepal nonetheless remembered gleaning from such sources information that Indians (which was as close to Nepal as most books addressed) had different attitudes towards time and that careful attention should be paid to use of the right and left hand. Although few took cultural types ideas deeply to heart, they deployed them in casual slights about the unwillingness of Nepali coworkers to make independent decisions or, more often, in relation to other expatriates. "Oh no, Hans is in charge of this project, you know what that means . . ." said one Canadian, stirring up a discussion of the rigid thinking and precision that those present associated with German colleagues. A source of humor as well as a form of critique, the stereotypes that expatriates often had before their overseas postings were reinforced and given scientific validity by cultural types research. The jokes about types— heavy-drinking Australians, the effete French, hierarchical Japanese—served as a shared source of camaraderie and were often spoken in front of their victims but rarely directed at Nepalis.

If Rajan Is Late to Work It Is Because . . .

The intercultural paradigms of Hofstede and Rapaille describe the kinds of conflicts expatriates might encounter coming to a hierarchy-accepting culture like Nepal from one resistant to hierarchy like the UK (Hofstede's PDI measure), but offer few explicit tools for responding to such dissonance. More practical guides for future expatriates are sometimes provided through seminars that include group activities designed to provide participants with a set of rules for interaction in a new cultural context. One of the most frequently used techniques is "cultural assimilators." These sets of scenarios and possible responses were produced as an explicit response to the perceived problems with "university-style" cross-cultural training. Developed in the 1950s out of the "critical incident technique" (Bhawuk and Brislin 2000: 8), assimilators describe an action "that is sufficiently complete in itself to permit inferences and predictions to be made about the person performing the act" (Flanagan 1954: 327). The act described is frequently an interaction between two people of explicitly different cultural backgrounds involving some kind of conflict or misunderstanding. Initially, these tools were developed to address specific national populations, and a number of researchers developed sets of questions for national groups in the 1960s and 1970s. These lists of "critical incidents" were gathered for places of military and strategic interest and anticipated a United States viewpoint as the neutral position from which the response was assumed. The first cultural assimilators were produced at the University of Illinois for the U.S. Navy, but now the format is ubiquitous in cross-cultural training settings and widely accepted as a useful tool for improving the cultural competency of workers.[6] Whereas scholarly interest in developing and researching new cultural assimilators has declined since those early days, the questions and methods developed by Harry Triandis (1972) and his colleagues are still widely used by cross-cultural trainers. In contemporary cross-cultural training workshops, one is likely to find groups engaging in discussions of questions drawn from a variety of national assimilators, online materials or scenarios about different countries created by the group leader.

Those who are given cross-cultural training using cultural assimilators are asked to select from a set of possible analyses of a situation, ideally discussing them with a small group of other trainees, and then to consider these options with the facilitator, who is tasked with explaining how some responses show a particular cultural misunderstanding or ethnocentrism. Some organizations rely exclusively on a testlike cultural assimilator that includes an answer key

An Exemplary Incident from the Cultural Assimilator and Alternative
Responses to It

Exemplary Incident
A professor was 20 minutes late for an appointment that he had made with
two of his graduate students. The students were looking at their watches when
the professor finally came into the room. The professor said, "I am terribly
sorry I am late."

Which one of the following is most likely in East Asia?

(a) The students might jokingly say, "Better late than never." (Go to page ii)

(b) The students might be very aggressive toward the professor in the
subsequent discussion. (Go to page iii)

(c) The students would say, "That's OK. We don't mind." (Go to page iv)

(d) The students would be very surprised at the professor's saying that he is
sorry. (Go to page v)

Alternative Responses
[p. ii]
You selected (a): "The students might jokingly say, 'Better late than never.'
" This is not the correct answer. It is not very likely that East Asian students
would joke with a professor in the classroom. (Go to page i)
[p. iii]
You selected (b): "The students might be very aggressive. . ." This is very
unlikely. It is unlikely for an East Asian student to be aggressive toward a
professor. In general, a person in a subordinate position rarely becomes
aggressive toward a person in a superordinate position. (Go to page i)
[p. iv]
You selected (c): "The students would say, 'That's OK. We don't mind.' "
This is the correct answer. Even when students are angry at a professor, they
usually do not express their feelings. However, if the students were late for
their appointment then the professor would be angry and would express his
impatience. (Go to the next incident)
[p.v]
You selected (d): "The students would be very surprised. . ." This is a wrong
answer. Being late is certainly thought of negatively in East Asia, and even the
professor would apologize to the students for his delay. (Go to page i)

Sample Cultural Assimilator for East Asia.

Source: Harrison (1992: 962). Copyright © 1992 by the American Psychological Association. Reproduced
with permission. The use of APA information does not imply endorsement by APA.

rather than the intervention of a human facilitator. Those participating in a cultural assimilator might be asked why a Greek woman reacted negatively to questions about her marital status or what one should deduce from seeing two men holding hands on the street in Mexico (Triandis 1977: 21). After the scene is described, participants are provided with four possible interpretations of the events or four possible responses to the situation. After participants give their answer, they are either told that their selection was correct and why, or informed that they misinterpreted the scenario and instructed to review the scene description and select again. Many people I spoke to in Nepal had been exposed to some activity like this. Those who were in group sessions remembered these as an opportunity to talk to other soon-to-be expatriates about their fears. They recounted that the scenarios were often merely jumping-off points for wider-ranging discussions about the possible repercussions of a cultural faux pas and their anxiety about their future homes. In recent years, more expatriates encounter cultural assimilators as written tests, with the answers also provided and additional information in a packet of materials to study at home.

For most, the memories of the content of these cultural assimilator tests seemed to fade into stereotypes and the cultural sensitivity they were designed to engender proved difficult for expatriates to apply when they reached their new home in Nepal. As one trainee recalled, "The thing I most remember is that Austrians are like coconuts and Americans are like peaches" (Lang 2004).[7] A woman I spoke to in Nepal described how her trainer took on the persona of a person in a different culture, with what she saw as an offensive caricature of accent and mannerisms, to demonstrate that what might be read as a gesture of affirmation by an American might mean something very different in another culture. "I felt like I was back in elementary school," complained another woman of her cultural training experience. She described a group activity in which different members were given cards representing different nations and characteristics to perform as they mimicked being in a dinner party environment. The most vociferous criticism of predeparture cross-cultural training came from a woman with a master's degree in psychology who found the techniques of those leading the class she attended a mockery of the profession: "It was like an encounter session—everyone asking how you feel." She described a session in which participants were placed in a circle, asked to discuss various potential cultural conflicts they might encounter, for example different attitudes towards workplace attire or the appropriateness of discussing salary among friends. They were then asked how they would react to different behaviors and harshly corrected regarding the right reactions to these encounters by their young facilitators, who in her estimation were likely college students. Several expatriates complained of the disconnect between these seminars and the obligations of their work. "There is just no point," remarked one employee recollecting these meetings, which he described as interminable. "I have never been in any of the types of situations we discussed in the group." Another person chimed in that he was frustrated with the "touchy-feely" character of these workshops and their dramatic contrast to the pressure to succeed and profit at any cost conveyed to him in other meetings. The disconnect of his work demands from these outsourced cultural training seminars was something he read as an indicator of how little value his employer actually gave to providing expatriates with cross-cultural training. As far as he was concerned, those tasks directly associated with his job were the "important stuff," whereas other activities were merely the employer "covering their butt" and a waste of very precious time when the family was preparing to leave for Nepal. While the *Global Relocation Trends 2009 Survey Report* suggests that 81 percent of companies provide cross-cultural training and 79 percent rate that training as having good or great value (GMAC 2009: 16), anecdotal evidence suggests otherwise (cf. Lang 2004).[8]

Anthropology and CCT

The utilization of anthropological research in the materials of cross-cultural training (CCT) highlights a more general epistemological challenge in business understandings of difference. When anthropology and other forms of cultural knowledge are integrated into these techniques, they are taken as "mere data"— paradigmatic nuggets of information to be inserted into the frameworks of cross-culture communications. Moments of intellectual shorthand or minor anecdotes authored by ethnographers within cross-cultural training become iconic statements. Texts written about a rural village in 1950 are retold as typical of the ways of all people in a country, for all time, and in every encounter. The writings of ethnographers are utilized and respected within cross-cultural circles, but they are taken as definitive descriptions and often further homogenized from their initial context, as when seventy-five-year-old research conducted as a means to gain colonial control over a given population is taken as material for the preparation of expatriates to go abroad in the twenty-first century.[9] All groups are stereotyped and made allochronic: put outside of time and change, they are presumed to be objects rather than subjects (Fabian 1983: 37). In a development-driven economy such as Nepal and with a predominance of aid workers within the expatriate community in Kathmandu, predeparture cultural training suggesting that "Others" exist outside of time and change creates specific problems for aid workers seeking to bring their professional obligations and cultural training into accord. Expatriate workers are simultaneously told unchanging "facts" about Nepal in their cultural briefing and charged with implementing wide-ranging societal changes as part of their job. In the disconnection of cultural training from professional preparation, expatriates are given two conflicting messages: "they are unique and different and do things their own way," via cultural types logics, and "we need to help them to be more like us," via the job assignment. Furthermore, without taking into account variables like class status or temporality, expatriates are in danger of generating offense when they take their culture lessons into the world and apply them to their coworkers, friends and household staff in the new country. Foreigners are rarely surprised that Americans do not come to their country driving covered wagons and wearing bonnets, but expatriate Westerners are often told to expect similar things from residents of their new posting. In cross-cultural training, expatriates are given rules for dealing with other cultures—do shake hands, don't point, never mention a co-worker's wife—but often not given context or reasons for these practices, making them exotic, the magical thinking of the Other. Furthermore, having focused on the radical difference between self and other, those engaged in this training can sometimes forget humanity, thus threatening to divorce their previous knowledge and morality from the new framework of cultural types (Geertz 1984: 86). Problems occur when the expatriate, having completed extensive cross-cultural training, concludes that previous thinking about humankind and civil behavior can be disregarded in this new realm; if the cultural assimilator does not say anything about a behavior, it must be acceptable abroad.

Un"crossing" Culture

The outsourcing of international employee preparation necessitates the transformation of culture into a distinct variable that can be obviated through the tools of cross-cultural training or erased as part of compensation. The market basket practices discussed in a previous chapter attempt to assign a remunerative amount to the conditions of geographic displacement, thus producing expatriates who are expected to be appropriate cultural actors through the goods they buy. The international citizen paradigm takes a different approach to the problem of culture—it deflects the problem onto the worker. The adventure and experience of living abroad is itself made the compensation and the result is a narrowed workforce of those "unencumbered" by children, family or community responsibilities. While extant research suggests that cross-cultural training is vital to expatriate success, this preparation is also quickly discarded or downplayed when international workers themselves come to be seen as expendable. In the training that is conducted, efficiency consistently trumps efficacy as the emphasis is placed on generalizable modes of expatriate preparation to enable outsourcing, even though this approach is deemed ineffective by researchers and participants alike. With the cultural types approach, one need not understand Bukubuku culture: one need only figure out in which of several dyadic pairs it is categorized, and compensate for coming from a "multi-active" culture into a "linear-active" culture by remembering not to interrupt people (Lewis 1996). The dissociations of workers from place and family, and culture from time and context, are made necessary by the restructuring of labor brought about by outsourcing—be it the outsourcing of expatriate training or the outsourcing of expatriate labor itself.

In the next section I turn to another essentialization of culture, the celebratory forms of cultural difference that are central modes of conviviality within Expatria. In Kathmandu many of the social events within the expatriate community focus in some way or another on culture, whether they are national holiday events, seminars on Nepali religion and customs or festivals celebrating the diversity of the group. These activities follow Richard Wilk's formulation of the "structure of common difference" (Wilk 1995), allotting a circumscribed space to the celebration of difference, making it palatable for a wide audience. At expatriate events in Kathmandu such as the International Food Fair or the Christmas Bazaar, different national cultures are allotted one dish, or one table, to display their distinctiveness. The result is a collection, a curio box of cultures (Stewart 1993), wherein each location is able to assert its particularity as long as it is confined to the realms of food, dress, crafts and the like. As with cross-cultural training and the market basket, culture is managed and controlled in such a way as to exclude business practice. Acceptable booths at the Christmas Bazaar must have national identifications; thus one would never see the Kodak booth or the Capitalism booth sharing space with Australia and France. Yet the point of these different codifications of culture is not merely that cultural essentialisms are bad or misrepresent some more true and authentic representation of difference. Instead, it is important to understand the reasoning behind such essentializations: By what logics is culture arrayed and displayed within the different arenas of global enterprise? What are the concerns that motivate attention to difference?

These are questions of structure and epistemology, but a further ethical question arises; what are the ramifications of these various understandings of culture and how are they deployed in Expatria? In examining the epistemologies of cultural knowledge within expatriate situations, one must ask questions about how such information is deployed in daily life, often in ways that are objectifying, and perhaps more important, about the variation in effect these objectifications have depending on the power a given community can exert against its definition by this global system of "curio culture." For the expatriate, what happens when the process of reification is reflected back on the self? Does this become a moment for deep reflection on essentialization and humanity or a means to turning difference into a game?

Perform Your Homeland—One per Table, Please

On a sunny December afternoon, the garden of the recreation facility was filled with groups of parents keeping half an eye on the various groups of children nearby. Older kids were playing ultimate Frisbee some distance from the café tables, while the younger children were engaged in less-structured games in the sandbox or with dolls. From the indoor restaurant area, a familiar song—albeit somewhat out of tune—came forth: "Happy Birthday to you, Happy Birthday to you. Happy Birthday, dear Stephanie . . ." Several of those present giggled at the enthusiastic, if off-key, performance of Stephanie's friends but clapped in celebration at the end of the song. This intervention provoked queries about who had a birthday coming up and a discussion about the birthday party held for children with birthdays during the month at one of the local international elementary schools. Soon the conversation turned to the question: "So how do you celebrate birthdays in Germany?" Oliver described the tradition of the candle ring, candles lit for each year of the child's life and burned during much of the day. An American asked about making wishes and blowing out candles, something Oliver had described his family doing, but he thought this was not traditional in Germany. Soon others were describing national birthday traditions, which birthdays were particularly marked in their country, songs and games that were associated with birthday celebrations. One Korean woman discussed how when she was a child, her mother had prepared special rice cakes for her birthday. "I buy those now, but my son also demands a birthday cake from Baskin Robbins. I guess that has become our tradition." The question "How does it happen in your country?" was an easy subject for small talk among expatriates, and even those who had lived abroad much of their lives enthusiastically talked about national traditions, including those they rarely practiced anymore. The most memorable of such "comparative practice" conversations occurred between two impeccably dressed women, and it was regarding farming practices in their home nations. It seemed remarkable to me that these women in high heels and tailored skirt-suits would be familiar with animal husbandry practices and crop rotations in their home countries, but national knowledge and the ability to represent one's homeland is a necessary skill in Expatria.

Cultural types paradigms for understanding difference focus exclusively on generalizable categories and expatriate training often emphasizes the hardships entailed in culture contact, yet in the everyday life of expatriates the uniqueness of culture is celebrated, albeit in ways that narrowly define the space available to express that distinctiveness. In the niches for culture generated within the expatriate social sphere, members are encouraged to display what makes their group special, although only if that can be expressed in the form of food, dance or art. Business, politics and beliefs are often excluded from such celebratory approaches to cultural display, either for their controversy or because such distinction is not perceived as "cultural." In a community with representatives from many different countries, "international" is a frequent framework for celebration. Most of the international schools in Kathmandu celebrate "International Day" or "UN Day" by asking students to come to class that day in their "national dress," and expatriate charity organizations often hold events using this framework to raise funds. These culture bazaars[10] act as discrete sites for the performance of difference in ways that both tame and commodify the potential chaos of difference. Through this formula, expatriates are able to communicate and laud their distinctiveness in a way that also displays the coherency of Expatria and its practices.

One of the largest and most regular instantiations of internationalism in expatriate Kathmandu is the Christmas Bazaar organized each year by two women's groups. Held in the garden of one of the large hotels in the city, the bazaar offers an opportunity for expatriates to do holiday gift shopping as well as to acquire decorations for the season. Several of the large local craft stores rent booths to sell their regular stock of handicrafts and pottery but also specially designed items adapted for the occasion, such as clay bowls decorated with Santa images and Christmas tree ornaments made using local papermaking practices. In addition, there are often as many as a dozen national booths, some officially sponsored by embassies, others created by national social groups and cohorts of motivated friends from the same country. These often depict the holiday traditions of their nation using stock images provided by their embassy, supplemented by personal items brought by participants. The German booth is a favorite attraction, both for the elaborate crafts display and the Christmas cakes and sweets for sale. Children often enter the courtyard already begging for the fruit and spice cakes they remember from previous years and demand over time has grown to such a point that now the cakes are made to specification at a local bakery, rather than in the German women's homes. Some people assist in hosting displays not associated with their home country but with a place at which they were formerly posted. Crafts from several Southeast Asian countries are arrayed at a booth managed by the Malaysian spouse of a German diplomat, with help from several Australian and Dutch women who spent time in Indonesia and Brunei, and a Singaporean couple residing in Nepal for business. Although many of these national displays offer items for sale, with proceeds going to local charities, the attraction is as much about chatting with friends at their booths and showing off knowledge of crafts and customs.

Country-specific holidays are a frequent occasion for events and offer the opportunity for nationals to explain and perform their traditions. Australia Day is marked with a barbecue and dance in the embassy gardens, although in recent years the Anzac Day celebrations have been larger, perhaps given the better weather in April. In other circumstances Australians have openly discussed the ambivalent status of this military holiday, but in the context of a group conversation including many non-Australians, the occasion for celebration was quickly described to me as being "like Veteran's Day," enabling more time to focus on celebrating the large cans of Fosters and explaining the differences between Australian rules football and its American cousin. U.S. Thanksgiving, with its origins in a similar tense domestic conflict, is celebrated in Nepal with a football game at the U.S. recreational club. Often there is a flag or touch football game with the Peace Corps volunteers taking on all others, as well as NFL football on a projection TV in the main building.

The Embassy of Japan's celebration in Nepal of the Emperor's Birthday offers a more formal approach to national holidays, consisting of a reception of official guests and many photo opportunities to show the various heads of national missions shaking hands. I learned that more casual celebrations of the day take place outside of the embassy's official event, in the homes of diplomats and with a mainly Japanese invitee list.[11] The Japanese Embassy uses other occasions to include the public, such as cultural events and celebrations, although mainly expatriates attend. Taking advantage of the widespread interest in Japanese popular culture, the Japanese Chamber of Commerce in Nepal hosted a new event, "Japanese Festival—Sense of Cool Japan 2008," to display different art forms and foods. The attendees were both young upper-class Nepalis and expatriates who were regulars at such events. The ikebana demonstrations that were frequently held at the embassy drew almost exclusively from an expatriate audience, with the exception of Nepali royalty. At one demonstration that took place in 1999, the embassy invited one of the leading instructors of the Ichiyo School of flower arranging to demonstrate her techniques, including making a display from flowers that she brought from Japan and inviting several members of the audience on stage to try their own skills. The demonstration, held in the main public hall of the embassy, drew at least fifty people, all of whom signed the guest book on entering and passed by a security agent who inspected any large bags. After all were seated, the host, who was the spouse of one of the diplomatic officers, began, in English, by welcoming the guest of honor, Princess Shruti, and introducing the two visiting ikebana practitioners. After this, the lead artist immediately began designing a large arrangement while her assistant explained the principles of Japanese flower arranging in general and of her school in particular. These were simultaneously translated by the host, but also detailed in a handout offered to all at the beginning of the reception. The assistant and the master appeared to have done the demonstration many times, as the completion of the lecture and the arrangement were simultaneous. The crowd politely applauded both performances. After that, two guests were tutored in creating their own displays and then the group adjourned to an adjacent room for tea and cookies. The event was popular enough that two women, one Japanese and one European, who had been posted to Japan for several years and had studied flower arranging while there, took it upon themselves to organize several follow-up ikebana events focusing on using local flowers and information about where tools and equipment could be found in Kathmandu. The Japanese Embassy event was well publicized in the local papers and continued to be invoked at the more casual events that followed, with the embassy supplying English-language books on ikebana and pamphlets for the group. Often hosted by the cultural arm of an embassy, demonstrations of national culture occur nearly every week in Kathmandu and are an occasion both for recognizing the multinational character of the community and to celebrate difference in an enjoyable way.

Expatriates' own mode of "dealing with" culture is influenced not only by cross-cultural forms they learn in predeparture training but also by their work experience and professional obligations. The structure of expatriate cultural performances mimics those displayed in their professional lives, exemplified by the institution of the United Nations, which is at once an idealized expression of expected equality among nations as well as a significant employer of expatriates in Nepal. The parallelism of nation-states as well as the exclusivity of the nation-state as the embodiment of culture are often taken for granted and yet are more recent developments than often presumed (Nielsen 2011). The UN is a marker for how these assumptions were naturalized, as well as the effect of the naturalization of the nation-state form, yet it has also created a unified expectation for relations between states. The post–World War II era and the creation of the UN led to "a different global: a global of horizontalities and symmetries (one nation-state one vote)". In pointing to the proliferation of the UN as a form, Kelly and Kaplan call for a critical reexamination of the assumptions of this new way of viewing the international in order to better understand "the politics of community" (Kelly and Kaplan 2001: 4), and while their argument centers more on historical ramifications for former colonial states, they also provide a lens to explain the logic of expatriate sociality and the assumptions that underlie the horizontal symmetry performed in the culture bazaar. Bjarke Nielsen describes a somewhat later shift that results in similar formations for culture in his examination of UNESCO's shift from a celebration of shared civilization to cultural diversity of nation-states (Nielsen 2011: 277).

All expatriates, whether they work for the UN or not, participate in this system of national culture and horizontal symmetry. In their professional actions, development workers, business people and diplomats are operating within a paradigm, perhaps particularly in Nepal, that implicitly assumes a hierarchy of nations while at the same time claiming structural equality and respect for difference. The framework of expatriate professional action is premised on vertical assumptions about progress and advancement, while cultural diversity is celebrated as a horizontal form—a system that can only endure if the two are kept separate. Rhetorically, global business may venerate the diversity of the world, yet in conversations among executives, the quantifications of potential market share and consumer buying power exclude difference through the seemingly benign mechanisms of statistical comparison and "the bottom line." In the practices of cultural celebration that take place among expatriates, I see an acknowledgement of difference that gives permission to ignore culture in the more substantive aspects of business, diplomacy and development. Through the mechanisms of cultural horizontal symmetry, once a nation has been granted a booth to display their distinction, their culture has been sufficiently acknowledged so that one can get on with the universal operations of business and good governance.

The Right Kind of Culture

The International Food Festival, held as a charity function by a local expatriate group in Kathmandu, displays the United Nations model of horizontal symmetry, highlighting the global character of the community while raising money for a local hospital. This event brings together expatriates who design tables highlighting their home or former host countries with food often provided by a local restaurateur in Kathmandu specializing in that cuisine. Each colorfully decorated table offers one or two snacks for sale deemed typical of the country. Visitors are able to move from Thailand to Germany in just a few steps and, in exchange for a coupon purchased for 50 rupees, sample a dish from a foreign land. Both chefs and nationals are on hand to answer questions about preparation or local practices. There are also competitions for momo eating, beer drinking and cake mixing as well as a short dance review and artist on hand to paint children's faces, thus rounding out its "festival" character. This highly successful event emerged from a series of cooking classes offered by an expatriate social group that included both host nationals presenting their own cuisine and events cohosted by nationals and local chefs.

Expatriate social events in Nepal frequently follow the formula of passing on national culture through hands-on educational activities that serve to highlight formal symmetry among nations. They also enact an explicit or implicit comparison with "the normal" and demonstrate where and when culture is appropriately displayed in Expatria. One week may feature a lecture by a famous ikebana artist sponsored by the Japanese Embassy, then the next week the Alliance Française sponsors an art exhibit and after that the American Embassy presents a jazz trio. Such nation-sponsored performances show that each country is alike, except in this one they eat rice instead of pita or French bread. The performance of parity through parallel representation is key to the United Nations logic. The multiculturalism of the expatriate environment offers a claim to equality but threatens to "defer the problems that capital, (post)colonialism, and human diasporas pose to national identity ..." (Povinelli 2002: 29). Thus even though expatriates in Kathmandu are often in the country precisely because of a proclaimed inequality between Nepal and their home country and many expatriates themselves have complex relationships to a so-called home nation, nonetheless they perform difference as if all countries conform to their stereotypes. The frequent resort to costuming as a part of these events illustrates their explicitly performative character. It is important that everyone know that these are costumes, which are then taken off to assume the "normal" dress of expatriate life. I found this most explicitly displayed when a born-and-bred New Englander was happy to put on cowboy boots and a ten-gallon hat to perform an America with broader stereotypes than a bow tie might illustrate.

The world-of-nations model often evidenced in expatriate social settings also makes an appearance in expatriate homes. This curio mode of cultural display finds a literal representation in the collections gathered by expatriates as a means to narrate their mobility across space and time. Through bucolic landscape paintings, elaborately decorated plates or children's dolls, expatriate families often acquire one particular object from each posting to symbolize their journey. Prominently displayed on the wall of one expatriate home in Kathmandu was a Plexiglas box containing ceremonial knives from the many African countries to which the family had been posted. Each small blade had a label describing from what "tribe" it came, although more often than not these "tribes" were countries. The collection had been assembled into this formal display, and several items added, as a parting gift to the Connelly family by one of the husband's local partners, given they were not anticipating returning to Africa. This large and fragile display of authenticity and mobility, along with their collection of Christmas decorations, was a bulky item in their shipping allowance. Another couple collected oil paintings of farming scenes from the various places their family had lived, a habit picked up in Southeast Asia that had continued across the globe. Although the paintings had been easy to acquire in Indonesia and Malaysia, the couple had to commission a Kathmandu artist to create images that fit into the theme of the collection and were similar in size to those already displayed. Scrapbooks of photos of a current posting might be of interest to a home audience, but these collections of curios served as a biographic narrative of a family's journey for an expatriate audience. Displays of these physical manifestations of a mobile life were often placed in an entryway and were a means of prompting a conversation about the locations where the family had lived, when and for how long, thus inserting them into the shared practices of Expatria. Discussion of the collection often generated comparisons or potential linkages, as inquirers tried to discover shared friendships or affirm rumors about the difficulty of life at a particular post. Like culture shows and international festivals, these carefully curated narratives of travel conformed to the representational model, ensuring one item per location and demanding a uniformity of structure across the diverse sites of posting. The curio model of culture evidenced in these expatriate practices appears in official realms as a structural convenience; yet the entailed assumptions about the ease of "dealing with" difference through these gestures seeps into professional practices.

In the expatriate performance of difference, the community celebrates managed diversity as a form of culturalism. In "The Work of Corporate Culture," Avery Gordon examines the corporate practices relating to diversity as a management technique that creates modular and impermanent forms of difference. She observes in the workings of professional addresses to culture a form of liberal racism that in the guise of promoting workplace diversity and equality surreptitiously remakes culture itself in ways convenient to the operation of business (Gordon 1995: 23). This is very similar to expatriates' performances of difference, but in this setting it can be difficult to determine who is doing the objectifying and who is being objectified by these processes. In the modes of expatriate selection, training and compensation, international workers are indoctrinated into the modes of managing difference, as both objects of the codification and future agents. Through culture shows and national celebrations, expatriates translate these processes into their own practices. The essentializations of masculine versus feminine, prominent in cultural types literature, are not the categories of the culture show; instead one learns which countries eat spicy food and who prefers bland cuisine. Yet among these global middlemen, there is a presumption that this is a culture game—a recreational celebration that need have little reflection upon themselves as the represented. The need to stand in this somewhat ironic relationship to identity, in which one distances such social displays of culture from the role culture plays in business, assumes that such essentialisms apply deeply to others but not the self. Yet this claim can be difficult to sustain in Expatria. In this environment, expatriates must on the one hand recognize the absurdity of cross-cultural training and on the other promote these techniques to their Nepali colleagues as normative modern practices.

Conclusion

This chapter looks at several approaches to managing difference that are applied to, by and for the expatriate worker under the aegis of cultural training and celebratory addresses to diversity. The shift to training workers to deal with an abstract "culture" is necessitated by the move to outsourced training, yet the approach to culture put forth by cultural competency approaches eliminates all the distinctions that are necessary for expatriate work and the social actions of Expatria. While understanding that one is moving from a reactive to a multiactive culture (Lewis 1996) may facilitate improved workplace communication, it has limited value in helping expatriates either to tailor their projects to local conditions or to communicate with their coworkers. Although a cultural type model like Geert Hofstede's claims to be very practical in providing an insight into the "reptilian brain" of various nations, its prescriptions on how to get people to buy U.S. goods or managers to lead a diverse workforce rarely are easily translated to the needs of expatriates in Nepal. Instead, a different set of cultural understandings is necessary for success in ventures such as inducing a local population to improve hygiene through hand washing, or transforming a women's empowerment program designed in Geneva to work in a rural village in Eastern Nepal. The challenges of making different diplomatic, development and business agendas work globally can rarely be reduced to a project of linguistic translation; they often require more dramatic transformations and a dialogic element that goes beyond the "add culture and stir" method that is utilized when diversity is outsourced. The operation of global business prescribes a globally applicable paradigm for action wherein culture must be made into a circumscribed category such that each different location can be plugged into an overarching system. Richard Wilk has termed a similar phenomenon "structures of common difference," which he describes in his examination of beauty pageants in Belize as "a common set of formats and structures that mediate between cultures . . . that put diversity into a common frame and scale it along a limited number of dimensions . . ." (Wilk 1995: 111). Whereas Wilk, with a gesture to Appadurai's "global localities" (Appadurai 1996), sees these as dimensions of celebration, an attitude seen in the international celebrations of expatriates, I suggest that part of the work these celebrations enact is the confinement of culture. While a multicultural buffet is a welcome form of diversity in Expatria, within the workplace any eruption of culture is a problem, both because of its multiplicity and in the ways in which it threatens to intrude upon what are presumed acultural workplace practices.

The outsourcing of expatriate training requires workers to be prepared for culture, without reference to any particular culture or place. In the same way, the development projects that draw many to Nepal for work are often planned in a central location and only later is specificity addressed as the project is deployed on the ground. The codification of culture found in the cultural competency rhetoric or in the cultural displays explored by Wilk has an essentializing effect that is disturbing to what anthropologists see as a more complex role for difference in the world. In the management of culture, there is more than bad anthropology at stake—there is a transformation wherein difference itself becomes the possession of the corporation, controlled by the logics of management and efficiency (Gordon 1995: 23).

The repercussions of this can be disheartening. The first is a redefinition of all that does not fit into the space allowed for culture as deviant. Local practices that cannot be or are not accounted for within a project's understanding of culture become labeled as laziness, backwardness or resistance. There is a divide between the "right" kind of culture, for instance what is seen at festivals, and the "wrong" kind, one that maintains values or beliefs incompatible with modernity or neoliberalism (Nielsen 2011: 279). While Nepali culture is interesting when it is about dances or food, when Nepali coworkers discuss their attitudes towards work hours or gender roles, it is classified as intolerant or in need of reform to produce a more mature society. With a place made for culture in its curio form, culture that refuses to stay in its place is matter out of place (Douglas 1966). This is not merely a story of the culture of the Other being codified but also about what is not allowed into the category of culture, particularly the impossibility of business norms being considered cultural. Civilizational logics return, but in more coded language, since diversity is accorded its due in curio form. Practices deemed antithetical to the normal operations of international organizations are categorized not as diversity but as deviant, while best practices and neoliberal instrumentalism are seen as outside of the realm of culture (Ong 2006: 228). While expatriates are instructed to accommodate the religious holidays of their local employees, these exceptions may only fit within the bounds of the structure allowed for difference. "Global best practices" are excluded from cultural analysis and instead presumed to be merely the universal best way. Culture is also claimed by business, not only in its codification but as it becomes a part of one's job. "Representing" becomes a necessity for employees like John, and whereas one might otherwise be asked to avoid distinction, "now you're expected to contribute it generously to the corporate mission" (Gordon 1995: 18). The requirement is to display one's own diversity, but only within the globalized grammar of business. In general, managerialism promotes the incorporation of the culture—as well as other forms of private life as seen in Chapter 2—in a way that can be oppressive, yet for expatriates the demand that one bring everything to the job is familiar from the structures of compensation and control that define expatriate labor. John, in his "Indianness," exemplified that performing culture is expected when it contributes to the needs of the employer.

In viewing culture as a necessary evil to be overcome through management, the practices of both training and everyday expatriate social interaction subscribe to the idea of culture as a singular variable, one that can be accounted for and counted. This understanding of culture is still very much embedded in a nation state model. The formal horizontalities and symmetries that are part and parcel of the practice of international business and diplomacy limit what can be allowed to have culture and thus deviate from an unexplored global norm (Kelly and Kaplan 2001: 4; Hindman 2009a). What Kelly and Kaplan call the "United Nations utopia" (2001: 15, 111) is not only metaphoric practice but also structural reality in Nepal. In conclusion, I want to suggest that this United Nations utopia has deeply ingrained itself into the globalized world and accommodations for cultural difference. This situation offends many in the academy, including myself, and the desire to proclaim "Adieu, Culture," as one observes the concept being reduced to an accessory, is great (Trouillot 2002: 54). The "culture discourse" is now used more often to serve racists and essentialist projects—for purposes of "quarantine" (58)—above all else. Yet anthropologists cannot lay claim to culture as "our" term anymore, if it ever was ours. It seems incumbent upon scholars to understand how the term, as any emic term, is used outside the academy, not only as an expansion of social science knowledge but also as it "affects the very location and organization of our working lives in the university . . . It's time to know something more about what is actually happening in that corporate world" (Watkins 1995: 2).

6 Living in Expatria

Institutions and the Mobile Community

IN CONDUCTING ETHNOGRAPHIC RESEARCH with a moving population, I faced a challenge common to many expatriates—how to find "my people." The rise of interest in mobile populations has been accompanied by a realization that research on moving people presents practical challenges not encountered by the "village" ethnographer (cf. Marcus 1995; Burawoy 2000; Büscher, Urry, and Witchger 2010; D'Andrea, Ciolfi, and Gray 2011). While trying to study expatriates in Nepal, I was enmeshed in the constant comings and goings of members of the community, and returning to "fieldwork" often meant establishing an entirely new network of connections and collaborations. Over the ten years most of the research on this project was conducted, I can recall only three people who were in Kathmandu over the entire time, all having unusual circumstances that kept them in-country while still within the expatriate circle. What was consistent was the institutions of Expatria: visiting Kathmandu's British School, the American Club or a meeting of the United Nations Women's Organization quickly put me in contact with a new cohort of expatriates. This chapter explores how expatriates use institutions to create coherence across their multiple moves, and how the nature and utilization of organizations is—or at times is not—changing as the population of those working in Kathmandu transforms.

Unfamiliar faces were common at the Tuesday night bridge group, and usually it was only moments before these newcomers found a connection with one of the regular attendees. Although the group met in the British Embassy Club, also known as the Sterling Club, it drew from all nationalities and all skill levels. Whether they had been invited by someone or just heard from others of the welcoming, convivial group, new players were always well-received on the condition they were willing to abide by the house rule that the losers buy a round for their table. Introductions almost inevitably began with a history of past postings as well as the visitor's past bridge experience. It rarely took more than one or two iterations of mobility to find a connection: shouts rang out across the room about a notoriously bad player at a regular game in Karachi who had not understood a Blackwood Convention bid; or a work-related tie surfaced as one new player found out that his ad hoc partner for the evening had played bridge in Auckland with his former boss. Newcomers quickly found connections and by the end of the evening, all were exchanging stories about bridge groups in which they had participated around the world and the idiosyncrasies of play at each posting.

At my table one evening, connections were being made at the expense of a bridge player who had gained worldwide notoriety for her temper. The woman, a ranked bridge player, joined casual games like the one at the Sterling Club and then proceeded to berate those she was paired with about their poor bidding. Around the table, people exchanged stories of her tirades in Kathmandu, New Delhi and Dhaka, and two of those playing nearby had first-hand experience with her outbursts. She was currently living in Nepal and those present were happy to have the opportunity to complain about her on this rare occasion when she was not in attendance. Yet the evening was not exclusively about bridge or problematic players, and the conversation drifted to a play soon to be performed by a local expatriate drama group as well as a new restaurant that was promising real Italian-style pizza. Regulars and newcomers alike were enthused to learn about the local gossip and tips on life in Kathmandu.

Although some organizations exist that seek to connect expatriates regardless of interests or nationality, for example InterNations, the venues that expatriates most often seek out at a new posting focus on some commonality and are grounded not in virtual connections but regular face-to-face meetings. In Kathmandu, the United Nations Women's Organization long served as the first stop for many expatriate families, but by 2000 its dominance was waning. Arriving at a new location, expatriates need only ask a few foreigners to find out where the bridge game, quilting group, international Christian church or Hash House Harriers meets in order to generate an instant community. While in large cities multiple organizations for each interest exist, in Kathmandu there is often only one group per activity, thus one needs to know only where and when a given interest group meets. Even in a small expatriate community, a diversity of organizations exist and whatever one's interest, it is likely that there is or has been a group that shares it. National women's groups, church organizations and sports groups can be found everywhere, while some clubs are particular to Kathmandu, such as Shiva's Slaves—a motorcycle touring club, less like their namesake Hell's Angels than a repair and riding companionship exchange. The expectation of parallel social networks in different locations allows expatriates to be confident that they can maintain consistent everyday life patterns across postings and participate in similar hobbies and community groups.

The sociality engendered by local meetings at the Sterling or Rotary Club is vital to making the constant movement of expatriate life seem more like stability, yet it presents a very different sense of the mechanisms of stability than the paradigm of the international citizen proposed in human resources literatures. Through expatriate social organizations, mobile workers create community, but they also police the boundaries of Expatria. The result is something that is not quite an expatriate culture, but does exemplify the translocal connections of Expatria. The disjuncture between their physical mobility and the coherency provided by the institutions of expatriate life often goes unremarked by expatriates themselves until retirement or the end of their expatriate career. At this point, many families find themselves unable to go home, or unable to make home feel like home again. Instead, expatriates find themselves most comfortable with other expatriates and seek to live among them, even in their so-called home country.

"Expatria" is an attempt to capture the feeling of familiarity within geographic dispersion that is a part of what makes the experience of this transient life more like continuity than disjuncture. Yet like other moments of distinction and boundary making, the character and extent of Expatria is most recognizable at its margins (Barth 1969). In the desire to distance itself from other populations of foreigners in Kathmandu, Expatria encompasses the structures and modes of employment that bring workers to Nepal, and that make the group distinct from the population of long-term residents, spiritual seekers, and tourists who are unwilling to leave a place they love. It is Expatria that many who follow this life find difficult to leave and when they relinquish the mobile life, they often experience dissonance greater than any they encountered in their moves. One sees the jarring effects of repatriation in the frequent overseas retirement of former expatriates who find that the home that they had desired to return to is not as they anticipated. At the other end of the age spectrum are the challenges faced by children of expatriates who return home for higher education. Many flock to organizations designed to support "third culture kids," such as "Global Nomad" clubs that exist at many colleges and universities or organizations such as the Foreign Service Youth Foundation. Either as students or retirees, expatriates become more aware of the unusual community of Expatria at precisely the moment they leave its despatialized confines. Expatria is a difficult place to leave behind.

This chapter explores different types of expatriate social organizations that contribute to the production of coherency within this transient population and how these organizations are used by employers, entrepreneurs and expatriates themselves. In part, this lens on the expatriate life introduces a more fine-grained view of the everyday life of expatriates, the mundane concerns of friendships and recreation, but there is also a wider claim about how various "local" concerns—particularities of time, space and economy—have shaped and continue to shape the utility of different forms of social organizations for the expatriate community in Nepal. The focus on organizations also brings to the fore issues present throughout this book: how overseas labor is changing and how the changes in employment influence the social world of mobile laborers.

In the 1990s, globalization was anticipated to make the world better-connected in ways that would obviate the difficulty of overseas postings, yet few now believe the rapid homogenization that was feared by some and longed for by others is coming to pass. The present decade seems marked by the rise of social media and the use of web-based platforms to bring people together. For expatriates, both of these techniques of overcoming space and division have not brought the transformations expected by pundits or their employers. Instead, forms of connection, including the Internet, have intersected with changing gender and labor expectations to bring about unintended new practices of expatriate life. The on-the-ground experience of globalization and social networking also plays out very differently in Kathmandu, with its eighty-eight hours of weekly load-shedding and intermittent interruptions in Internet connections. Metropolitan headquarters can carry on under the assumption that expatriate workers can keep up with the latest events through Hulu or BBC iPlayer, but on the ground one quickly discovers that those services are blocked in Nepal for copyright reasons. For example, the introduction of electronic books was celebrated by many tourists and expatriates in Nepal as a way to get recent books and periodicals often difficult to acquire, but Amazon charges additional fees to many overseas users, even for books offered for free in the United States, and the wireless network that allows users to download material directly to the Kindle is unavailable in Nepal.[1] The connections facilitated by technologies have not, in the end, produced the erasure of displacement initially envisioned, but instead have produced new oppor-

tunities for entrepreneurialism and expatriate involvement in generating expertise that was once the exclusive domain of human resource professionals.

The use of online platforms by expatriates to promote their own businesses
came as somewhat of a surprise to business scholars, but also it is the product
of changes in expatriate labor in part predicted by new business theories. The
nature of overseas labor is changing and the population of mobile professionals
in Kathmandu has transformed over the last decade. For example, one of the
most prominent forms of expatriate sociality—the women's social club—finds
itself in transition due to the rise of dual-career families and increased numbers of short-term male expatriates in Nepal. But the social activities of expatriates also include practices lamented as lost in contemporary social science
literature: civil society activities and devotion to the community mourned as
abandoned by those who see social networking as bringing about the decline of
face-to-face sociality (e.g., Lanier 2010; Carr 2011; Turkle 2011). The desire to
produce forms of expatriate sociality, whether virtual or face-to-face, has had
unpredictable outcomes for both expatriates themselves and those who seek to
manage their overseas lives, particularly at a moment when the makeup of the
community is changing, perhaps to such a degree that it is difficult to call it a
community anymore.

From the Newsletter to the Newsgroup:
Making a Proprietary Expatria

Expatria was a "virtual community" before the phrase was commonplace. Yet
as technologies like the Internet make it possible for larger numbers of people
to be involved in supralocal, despatialized communities, expatriates themselves
are exhibiting less interest in utilizing computer-mediated communication to
establish social connections, although they find much value in other uses. In
this section, I begin with the non-computer-mediated techniques used by expatriate families to connect with one another, exploring what needs families
living overseas were able to fulfill by connecting with other expatriates through
newsletters, books and face-to-face meetings. Initially, computer-mediated
technologies merely served to facilitate the same types of exchanges that had
previously taken place on paper or in person. As access to technology and the
variety of modes of connection expanded, new formats for information exchange developed. This expansion looked far greater online than it did in places
like Kathmandu, which still experienced, and continue to experience, a vast
digital divide. Thus while metropole-dwellers such as employers and potential
expatriates saw a thriving community online, this medium was utilized mainly

by those who were not actually abroad. Yet this is not a story of how new technologies led to new forms of expatriate community, but how transformations in gender roles, an expansion of those seeking overseas work, new categories of transnational labor and the development of new expertise in transnational labor management intersected with these computer technologies. I argue that the capacity of expatriates to connect transnationally preceded the Internet and thus it is important to consider the "link between historically constituted sociocultural practices within and outside of mediated communication . . ."(Wilson and Peterson 2002: 453).

Communication among expatriates previous to its computer mediation was mainly between those who shared a common interest or a common employer. Shell Oil, with its large number of mobile employees, has a long history of networks among its expatriate professionals as well as a well-archived collection of materials about its employment practices and the lives of its workers abroad in what is now known as the Expatriate Archive Centre. The enclavic zones in which oil-refining families lived and the discrete number of locations for posting enabled the company to produce a sense of a transnational Shell community as early as the 1950s, as discussed in Chapter 1 (see also Shell Ladies' Project 1993; Gordon 2008). There were also interest-group connections between English-language church groups, in part facilitated by visiting missionaries who acted as messengers for exchanges between international churches. Thus, church newsletters would discuss where former expatriate members were now posted and the news of their new church activities. Organizations such as the Hash House Harriers, established for recreational purposes under European colonial rule for officers in Southeast Asia, found new life as centers for postcolonial activities for international workers and their families (Lyons 1992). The published materials from these groups circulated within a tight network, and awareness of geographically dispersed groups participating in the same activities gave participants a sense of a larger imagined community (Anderson 1991). By the late 1980s, many local expatriate organizations were publishing print newsletters for interested parties to be circulated within a given country. Bulletins for national groups, such as the *Yank and Yeti* for Americans in Nepal, rarely circulated outside the posting. The value of such publications was in their distribution of local and timely information about community events, and in a place like Kathmandu without a viable postal service, they would appear at known expatriate venues to be picked up by interested parties or subscribers. There was some overseas circulation, as when copies of the UN Women's Organization (UNWO) magazine, *The Mirror*, or the *Yank and Yeti* would be passed to those soon to be posted to Nepal, to give them a sense of the community. Without the electronic connections facilitated by the Internet, printed pamphlets hand-carried or passed through diplomatic mail were one of the few means expatriates had of understanding the lives of others in similar positions or of life in a new posting.

One of the first newsletters to target an audience beyond a single employer or location was the *Spouses' Underground Newsletter* (*SUN*). The *SUN* emerged to respond to some of the same concerns that produced the Shell Ladies' Project in the early 1990s. While the Shell Ladies' Project collected stories of Shell spouses in the books *Life on the Move* (1993) and *Life Now* (1996), the *SUN* was an informal photocopied collection of writings from expatriate families affiliated with a diverse set of employers about their frustrations and enjoyment of life overseas. The six-to-ten-page pamphlets were mailed to subscribers around the world and circulated (and recopied) as people moved about their travels. So-called "stitch and bitch" groups had long provided face-to-face outlets for expatriate spouses to complain about their frustration with overseas life, but these new print venues were transforming these complaints into a literary genre and giving authors an audience that extended outside their own posting. The *SUN* often featured letters from spouses who lauded the newsletter, explaining how they waited patiently for each copy to arrive and how the *SUN* was the first time they realized there were others who shared their feelings. Many of those who were contributors to the *SUN* and the Shell Ladies' Project began to view their activities in a more professional light, changing their identity from trailing spouse to creative writer or editor and viewing their time abroad as an opportunity to develop a voice and an audience.

The first Internet-based expatriate institutions sought to provide online sites where a dispersed, sympathetic audience might enjoy stories like those in the *SUN* as well as an outlet for those with literary hopes and experiences of mobile life and work. Venues such as the *SUN* had utilized expatriate spouses not merely as content generators but also as marketers who, through this process, developed the entrepreneurial skills to expand the readership of the newsletter and attract sponsors. Expatriate spouses continued to be predominant in the new online formats as readers, authors and publishers.[2] More and more trailing spouses were seeking opportunities in the 1990s to do independent work, as reserved positions for foreign service or business spouses were far fewer than the number of those interested in working while their partner pursued an overseas career. Many of those spouses participating in these print and eventually online collections of expatriate writings began to consider writing and publishing as a profession, rather than just an opportunity to share complaints with other expatriates.

In the 1990s, a few electronic mailing lists (or listservs) began to emerge to disseminate letters and announcements to interested expatriates. At this point, most were based on email circulation or a bulletin board format and were country-specific. These electronic mailing lists were often managed by a local expatriate who collected the email addresses of local expatriate families and circulated messages to all those who subscribed. Country-specific lists such as "lista expatriate," a list based in Lima, Peru, were designed to "hold friendly and open discussions in english [sic] and to share information of interest to the expatriate community. content [sic] might include: listings of coming events, job postings, buy-and-sell ads, changes to the immigration code, questions and answers, options and discussion, and much more" (Larue 1998). Daily emails would arrive to subscribers describing a list of items being sold by a departing expatriate, sharing a joke, announcing a school play or providing positive comments about a household worker who was now available for hire by other expatriates. Similar information also existed in bulletin board format, with information arranged around topics such as "for sale," "upcoming events," "humor," and "services," where participants listed their announcements or contributed to threaded discussions about a given location. Although many cities across the world had some forum like this, use of the Internet in Nepal was still not widespread in the 1990s and no similar institution existed for Kathmandu.[3]

Use of these forums by career expatriates and their families was short-lived and by 2000 few of these lists survived, even in an updated technological form. The problems that occurred in lists such as "lista expatriate" in Peru or "Expat Brussels" were the same concerns that seemed to plague other web-based interest groups. Different participants saw different information as worthy of placement on the list. Some welcomed the lively debate over which local team was superior, others saw such postings as superfluous. Political arguments and specialist debates often extended for multiple emails until administrators intervened. Some lists were able to continue until the early 2000s with strict regulations on what postings were allowed, and most confined themselves to announcements of events and items for sale, but the talk of such sites as a "community" had already receded.

Selling the Expatriate Community to Itself

The late 1990s saw new technological means and content genres vying for expatriate attention online, many of which went beyond specific interests or countries to focus on providing services to a global expatriate community. Several "e-groups" and chat rooms were developed through America Online (AOL) in this period focused on the concerns of expatriates and providing a space for generalized discussions of the challenges of life abroad. Although the subject matter was closer to that of the *SUN* than of the listservs, the email format encouraged a different genre of communication. "Spouses-expat" and "expat chat" were lists where potential expatriates and their spouses contacted those already experienced in life abroad to ask questions about what they might expect. At the time, many expatriates on these sites were just beginning to engage with the Internet and computer-mediated communication. The instigators of these fora were often retired expatriates, former leaders in expatriate organizations in a posting or foreign service spouses temporarily posted to their home country. The lack of viable access to the web prevented many posted to places like Nepal from participating in these sites, thus those exchanging information were often not abroad but former expatriates talking to future expatriates. Such arenas produced a new awareness among those who had left expatriate life that their knowledge was valuable. For this population, as well as their interlocutors, web-based communication fulfilled a need; just as those about to be posted sought information, returnees were often longing for the sociality they experienced in Expatria. The population less common in these fora was current expatriates, particularly those residing in the non-West. Yet these direct—former to future—expatriate venues had competition from a newly emerging professional advice arena.

An assortment of information for expatriates was developing simultaneously under the guidance of entrepreneurs hoping to sell their services and knowledge of expatriates directly to employers. Expat-Repat and Expat Forum offered discussion boards and listservs structurally similar to the older national bulletin boards, but these lists were hosted by independent human resources professionals and others, including psychologists, cross-cultural trainers, relocation specialists and business coaches.[4] These chat-style lists often served as the front door to a larger set of fee-based services provided by the expanding expatriate services industry. Public postings discussed the concerns of expatriates about professional development and family safety, with general responses mentioning publically available materials, while other postings directed readers to offerings of their businesses and the individualized support services they could provide for a fee. It was often difficult to distinguish which messages were by professionals in the employ of human resource agencies and which were from concerned expatriates until one reached the end of the post, where an author would list his or her affiliation. At times, professional services would copy advice from public boards to post on their own sites.

Expat Spouses E-Groups was one of the most active of the broad public-audience listservs in the mid to late 1990s, and their development tells a typical story of how what began as a peer-to-peer exchange of advice became a private, specialized-service enterprise. There was activity on Expat Spouses E-Groups every few hours in the early part of the site's life and participants were quick to respond to any new posting. The tone of most of the emails sent to the list was informal and friendly, replicating the style of face-to-face conversations among expatriate spouses. Many of those active on the list were either retired expatriates or expatriates posted in their home countries for a period. One frequent genre of posting was from those about to move to a new posting, asking what experienced expatriates found they missed while abroad and how they packed everything into their moving allotment. A new inquiry would usually receive three-to-four responses from the most active participants, depending on how many other messages arrived on a given day. Some posters presented general questions about what to expect from a first overseas job; others sent in more locally specific questions about the cost of a particular food in Hong Kong or the quality of schools in Singapore. Responses varied from brief messages of support—"hang in there lori"—to multipage essays. Some questions invited solutions to specific problems, such as getting special British foods abroad, and readers wrote back with suggestions such as "Have you seen or heard of 3ex.com. They are the most excellent internet company in the world." The majority of responses took a more letterlike form, with authors devoting three-to-five paragraphs to asking clarifying questions describing their own experiences abroad and offering support and recommendations. These more extended responses often began with an introduction to the author's personal history of expatriate travel, as a means of both establishing rapport and demonstrating the authority behind their recommendations. The practical advice was usually accompanied by affirming statements about how others had survived such trials and a request that the questioner keep in touch and let the group know how things turned out. The following appeared in one exchange about the challenges of moving to a hot climate, and concerns about both loneliness and appropriate clothing for Abu Dhabi from a regular forum participant:

> Having survived a hot climate for five years in a place where everyone is at least
> 10 inches shorter than I am, I can recommend stocking up on clothes before

you leave. Check with the embassy first and see if shorts and sleeveless are allowed . . . One other thing to look into before you go. Shoes! We don't think of
things like this often because we just assume that we can go out and buy what
we need, and everyone needs shoes right! But are you used to wearing shoes that
you must walk in, every day, in a hot climate on uneven surfaces? I wasn't, all my
shoes were more suited to in and out of the car, not miles on foot in unfamiliar
territory. My best find was a kind of German walking shoe call Rieker . . . That's
my piece of advice for anyone going anywhere actually. You are going to walk a
lot, be prepared. (Spouses-expat@egroups.com 06, May 1999)[5]

Such essay-length responses were common contributions from one or more
of a half-dozen regular group participants, and despite the urging to keep in
touch, questioners often disappeared from the list after a brief "thank you"
message once their discrete question was answered.

Over the course of Expat Spouses E-Groups' brief history, the types of participants and their contributions changed. After the initial months, several participants began emerging as leaders of the group, and these women and men
began including within their postings information about their own efforts to
formalize their advice for expatriates. Some mentioned books they had written
or planned to write, while others pointed participants to newsletters or other
Internet groups they had created. For example, one contributor, who initially
introduced himself as a long-time expatriate, after several months began including information about the international moving company he owned in his
signature line. Sometimes respondents would encourage a particularly insight-
ful writer to codify and distribute his or her advice in some way—noting that
they had long suffered without any "rule book" or person from "our side" offering ideas.

Despite encouragements to formalize respondents' ideas, explicit commer-
cialism was discouraged on the list. A controversy came to the fore when one
woman posted an extensive survey to Expat Spouses E-Groups and asked participants to respond to her directly, rather than to the list. In her initial posting
she noted that she had previously been an expatriate herself but was hoping to
"make this better" by creating workshops for expatriates. Her survey prompted
public criticism of the questions as well as hostility from contributors who
felt this type of posting was contradictory to the casual "coffee-hour-like" exchanges that were seen as the main mission of the group. Others asked what
she was planning to do with the information, and it was revealed that she was
working with others to build a new expatriate services company and that the

survey was part of her efforts to generate a statistical profile of expatriates and their problems for use in her new company. The survey was but the first posting to produce frustration that the list was being used to promote individual business objectives. Some sought to exclude promotional activities from the list entirely as extraneous to the objectives of the group, while others accepted commercial posts from recognized group members but not from those deemed outsiders. The new attention to commercial opportunities for expatriate services to some degree increased the quality and detail of postings, as authors sought to make a name for themselves and demonstrate the quality of the services they would eventually be providing for a fee.

The exchanges found at Expat Spouses E-Groups provided general support and specific information about posting destinations, information expatriates were rarely receiving from their employers. These online venues for expatriate communication were emerging similtaneous to the vociferous conversations in international human resources about the reasons for expatriate failure. This scholarly debate, as previously discussed, largely placed blame for the ineffectiveness of expatriate employees on family resistance to overseas posting and spousal unhappiness (Fukuda, Chu, and Chu 1994; Harzing 1995; Swaak 1995; Forster 1997). Yet much of this research focused on quantifying the costs of the problem and hypothesizing its causes, with only brief concluding sections devoted to potential remedies. Those who did propose solutions often called for greater corporate attention to socialization and the need to foster strong ties and regular contact between home and host countries, promoting both professional and personal connections while abroad. Yet there was not, as of the mid to late 1990s, much address to how computer technology might facilitate this. Instead the academic field of human resources management was lauding the potential for new computer programs, such as Expatriate Software for Windows and the Global Expatriate Management System, to simplify expatriate selection and compensation. The world of chat groups and listservs was not a part of human resources analysis. Even in professional publications addressed to those managing overseas personnel, such as *HRFocus* and *Personnel Journal*, there was little attention to online resources or existing information exchange and support forums. A 1998 *HRFocus* article on expatriate resources has a short section on helpful websites, but its main recommendations are not expatriate-specific sites but Berlitz and Atlas Van Lines ("HRFocus Special Report on Expatriate Management" 1998: S11). The connection between online venues peopled by anxious expatriate families and the call for more expatriate support by human resources professionals had not yet occurred.

By the middle of 1999, Expat Spouses E-Groups appeared to have more participants seeking to promote their own businesses than new contributors, and the half-dozen service providers each felt the need to respond to new emails by expounding their own philosophy. The group's organizer, who from the list's inception had been working to found an expatriate services company, had successfully established her expatriate services business, with its own distinct website. With several months' notice, she closed Expat Spouses E-Groups and created a new porthole for spouse and family exchanges on her own website.[6] By this point, her company had quite a few competitors, including one that managed a similar listserv, although it had proclaimed from its inception its association with a corporate sponsor. At least five frequent contributors to Expat Spouses E-Groups had, during the group's history, formed their own corporations, written books on expatriate support or been a part of forming fee-based websites for expatriates. The originator of Expat Spouses E-Groups was able to recruit several of the regular participants as consultants on her website, which continues to offer a wide variety of information to potential expatriates, including essays on various locations and specific problems, subsidizing this information with advertisements for services. These former expatriates and expatriate spouses were producing new arenas to support expatriate workers, but rather than forming alliances with human resources agencies, many of them linked with businesses that provided services for a general audience that could find a new market in expatriates such as mail-forwarding services, movers, online banks and mail-order retailers such as Amazon and L.L.Bean, which supported their websites with advertisements and subsidized mentions in articles.

The demographic of people who participated in the subsequent website, Expat Exchange, was quite different from the contributors to Expat Spouses E-Groups. Although some of the same experts offered formal essays and information on various locations, most of those who posted questions to the subject-driven public forums that replaced the listserv were not career expatriates. Instead, many posters were seeking work abroad, asking how to get work visas in various locations, housing costs and the like, and this trend has only grown among the current participants in Expat Exchange. Expat Forums, Expatriate Network, Expatriate Expert, Living Abroad and Tales from a Small Planet are all large expatriate websites with venues for discussion among expatriates, but most of the open forums are crowded with thinly disguised mail-order bride solicitations, short queries asking "how can I get a job in Australia" posted to every website or announcements of opportunities to teach English abroad. Few posts actually receive personal responses and there is little in the way of ongoing dialogue or repeat forum participation. Many websites have moved their articles behind membership-only or for-fee partitions. Others keep much of their content free through a combination of banner ads and the sponsorship of expatriate service providers. Some of the previously public websites that grew out of the early message boards and groups have now disappeared, having been made a part of expatriate services companies that now offer access only to those whose companies are using their services.

The electronic venues visited by expatriates in the mid to late 1990s and early 2000s presented a diversity of services and opportunities for those living abroad. At that time, expatriate websites were still rare and competing formats and user knowledge contributed to a proliferation of venues and uses for electronic communication between expatriates and those interested in their lives. Meanwhile, those responsible for mediating expatriate employment saw promise in technology as a means to obviate the problems of living abroad, but they struggled to figure out how. International human resources scholarship looked to online networks, not as a means to obviate failure or provide services, but as a means to reduce overseas pay through improved data or to administer testing programs to potential expatriates. Direct expatriate managers continued to provide services individually to those they employed, but anticipated that support previously provided to workers overseas via telephone, mail or before departure could now be supplied through the intervention of computers and undersea cable. These same technologies, they hoped, would also negate many of the concerns and complaints of expatriate families about a lack of information and communication. Opinions varied as to whether the capacity of electronic communication to link people worldwide would increase the number of expatriates as more businesses were globally invested, or whether these technologies would make such travel no longer necessary. Either way, it was predicted that the Internet would make expatriates happier (and less expensive) as the hardships of overseas life diminished.

The Expat Side of the Web

There was little attention paid by employers to how computer technologies were enacting other changes in expatriate life and the management of international employees. In the rise of Internet-based communication for expatriates, there was more than a technological revolution. The possibilities of long-distance connection and international communication afforded by network infrastructure did provide the opportunities for international families to keep in touch with friends and relatives across the globe. But many found that the expectations of the electronic revolution outstripped the realities of access, and expatriates in places like Nepal did not experience the promised seamlessness of connection. The digital divide between home country services and posting location further exacerbated expatriate frustration with cosmopolitan assumptions, as computers began to play a greater role in expatriate support services, as well as daily office life. Now the home office expected all communication to take place online and in real time, a challenge in Nepal with a ten-and-three-quarters-of-an-hour time difference to the U.S. East Coast as well as the problems of frequent power outages and phone lines that often went out of service, either due to natural causes or political conflict. The immediacy of the web that appeared obvious at the home office seemed less so from Kathmandu.

More significantly for the world of Expatria in Nepal, these technological innovations were occurring at the same time as a shift in the demands of overseas families as well as new attitudes in the international human resources industry. Web-based technologies offered entrepreneurial opportunities, both inside and outside the expatriate services industries, and a mechanism for creating careers that could be conducted from abroad—if the technology could be made reliable. Women who found their independent careers suspended as a result of a husband's overseas placement saw in the Internet an opportunity to maintain or establish their own jobs—work that could avoid the practical difficulties of distance and visa regulations. Through correspondence on listservs, many began to establish themselves as expatriate experts, learning ways to promote their experience as spouses as a salable commodity. Others merely used computers and email to generate consulting jobs in their own field of expertise or emailed their creative writing to potential publishers. In addition to benefitting expatriate spouses and retirees seeking to market themselves as expatriate experts, computer connectivity opened up awareness of expatriates to many companies, which began to use the Internet to appeal directly to overseas workers. Expatriates learned through the web how to access services enjoyed by their compatriots at home, such as remote college and career counseling or financial planning, and began to make demands of their employers to sponsor these services. Yet this also produced a new hierarchy of desirable postings among expatriates, as home offices anticipated the availability of mail-order services and the potential of spousal employment by virtual means, with limited awareness of how this was still impractical in places like Nepal.

The beginning of the new millennium saw a proliferation of services marketed directly to overseas workers via the Internet: financial companies offering bill-paying services, shipping companies promising to deliver familiar goods worldwide,[7] moving companies and twenty-four-hour crisis chat lines. Although some of these were associated with expatriate service providers, more frequently they were merely companies that became aware of how they might find a niche market in expatriates. Many nation-specific companies sprang up offering to ship national foods abroad or to facilitate transactions in a home nation. Again, Nepal's infrastructure problems, poor mail service and reputation for graft often ensured such promises were unfulfilled for those posted to Kathmandu.

As user-generated sites retreated behind private walls, many became disenchanted with the venues. In the late 1990s, several of the listservs and bulletin boards had begun to describe themselves as a community, as relationships between individual posters developed. When those sites were taken over by third-party providers or new platforms to manage the sites were introduced, complaints quickly arose that the community was being destroyed.[8] The websites and discussion groups that continued to offer public access dramatically changed the subject matter they addressed, with most postings describing concerns that would have previously been irrelevant for those with expatriate packages. The fear of corporate control of expatriate websites meant that several discussion sites were initially opposed to monitoring of any kind, but eventually had to succumb as the contributions began to consist mainly of people looking for marriage partners.

Thus, it should not be surprising that I did not meet many expatriates in Nepal who had found useful data on these websites.[9] A few expatriates mentioned seeking information about the countries where they might be posted next, but several others said that they were still uncomfortable with the Internet. One woman described having posted a question on an expatriate discussion group regarding the availability of goods in a place where she was going to be living, "but no one ever responded . . . it was all porn stuff." One employee mentioned that he received information on expatriate life by email: "It is some stupid service they have me subscribed to," he added, noting that it was part of his "wellness package" and inquiring if I could help him get the mailings cancelled. Those who frequently used email and visited websites did many of the same things one might expect of a nonexpatriate, such as researching colleges for their children and looking up information online. For many expatriates in Nepal, email was an important way to keep in contact with friends from past postings or family members at home. But there was resistance to computers and the Internet among traditional package expatriates, both to the technology and to the rise of non-face-to-face communication. As one spouse in Nepal explained, she had little interest in sites like Facebook: "too many of my friends are already virtual."

Those managing expatriate life and employment anticipated that computers and connectivity would be tools to facilitate an erasure of space, hoping they would, if not obviate the idea of expatriates, at least reduce their expense and failure rate. They did not foresee the ways these technologies would intersect with the simultaneous occurrence of employment and gender-role transformations, nor did employers anticipate the ways that expatriates would utilize the medium to make themselves suppliers of expatriate services. The World Wide Web did not prove to be the panacea for erasing expatriate failure and in the end made the business of expatriate management more, rather than less, complex and conflicted. It is the face-to-face interactions that continue to produce community overseas, adopting familiar forms such as Boy Scouts and Lions Clubs.

Governing Expatria

The United Nations Women's Organization of Nepal (UNWO) has long held a position as the clearing house for information about expatriate life in Nepal and activities for foreigners living in Kathmandu. In the 1980s and 1990s, UNWO was the first stop for many new expatriate arrivals and served as my starting point each time I sought to rediscover the expatriate community in Kathmandu. This section explores how different organizations that address an expatriate audience in Nepal serve the community and how these groups and the populations of foreigners working in Kathmandu are changing in concert with one another. When being an expatriate in Nepal once meant being part of a population circulating around the world every three-to-five years, organizations like UNWO facilitated coherency in everyday practices to counter this constant movement, as well as providing an outlet for the time and talents of trailing spouses. As new pathways of movement now determine the work and domestic lives of foreigners laboring in Kathmandu, different organizations are called for and the labor of "incorporated wives" to keep them operating can no longer be assumed (Callan and Ardener 1984). As one of the board members of AWON, a similar women's organization, noted in 2012, "there aren't any nonworking women anymore." The expatriate women's clubs, she noted, are still supported by a few Nepali women like herself, but in her estimation, the organization will likely end operation soon, as "the expats really sustained the energy and were the reason for it existing. Now there are so many clubs and events, and with most of us women working, you have to choose carefully, what to attend and what to join." Currently, organizations like UNWO and AWON exist alongside Zumba groups and dart leagues, a diversity that reflects different forms of labor and thus different social needs of foreigners in Kathmandu. Examining these new social organizations provides a lens into how Expatria is changing. The boundaries of Expatria in Nepal are becoming more firmly established in some ways and in other ways becoming unfixed, changes that reflect shifts in expatriate employment practices, conditions in Nepal, global economic and political transformations as well as alterations in the gendered division of labor in situations of overseas employment.

Although not the oldest expatriate social organization in Kathmandu, the United Nations Women's Organization (UNWO) is the most traditional of the many organizations in Nepal and the changes in its activities and membership present a stark illustration of how expatriate Nepal is changing. UNWO is loosely affiliated with a larger set of United Nations Women's Guilds and has a large dues-paying membership of both Nepalis and expatriates from across the world. Overarching women's organizations like these exist in many expatriate communities across the globe. This type of formal organization is central to the formation and delineation of Expatria in its various hubs across the world. By providing durable structures, it enables a perpetuation of tradition and provides a site for recording the history of a transient community. As one president of UNWO noted, providing support for new arrivals to Nepal is "a very important part of UNWO's responsibility here just like other UN Women's Organizations around the world" (Piper 2009: 3). Given that these international women's organizations are analogous in every given posting city, they are a familiar initial contact point for those arriving at a new posting. By providing information for new arrivals and monthly event calendars, organizations like UNWO serve the expatriate community by creating a supportive point of entry that can be recognized regardless of location. They provide an immediate set of vetted service providers and potential friends in the new home, making the process of arriving at a new posting not so alien. Groups like UNWO often serve as starting points for visitors who will likely eventually focus their social energies elsewhere. As formal and freestanding polities, they offer an open door to those with no entrée into other social networks.

An example of the services provided by UNWO is the welcome kit that can be loaned to new arrivals. Depending on what arrangements have been made with an employer and the local housing situation, expatriates often arrive in Kathmandu with little other than their luggage and must wait from a few days to as long as a few months for a larger shipment of household goods to be delivered. Under the aegis of UNWO's hospitality committee, the organization has a collection of pots, pans, sheets, towels and the like that can be loaned to families to tide them over until their own housewares arrive. When one UNWO board member tracked down the location of the UNWO welcome kit for a newcomer, she found a motley collection of camping silverware and sheets that had become grey through the harsh washing conditions of Nepal. Despite exchanging laughs over the paltry collection, the receivers of the kit celebrated finally being able to cook a meal at home after weeks of eating out. From monthly teas welcoming new arrivals to Kathmandu, to mentoring programs linking incoming women with those with several years of in-country experience, to introducing families with children of a similar age, UNWO works to address the needs and concerns of new arrivals.

The Mirror Magazine, published by UNWO, provides information to the expatriate community in Nepal, and its format would be familiar to expatriates from similar mailings generated in different postings. One of the most utilized sections of the magazine, which has not been available online, is the calendar section announcing events, including official board meetings, newcomers' teas, national holidays that might be unfamiliar to foreigners, school holidays and meetings of affiliated organizations and clubs. The Mirror includes a section titled Ke Garne? listing other local expatriate organizations, including the International Women's Sewing Group, Kathmandu Association of Mothers and Babies International, the British Council, Toastmasters and other national and interest-oriented groups.[10] A typical issue of The Mirror also includes a short article from the current president of the organization, reports from events that took place in previous months, often an article providing information about a Nepali tradition or holiday, a story about the impact of a local aid organization, a book review and a recipe. Almost as important as these articles are the advertisements that list medical clinics, beauty parlors, shops and restaurants that, by implication, are appropriate for expatriates. More space in the magazine is taken up by announcement of opportunities outside of UNWO than by listing its own events, a fact in keeping with the mission to facilitate connection within the community.

UNWO is in the model of benevolent women's ancillary groups, with a focus on charity work and a highly structured bureaucracy. The board of directors forms the core of UNWO and consists of presidents, vice presidents, treasurers and representatives from the various committees, which include the education, hospitality, membership, welfare, fundraising and programs committees. At board meetings I attended in the 1990s, the tone was quite formal, with occasional references to Robert's Rules of Order and strict compliance with the agenda. Participants took their titles and responsibilities very seriously and often invoked the importance of their duties and their responsibility for the legacy of the organization. The active membership of UNWO has changed over the years: in the 1990s it was very international, involving women from across the globe, whereas currently the organization struggles to fill board positions and, at many events, more than half the attendees are Nepalis. The multinational character of the group meant that even though English was the language of the organization, few spoke it as a first language and any social event soon broke down along linguistic lines. In addition, the self-imposed definition of UNWO as a charity organization devoted to remedies for the poverty in its host country resulted in social events that were rather somber. The disparate goals of the organization became apparent, for instance, when a cooking demonstration induced guilt through a preceding discussion by the hospitality committee chairperson about the hospital equipment to be funded by donations collected at the event.

UNWO exhibits a characteristic often associated with colonial socialities. Much of white female colonial social hierarchy mirrored the professional hierarchies of the male world of English governance. Englishwomen performed their own status dance within the volunteer organizations and charity activities to gain advancement for their partners, to reinforce social hierarchy within the British community and to display their superiority to those outside the community (Ballhatchet 1980; Callan and Ardener 1984; Strobel 1991). UNWO evidences similar manifestations of the transference of male authority onto wives, who deploy their husband's superior status in the board meetings and social gatherings. UNWO requires a percentage of its board members to be spouses of direct UN employees. Although that percentage has diminished in recent years as a result of changing UN employment policies, top positions like those of president and vice president are usually held by wives of high-ranking UN personnel. The women central to these organizations were vital to the functioning of the expatriate community in Kathmandu, and they defined themselves as community leaders because of their titles and involvement.

Historically, many women in UNWO saw their participation in women's organizations as an extension of their husbands' workplace obligations, both in terms of the merit their partners attained from their participation and the parallelism of their charity activities with the diplomatic and aid activities their husbands were pursuing as a career. Leadership in the organization was seen as a duty, albeit one that could be pleasurable at times. One of the board members of UNWO in 1999 remarked on her feeling of responsibility to participate, not-ing that "there aren't so many of us [direct UN employee spouses] anymore" and that her husband's position obligated her to run for board membership. This approach to UNWO as an obligation, either because of the status of one's spouse or out of a sense of noblesse oblige, contrasted with the attitude of a certain diplomatic spouse resisting regular participation in these organizations. She felt that since she was not getting paid to be a diplomatic spouse, she should not have to take on these roles and that furthermore her time could be better spent in promoting her own career or in "real" charity activities, unlike those she perceived as social events masquerading as charity in women's groups. She further criticized participants, noting that "all the charity things are done with a sort of superior attitude—like these women have something to prove."

In 1994, when I first encountered UNWO, its board consisted mainly of European and American women, with a few Southeast Asian spouses, Indian and Nepali women filling less prominent positions. The organization held many social activities that also raised funds for women's and children's causes, such as a scholarship fund for rural girls and contributions to a local orphan-age. The organization had a strongly positive reputation in the community, even among those who were not participants, less for their outreach in Nepal than for the services they provided to expatriates. When I returned to Nepal in 1997, UNWO had undergone a decline in its reputation. The president of the organization, Barbie, had been in place for several years and was disliked by many expatriate women. Their vociferous criticisms were in part on account of her leadership style and organizational choices, but also included some ad hominem attacks that reflected new tensions within the community. She was accused of implementing a "Manila Mafia," as many leadership positions in the organization as well as project heads were chosen from her cohort of friends from the Philippines. The regional term for her collection of friends also indexed a hostility to their marital histories as well. Many of the women were second wives of European men working in the UN or other diplomatic organizations. One German woman, Greta, tied her anger at this group to a personal experience: a close friend of hers, another expatriate spouse, had found out about her husband's affair with a local woman on his staff dur-ing their posting to Southeast Asia. Greta reported that when her friend had confronted the husband, he divorced her nearly overnight and married the younger local woman, "stranding her in this place—she didn't have her own money and had to call her parents for help getting back to Germany." Greta's story found widespread resonance and many claimed to have heard of similar events, and the anger of these "first wives" was often transferred to the UNWO president and her friends.

Barbie had done significant work to transform UNWO over the three years of her leadership. She had expanded and regularized the organization's charity activities, integrating more closely with the UN's aid work and agenda, including hosting the UN Women's Day, bringing in international speakers and generating enough funds to sustain three scholarships for women seeking nursing training. The same debates that occurred within the UN's development branches were played out in UNWO's board meetings: discussions of self-help and sustainability, concerns over the corruption of local officials and prioritization of needs of the population. While the budget controlled by UNWO was dwarfed by those of formal aid agencies, the conversations around its allocation were vociferous and well-researched. Information from the activities of the aid agencies flowed into the women's organization and vice versa, as was the case when one wife was able to influence her husband's organization to start a new health campaign for girls that had been rejected as a priority by UNWO.

Many disliked the formality Barbie brought to the organization, a fact well known to her. By her own account, she considered herself a businesswoman and hoped to run UNWO like a business. There were barriers to this within the organization, as several of the subcommittees had long-standing leaders who were reluctant to change their ways. Several UNWO projects were championed by Western women who had been in the organization for a dozen or more years. These leaders were once expatriate spouses, one of whom had decided to retire to Kathmandu when her husband had died soon after their Nepal posting. Another had experienced the same fate as Greta's friend, having been left in Nepal by her husband, who married a Nepali woman and left the country for the next posting while she remained behind. These two women had been mainstays of UNWO, attending every event and maintaining their long-standing roles in the organization, and Barbie found leaving them to their own devices the easiest approach. Barbie continued to run UNWO for several years, but had left by the time I returned to Nepal in 1999.

By this point, UNWO had become a less central part of the expatriate community. Although *The Mirror* and the *Newcomers Guide* were still important resources, fewer expatriate spouses were joining UNWO on arrival and attendance at their large charity social events had declined to such a point that several had been discontinued. Although the president of the organization was still the wife of a UN employee and the Western women who had become long-term residents of Nepal continued their projects, nearly all of the other leadership positions were held by Nepalis or were unstaffed. There were two groups of Nepali women participating in UNWO: spouses of the political elite, especially those associated with the former ruling Rana family, and a large cohort of local entrepreneurs. Many of these businesswomen had expatriates as a significant portion of their clientele; thus the stores and restaurants that advertised in *The Mirror* were now represented on UNWO's board. The Nepali women active in UNWO have become central to the charity projects of the organization. While expatriates often tried to cast the Nepalis as "native informants" about underdevelopment and poverty in the country, the elite Nepalis found in UNWO a venue to express their attitudes to helping their fellow Nepalis and deployed in their activities a particular form of civilizational discourse that has fallen into disfavor among expatriates with the rise of a democratic Nepal (Pigg 1992). Some Western women I talked to were reluctant to participate in the UNWO board, claiming too much of the business was conducted in Nepali. While I did not observe this in my own board meeting attendance, the rumor was enough to keep many away. In addition, this was also the period when fewer trailing spouses existed in the community, as long-term postings in organizations were declining.

By 1999, AWON had ascended as a more popular venue for those interested in participating in an expatriate women's social organization. Predating UNWO, having been formed by the spouses of some of the first American workers in Nepal, AWON at its inception in 1955 stood for American Women of Nepal. The organization for most of its history has had a connection with the official U.S. Mission, although recently for legal reasons and to emphasize the international and working character of the group, the name was changed to Active Women of Nepal, preserving the acronym. In the past AWON's association with the United States was formalized by the automatic appointment of the spouse of the U.S. ambassador to be the president of AWON, a position that many ambassador's wives had embraced, but which had been made problematic by the appointment of several female ambassadors from the United States. UNWO and AWON at times acted in consort, sometimes in competition, and although they shared many of the same functions, by 1999 the character of the two groups had diverged significantly.

AWON in its public representation was a much more casual affair, and its name transformation was intended to point to the participatory nature of its events as well as to emphasize the networking possibilities of the organization, making it appeal to trailing spouses with career aspirations. With more than fifty years of history, AWON has established several long-standing institutions that have persisted through the changes in both Nepal and the expatriate community. The English-language library, once a book exchange among expatriates, is now a freestanding and independently functioning institution used by local schoolchildren. The Kalimati Clinic, which was initially founded to provide health care and vaccinations for expatriate household staff, now focuses mainly on providing low-cost health care to local residents of the area and outreach programs across the country on preventative care. Although AWON activities continue to raise money for these enterprises, the clinic and AWON Library are also significantly independent from the organization and are run by paid Nepali professionals. AWON's fundraising activities emphasize the social character of the events, attracting large groups of expatriates as well as resident foreigners to annual gatherings such as karaoke night, a masquerade ball and a silent auction. There have also been a wide range of unofficial AWON events stemming from friendships among AWON members. The mention of a longing for board games at a 1997 AWON officers' meeting generated an offer from one member to host a bimonthly event at her house. AWON's charity activities now have a higher profile than those of UNWO, yet less discussion of charity took place at board meetings. Instead, the Nepali staff might submit a report to the meeting about activities and expenses at the clinic, which was always approved with little comment. Many AWON activities often took place at night with entire families participating in gatherings such as '50s Night. Amid poodle skirts and Elvis impersonators, a substantial amount of money was raised to support the various social services of the organization. While the leadership of the organization continues to consist of expatriate wives, regular participants also include Western independent businesspeople, resident foreigners, male trailing spouses and an increasing number of female Nepali entrepreneurs.

Associations of Avocation

Over coffee around an outdoor table at the American Club in Kathmandu in 1997, several women had gathered, some fresh from dropping children off at school, others still in athletic gear from the morning aerobics class held at the Club. Disparate groups of foreigners are found at Phora Durbar, the more common name for the American Recreation Club, a name that acts as a reminder of its history as a Rana royal palace. On any given day at Phora, there are those sharing morning coffee, early morning exercise partners meeting up, business lunches, evening film showings and teen dance parties. The women gathered there this morning were regulars, although what they seemed to share most was a schedule that allowed them to meet for coffee at Phora at 10:00 A.M on Tuesdays and Thursdays. My attendance at this unofficial gathering of friends was generated by the sort of follow-on invitation that was extremely common at expatriate social gatherings—and this coffee gathering generated yet another. Among many other things, we were discussing the various errands and meetings that framed the remainder of the day for those present. Some expressed frustration about the various tasks that had to be done, things to be picked up at the cleaners, appointments with a tailor about a child's dance recital outfit or attempts to refill household gas containers during the shortage at that time. When I confessed few plans for the remainder of the morning, one woman quickly proffered an invitation: "Why don't you come with me to the quilting group—we can have lunch afterward." My protests of a lack of quilting knowledge or skill did not deter my friend; she noted that most of those who attend are poor seamstresses themselves, that there is always cutting work to do, that there are members always willing to teach a newcomer or, if nothing else, I could just keep her company. As a culminating argument, she noted that the group was producing quilts and toys for the local orphanage.

There were a dozen women at the quilting group when we arrived, most of whom were older than those at the Phora gathering—fifty to sixty rather than the thirty-to-forty-age group who shared coffee. The one exception, other than myself, was the teenage daughter of a participant who was visiting her parents, having taken some time off from college to explore Nepal while her parents were posted there. I was one of several novices delegated the task of cutting squares of fabric from remnants collected by the women, either through donations or leftovers from their own sewing and tailoring projects. The group had different stories of expatriate life—some were nearing retirement from a lifetime of overseas postings, others returning to living abroad after a hiatus while their children were in high school. There were residents of nearly a dozen different countries, including Japan, Australia, the United States and Germany. Conversation was loosely focused on the task at hand, and there was an eagerness to introduce those unfamiliar to the craft of quilting.

Most of the women there were regular attendees who made this gathering part of their weekly schedule. Some used the meeting as an opportunity to consult others about local shopping venues, other craft projects or the conditions at other cities to which they might be reposted. Many of the exchanges consisted of what in Nepali would be termed *guff-suff*—idle gossip and trivial discussions enjoyed by friends. This group had no particular name, although it sometimes allied itself with the International Women's Sewing Group. It was a genre quite familiar to most of those present, who had participated in similar groups else-where, and comparisons to craft projects made for charity auctions at other postings were frequently mentioned. One woman compared Kathmandu's quilt-ing group to an event she had attended in Indonesia where women knitted items for sale at an annual craft bazaar, with the profits going to a local women's shelter.

This quilting group was just one of dozens of similar organizations, most of them informal and publicized only locally, that were a daily part of expatriate life in Nepal in the 1990s. They were sometimes centered on a shared interest in an activity such as running, quilting, singing or games, but just as often these groups consisted of people whose schedules simply allowed them to show up at the same place, at the same time. While most groups were informal and name-less, there were also a number of international organizations such as the Lions Club, Boy Scouts and Hash House Harriers that held meetings in Kathmandu. The central activity or hobby that might give shape to the gathering often was secondary to the relationships that brought people together. There was a re-markable diversity of skills and interests held by expatriates in Nepal, ones they had often picked up at past postings. In a twist on the idea of "time-space compression" (Harvey 1990), the expatriate condition often produces acceler-ated friendships and opportunities to develop accelerated expertise, at least in relation to home country norms. A novice runner might find himself joining a running group in one location, be named vice president of the running club in the next posting and form his own organization just a few years later at a site lacking one. One woman in Nepal learned about the history and craft of Turk-ish carpet making while posted to Istanbul, continued her education by tak-ing courses in the UK and found herself in Nepal teaching classes and leading tours to carpet-producing areas of the Middle East; her transformation from novice to teacher took just four years. These interest-based groups usually had significant stability and longevity in Nepal, with the attachment to a particular day, time and location of meeting persisting even as the participants continu-ally turned over—thus for years Tuesday night has been the night for bridge at the Sterling Club in Kathmandu. These organizations also produced a sense of consistency for expatriates as well. The ability to continue an activity across several postings was often a part of a family's self-narration of their history and identity. As one woman described it, "Wherever I am, I am the choir leader." Children could identify as "soccer goalies," or couples as "bridge champions," even if they did not know where they would be living in six weeks.

The way in which these organizations provided continuity appeared to be especially significant for families with children and those with a strong religious life. Many families described their story of international moves as moves between various international church congregations as much as between countries. After church services held at an international school auditorium, congregants would often exchange stories about where they had attended church at past postings and events held in other locations that they hoped to replicate in Nepal. Through these exchanges, one had a sense of a global field of connection, of disparate spots across the world where a population might find communion. The Sunday bulletin at the International Church of Nepal listed where past congregants were now posted and what church they were attending. The ability to expect certain familiar structures and affiliations regardless of where the next posting took them was cited by many expatriates as a source of comfort, although many expressed anxiety as to whether the new church, or tennis club, or bridge group, would be as good as the last one. In this, I see a manifestation of Expatria, but also an instance of its limits. The awareness of similar institutions worldwide was valued by those about to move, but for most it was the mundane exchanges that defined the daily life of expatriates in Nepal, with clubs only facilitating their connection. Families relished their church group, their dinner club, or their tennis team for its individuality, with the parallelism of institutions only mentioned during moments of arrival and departure.

Families also valued the availability of an expatriate network beyond Kathmandu in the activities of international schools, especially Lincoln School and the British School. Many parents were less concerned about the activities and goods that were absent from their own lives as a part of expatriate living than about the possibility that their children might be missing out on some key experience (see Hindman 2007b). Although several schools exist in Kathmandu for the international community, Lincoln School is the largest and most respected. Based on an American education system and originally formed to serve official U.S. government employee families, Lincoln now provides a K-12 education to a wide range of expatriate and elite Nepali children. For some parents, Lincoln School's membership in SAISA, the South Asian Inter-Scholastic Association, is one of the school's greatest assets. Through SAISA, Lincoln School students are able to compete in basketball tournaments, arts events and a variety of exchange activities. At least a few times every year, a group of Lincoln School students heads off to Lahore, Dhaka or Colombo to compete in a sports tournament, perform in a band concert or participate in a Model UN event. These exchanges are seen by parents as a valuable normalizing experience. The entire school often participates in send-off parties and decorates the grounds to celebrate the return of a triumphant team. For students, it is also a welcome break from the insularity of the Lincoln School environment and an opportunity to meet peers at other institutions. With only three hundred students across fourteen class years, it is easy to become bored with one's classmates and a SAISA trip is often an opportunity to meet new friends or romantic partners, and the dances that often accompany the trips promote this.

Lincoln School basketball tournaments, Tuesday night bridge gatherings, Thursday afternoon quilting groups and Wednesday morning coffee klatches have been the mainstays of expatriate social life in Kathmandu. These activities share similar characteristics: they are centered around a particular activity, have a consistent population of attendees (at least insofar as there is consistency in the expatriate population) and have a history that often extends beyond the tenure of any individual participant. Many activities are found in every posting and some have an official transnational connection through an overarching entity like the Alliance Française or Toastmasters, but more often the connection between Kathmandu's yoga group and the one in Kyoto is in the rumors and exchanges of individual expatriates. I cluster these activities under the label of associations of avocation not only for a felt similarity in the role they perform in expatriate life but also to signal a tension between global connections and local manifestations. Thus, while schoolchildren were thrilled to participate in South Asian regional basketball tournaments, one woman expressed her lack of interest in attending a bridge event in a neighboring country, noting that she traveled a lot as an expatriate and that she already had enough long-distance relationships to sustain as a part of living abroad. Bridge night for her was about immediate, face-to-face interactions and the group of people who came out every Tuesday to play.

Associations of avocation highlight the difficulty of standardizing the world of expatriates. Transformations in overseas labor and the rise of professional, often subcontracted, labor management reveal fissures in the capacity to generalize the expatriate experience across different locations. Human resources professionals and cross-cultural trainers seek to assist the abstract expatriate and to do so from the metropole, yet many of the daily activities and frustrations of families living in Nepal are invisible from their position. Tuesday night bridge at the Sterling Club has no website, there is no blog of their activities or record of weekly attendance. Likewise, the struggles to find cooking gas or dissatisfaction with the sixth-grade teacher at Lincoln School cannot be ascertained from abroad. For many who participate in expatriate social activities in Nepal, it is the face-to-face intimacy and separation from formal structures that is the attraction of such events.

Happiness, sociability and becoming established in a new location are seen as key variables in generating successful expatriate postings; yet manufacturing these through rationalizing techniques is often unsuccessful. In the quest for best practices within expatriate management, the world of overseas workers is subdivided to accommodate service-providing professionals—rather than the needs of expatriates themselves. Expatriates are provided with one set of resources to assist with spousal career issues, while a second agency assists with emotional support and a third service provider may address education and family adaptation. Each of these agencies seeks to rationalize and maximize what is under its charge, and while each may produce effective, auditable results, no one attends to the intersection of these domains. Although rarely seen as such, one of the perks offered to expatriates as part of their overseas package is "carework"—some form of emotional support deemed necessary by employers to assuage the displacement from their homeland social networks. But in places like Nepal, the turn to professional management has meant that such carework is provided at a distance. Carework is difficult to offshore, as many globalization scholars have noted, and seeking to manage expatriate sociality remotely has had little success (Ehrenreich and Hochschild 2002; Sassen 2006a, 2006b; Misra, Woodring, and Merz 2006). While migrants from the Global South move to the urban Global North to provide proximate care for elites in the metropole, expatriates are elites moved to the Global South, and although they are provisioned with local care workers in the form of nannies, maids and drivers, other forms of caring are necessary—best friends, bridge partners and running buddies—that require proximity. Saskia Sassen's work on the global city notes how the urban elite are tied to the migrant underclass service providers by the demand that both be present in the city to do their job, making place of on-going importance for these populations (Sassen 2006a). Although the economics are very different, for expatriates in Nepal, best friends are not offshorable, but must be physically present to serve their role. Although online forums exist for bridge, and Skype can connect people in real-time conversations around the world, in Nepal these do not (and often due to technological limits can not) substitute for Tuesdays at the Sterling Club.

Women's Clubs for Men

An expatriate women's club can still be found in nearly every major city around the world and their support and social events are still sought out by many enmeshed in the expatriate circuit, in Nepal and elsewhere. Yet numerous changes are transforming the role these organizations play for expatriates as well as the

membership and activities of such groups. These changes, along with the related shifts in the form of family deployment and the nature of expatriate jobs,
have altered the expectations of new arrivals such that they find little of appeal
in the offerings of traditional women's groups. Since 2000, more and more elite
foreign workers are deployed alone and expect their posting in Nepal to be
brief. Fewer and fewer workers in Nepal consider themselves professional expatriates, instead identifying with an employer or career that may or may not
involve future overseas postings. The labor of spouses can no longer be taken
for granted as an uncompensated benefit by employers. These transformations
are products of the changing character of labor and its global deployment, as
well as of the turn towards outsourcing the management of expatriates, but
these transformations intersect with a wide set of processes. The rise of political
violence and instability in Nepal, changing family dynamics around the world
brought about by gendered labor demands in the global economy, new technologies of connectivity and transnational business opportunities are all also
exerting an effect on how foreigners live and work in Nepal. Women's clubs thus
find themselves with different roles to play in serving this new demographic of
expatriates in Kathmandu, and new organizations are being formed that suit
the life of these foreigners working in Nepal.

Foreigners arriving to work in Nepal under the new regime of employment
find themselves living in a style previously unseen in Kathmandu but familiar
from other forms of overseas life. The gated worlds often associated with expatriates—the self-contained compounds common in the Middle East as spaces
for foreigners—were not common in Kathmandu (cf. Low 2003). Rather, in
clusters and clumps, foreigners occupied neighborhoods across the city and
spent many hours each day being chauffeured around the city through horrible
traffic to various shops, appointments and meetings. The rise of single, short-
term, elite transnational laborers has made the homes that served as the nodes
of this life no longer appropriate or of interest. In their place, a few residence
hotels have been created and employers are developing relationships with these
and other hotels to house their contract employees. In these living arrangements, expatriates are often able to eat, shop and recreate all within the grounds
of the hotel (Hindman 2011). Microcommunities emerge within these hotels,
like the Antigone, where small groups of expatriates share meals and commute
to their jobs in company-provided shuttles. With only a few months to spend
in Nepal and little incentive to leave the well-appointed, Western-style accommodations, most confine themselves to the hotel pool and ad hoc gatherings to
watch satellite TV.

Those who do venture out of the hotels seek a different preexisting community for sociality in Kathmandu, the ample tourist zone. Although expatriate workers are politically and economically quite different from the young backpack tourists who are the dominant population of Thamel, the major site for budget tourism in Kathmandu, the facilities offered for tourists there appeal to short-term expatriates as well. Many seek out the Thamel bars showing bootleg American movies on a wide-screen TV on weekends. A wide variety of restaurants also offer a break from the hotel buffet where many single expatriate workers eat twice daily. On weekend nights, the more upscale bars host karaoke nights and poker tournaments that are populated by short-term workers, U.S. Marine Security Guards, a few Peace Corps people in town or students on study-abroad programs. Short-term expatriates not only merge with the tourist population but also seek out some of the same activities as tourists. Although several short-term workers I spoke with rejected the idea of seeing the sights of Kathmandu, a few more adventurous types thought it would be unfortunate to "come all this way and not see the Monkey Temple" or the other major sights of the city. Moving away from career expatriates to short-term workers or international citizens was expected by the international human resources literature to bring not only savings but also more-locally engaged workers. If Alan and John are any indication, the opposite appears to be the case. Replacing career expatriates with independent contractors posted abroad for short periods results in workers who have little need or incentive to interact with local populations and instead are able live in non-places such as the Antigone Hotel (Augé 1995). Even the everyday errands required by expatriate life and facilitated by the AWON/UNWO *Newcomers Guide*, such as buying propane and finding a barber, are no longer necessary in the enclavic life of the transient protean expatriate.

The decline of expatriate women's organizations in Kathmandu and elsewhere is not exclusively about the shifting priorities of members or a globalizing world no longer in need of such institutions, but about the decline of package expatriate employment. If they once played a role in organizing the social lives of expatriates and producing a sense of an expatriate community that can be found across the world, that way of life is less common. To many, these institutions look like legacies of colonial forms, outlets for bored housewives and venues for entrenching social hierarchies; and thus one might assume that their decline indexes the decline of such forms of elitism. While this may be the case, there are new polities interested in such status-making institutions that are stepping into the void, including elite Nepalis, and new forms of overseas placement are generating different institutions. By 2007, one was more likely to find a large group of expatriate workers gathering on Saturday morning for a Hash House Harriers event than a Thursday afternoon tea. To understand the shifts in UNWO and AWON, one needs to see a complex field of changing family structures, employment philosophies, political events, technological advancements, global business and even the shifts in experiences of travel and space.

Whither Expatria?

Like other newcomers to Expatria, I was first introduced to the world of expatriate Nepal through organizations such as UNWO and club meetings. Having regular times and structure, they seemed the ideal starting point to begin research on the life of expatriate in Nepal. The repressed Malinowski in me hoped at these events to discover "the rules and regularities of native custom" (Malinowski [1922] 1984: 17). Furthermore, it was easy to arrive at a newcomers' coffee—in spite of declaring that I was researching expatriates—and meet many people willing to talk about their lives. In the 1990s, these organizations were filled with people exchanging ideas about the challenges of living abroad and the changing world of overseas employment, and an intrusive anthropologist asking where someone had lived previously was given a welcome reception. Despite lacking a village headman or a central hut, group meetings provided a starting point for meeting expatriates, and formal meetings often led to other forms of sociality, eventually leading to the more subtle "imponderabilia of actual life" (24). Even as I attempted to wear my metaphorical "Anthropologist at Work" button—reminding people of my research motivations—because I am a white woman that warning was often forgotten. Over time, I came to worry less about how I was understood within expatriate circles and focused more on observing the changing character of these organizations. Through the shifts in social organizations I became aware of shifts in employment and in the overall expatriate population, watching Expatria in Nepal change over the years.

Expatria is a social unit, but its limits are determined by labor, especially the expatriate package and pathway. Although visa laws, college admissions standards, employment policy and health care concerns were central to the everyday concerns of expatriates, they escaped the bounds of "expatriate culture." The boundary between work and leisure is elided in expatriate life, with families displaced for the work of one member. Divisions like public/private are irrelevant in this setting. Rather than the "cultural rules" that an anthropologist might hope to find, expatriate lives are governed by material objects and conceptual practices drawn from a motley collection of arenas. The unsurprising revelation that expatriates are not rigid followers of either home or host country logics was thus only the first of many dualities that fell as I attempted to understand Expatria. Like the unexpected twists and turns in expatriate use of the Internet, I found that new logics continually revealed themselves and had to be negotiated by the mediating actions of those living the expatriate life—as well as a changing population and practices that existed under the umbrella of Expatria.

Clubs and websites may not hold the "code" to unlock expatriate culture, yet their workings reveal the special challenges faced by people who move every few years and as a result are required to create and recreate personal and professional narratives. They also show the difficulties entailed in understanding how the social activities connect to changes in expatriate labor expectations. Yet limiting life to a cultural code—be it Nepali, Australian or Expatriate—participates in the same process of typologization that underlies the techniques of intercultural communication, which poorly prepare overseas workers for life abroad (Rapaille 2006). Scholars of international business expected that the connections afforded by the Internet would erase the difficulty of mobility, while those charged with expatriate management thought that the same technology would offer a cost-cutting solution to the demands of overseas workers. Expatriates did find use in the connections afforded by online communication, but more to replace a local newspaper or as a setting for exchanging information on events and goods for sale. At the same time, entrepreneurs mined the developing web communities for business opportunities, either expanding their consumer base abroad or finding a way to turn their experiences as expatriates into businesses. The expectation that technology would have the same effect on expatriates in Nepal as in the Netherlands presumed a global flattening that has still not come to pass. In addition, many in the metropole saw only what web-based technologies offered them in the home office, unable to relate these technologies to other changes in labor and gender roles. In organizations such as AWON and UNWO, one can observe the dramatic changes that are taking place in the structures of expatriate employment that are having profound effects on the membership of such clubs. Thus, although UNWO continues to hold coffee hours and lend out newcomers' kits, the profiles of its board membership today and just ten years ago are very different.

To see these differences, it is necessary to look not only beyond the surface but also beyond the bounds of Expatria in Nepal to the shifting network in which it must constantly be produced. The institutions of expatriate life, from

Sunday school groups to the bulletin board of Expat Exchange, thus provide neither a set of rules nor an absolute boundary for the community. Instead, they act as a company water cooler for a group that can never have one—a site where conversations about diverse topics bounce off one another and proceed, albeit transformed, on their way. As a dense node of association, expatriate institutions do provide correctives to many assumptions about what matters for expatriates and destabilize an understanding of this life as one defined by nation, employment, family or any other singular pathway. Through these organizations, the simplistic narrative of this world as one defined by transitoriness is undermined, as those who seek to return "home" after a career overseas find. Yet the changes in these organizations leave unsettled the issue of expatriate culture, expatriate community and Expatria itself.

Conclusion

Kathmandu's Twenty-First-Century Expatria

THIS BOOK HAS EXAMINED the shifting character of expatriate workers and families in Nepal between 1990 and 2012 through the lens of their labor as mid-level global professionals and the bureaucratic transformations inflicted upon them—and often by them—in Nepal. In displacing two significant dyads—public/private and global/local—I have sought to present a story that juxtaposes centrally determined best practices and everyday life among foreign workers and their interlocutors in Kathmandu. While accepting many of the critiques of global business and development put forth by anthropology and other humanist fields, in *Mediating the Global* I have brought to the fore the institutional, technical and financial impingements upon the life of expatriates. In examining the so-called best practices that are applied to expatriate workers, such as balance sheet compensation and flexpatriate employment, one observes moves of efficiency and neoliberalism that are familiar from other realms of business as well as from the projects of expatriate workers themselves. As a population caught between locations, changing philosophies and new practices, expatriates feel the negative repercussions of these policies, even as they seek to promote them. As a result, the package expatriate, once the norm of Expatria in Nepal, is in decline, with many new forms of precarious labor seeking to fill the spaces left behind. Local and international consultants, voluntourists and ex-military professionals now do the work once done by professional expatriates. Yet, in taking this not merely as a story of changing labor practices, but of how these interact with life beyond the office, this book shows how the new expatriate worker is also changing the social life of Expatria and the kind of work it is possible to do in Nepal, given a new class of experts and amateurs who are replacing the professional expatriate.

Shopping at the 1905 Farmers Market. Author photo, April 2012.

The Wednesday morning market that was held at the Summit Hotel is gone. In its stead are markets held on Saturday and Sunday, one in Kathmandu proper, another in Patan. The Saturday market is held on the grounds of the 1905 Restaurant, across the street from the U.S. recreational compound, Phora Durbar, and just a block from the entrance to the tourist district of Thamel. With a decline in the number of nonworking expatriate spouses, it became necessary to hold these markets on the weekend, although the sociality of the Summit market has been retained. A visit to the market often lasts all morning or, for some, into the afternoon, as friends meet up for coffee and segue into wine if the weather is good. There are still a few local farmers selling vegetables, often with a greater diversity of offerings than was true ten years ago and with promotional materials about their sustainable farming practices. They must compete for customers with a number of foreigners who have started organic farms in villages around the Kathmandu Valley. A German couple as well as a French-Nepali couple have both founded agricultural/tourism businesses that sell vegetables in the Saturday market as well as to local restaurants, and use the market to promote visits to their farms, describing a weekend stay as a way for stressed foreign workers in Kathmandu to escape the chaos of the city.

There is a symbiosis between these farmers and some of the local foreigner-run restaurants, which also sell products in the market such as salad dressing, cheese, sausages and even pâté.[1] There are also several tables selling crafts or products such as honey, tea and preserves that are a part of the work of an NGO. For example, one popular vendor sells low-sugar jams made by women who were rescued from abusive families, with the profits going to fund their rehabilitation. Looking out over the crowd, one finds it hard to distinguish between buyers and sellers. Most visitors or booth hosts are in their late twenties, frequently from Europe and residing in Nepal for a year or less. There are seemingly equal numbers of men and women. While some foreigners are working for long-standing organizations such as Save the Children, many are establishing their own charitable/entrepreneurial concerns, such as the agro-tourism pioneers. Leaving the farmers market, one encounters an exemplar of this new type of expatriate and expatriate employment. Carrying a bag of bread and

Crossing Kantipath from 1905 Farmers Market to Phora Durbar. Author photo, May 2012.

cheese, I was approached by a twenty-something German woman who wanted to know if I was familiar with Dogs of Kathmandu. The organization's table was hosted by two other young Europeans, a Korean-American and a Nepali who had lived most of his life in the United States. They sought donations for their neuter and vaccination program for street dogs. While some of those staffing the Dogs table were veterinarians in training who were volunteering in Nepal, others worked during the week for NGOs and contributed their time to the Dogs program on the weekends.

Although this new-style cohort of young, short-term European workers were the dominant population at the farmers market, they were not the only visitors. The package expatriates, of the type that predominated in Kathmandu in the 1990s, could also be seen conducting business. One Saturday morning, I followed a mother and child dodging cars to cross Kantipath to reach the farmers market on the grounds of the 1905 Restaurant. The mother, Mrs. Thomas, clutched her daughter's hand in one hand and had a bag of plastic shopping totes over her shoulder; her daughter carried a tennis racket on her back. Once they had survived the harrowing crossing, the mother congratulated herself: "It was smart of us to think about parking at Phora." She had left her car and driver behind the safe walls of the American recreational compound, thus taking advantage of secure and easy parking, even though the 1905 parking area was also filled with the blue-plated Pajero jeeps that indicate package expatriates.[2] The mother, safely across the street, turned around to look back at Phora and remarked, "It looks like the Stephensons had the same idea," recognizing a car of her friends going into the compound. A couple and their two children jumped out before the car went through the security check, as they intended to come to 1905 as well. Mrs. Thomas and her daughter did not wait for their friends, however, and strolled through the parking lot, trying to avoid the droppings left from the many crows that roosted in the trees overhead. Mrs. Thomas and I were headed to the same booth, one run by a middle-aged Italian man who was producing cheese with milk from his own organic dairy farm. On offer were his versions of mozzarella, Parmesan and several mild-flavored cheeses. "Should we set up a little cheese plate for the party tonight?" Mrs. Thomas asked her daughter, who assented this was a good idea. Her daughter seemed less invested in the cheese or the party than the attractive pictures of the farm animals on display. Mrs. Thomas continued pondering her menu, in part to herself, in part to the cheese vendor, debating how many balls of mozzarella they might want and what other uses they might have for cheese during the week. In the end, she decided that five balls of mozzarella, a small wedge of Parmesan and a piece of olive-flavored cheese would be sufficient. After the weighing of the two harder cheeses, and with the mozzarella at 400 Nepali rupees per ball, her total was 3200 rupees, almost $38 at the exchange rate at that time. While her daughter, following the "no plastic bags" practice that was a part of the market's environmental agenda, deposited the cheese in their tote bag, Mrs. Thomas rummaged in her purse for her wallet. Once she found it, she chuckled, turned to me to apologize for how long they were taking and then put her wallet back in her bag. "That's right," she commented to her daughter, "I need Dad's envelope." Her wallet contained U.S. dollars, useable at Phora Durbar and the commissary, but not here at the farmers market. She then pulled out an envelope made of rough handmade Nepali paper that contained her Nepali currency and was able to pay the Italian cheese maker for her purchases.

The scene at the 1905 farmers market reflects both the changes and the consistencies of life as a foreigner working in Nepal. While package expatriates like Mrs. Thomas continue to operate with foreign currency in their wallet, they mingle more frequently with a diverse array of foreigners. One of the most visible and regular crowds at the farmers market was a group of short-term aid workers and volunteers who often established themselves in a cluster in the garden and spent the entire day at 1905. All in their twenties and early thirties, they used the market as an excuse for extended sociality, as the women at the Summit had in earlier times. Of the nearly dozen friends who sat on cushions or napped on the well-tended grass, the majority were men working a year or less with an aid organization, most of whom intended afterward to go on to graduate study. Their conversations moved during the afternoon from politics in their home countries to their aspirations for the future or everyday challenges of life in Kathmandu. On one day after the market, most of the women had moved off to share a bottle of wine while the men clustered around the table over beer, debating the merits of *Freakonomics* (Levitt and Dubner 2005). This book was widely available in Kathmandu, and was featured in the bookstores in tourist areas as well as in academic shops less commonly visited by tourists. While all present agreed that the examples in the book were somewhat frivolous, one participant contended that the overall claims were nonetheless valid. The merits of the book seemed to provide an excuse to consider their futures after Nepal and how they might incorporate their experiences in Kathmandu into a future career, one that most of those involved anticipated would not involve travel to places like Nepal or aid work in any conventional sense. Like the examples in *Freakonomics*, the lives of both package and new-style expatriates in Nepal were not following the logics of traditional labor theory, and different groups were finding incentives not predicted by human resources professionals or their employers.

The More Things Change . . .

A comparison of the 1905 farmers market with the Summit one reveals that there has been a change in the population of foreigners living and working in Kathmandu. Yet what has changed about this group? Is it mere demography, labor or something more? Perhaps most important, why has this change taken place and what are its ramifications for both overseas elite workers and the labor they do in Kathmandu? Many of those at the farmers market in 2012 could trace their job to employers prominent in the 1990s: UN agencies, diplomatic staff and national development agencies like DFID, CIDA and GTZ, although this list now included Japan and South Korea's national development agencies, which were becoming more prominent (JICA and KOICA). New employers were to be found in business and finance, as well as local NGOs that employ foreigners like Dogs of Kathmandu. The array of faces at 1905 featured wealthy Nepalis and Indians, as well as many more East Asians and Africans than would have been present at the Summit. The marital status and age of those present had shifted dramatically as well, with a much younger crowd now dominating and single men and women outnumbering married couples. There were repercussions from this shift in the social lives of expatriates, so that meeting friends at restaurants now dominated over dinner parties at home and apartment life was more common than compounds and staff.

Time had changed also. With the presence of fewer nonworking spouses, daytime events had a smaller population of foreigners from which to draw. There was also a change in the perceptions of longer senses of temporality. Few of those at 1905, whether behind the table or in front of it, expected to continue along their current path for an entire career. Several foreign vendors skewed the average age of those present higher, as they were pursuing organic farming or pasta making in Nepal as a semiretirement career. Many of those buying goods saw their time in Nepal, whether working or volunteering, as a skill-obtaining sabbatical, one they anticipated leaving having gained the experience of working in a "third world" context. Several young professionals viewed working in Nepal as "paying it forward" for what they anticipated to be future employment in less-charitable industries. "I hope I can find a way to hold on to this experience," said a young British man who hoped to begin working in the financial industry in just a few weeks, as he joked about how he would likely be exploiting people in his future career and hoped he was gaining some good "karma" as a result of his low-paid internship in Kathmandu. Several people cited economic downturns in their home countries as reasons to come to Nepal, delaying their longer-term career while "giving back" at a time when jobs were difficult to find.

For those researching international human resources practices, this demographic shift might seem like a fulfillment of their predicted and prescribed transformation, this new population serving as their so-called international itinerants or flexpatriates. But this cohort of overseas professionals often worked in positions like those of the past generation of expatriate workers in Nepal, but at a lower salary and without the benefits that the package expatriates had enjoyed. And few of these new-style expatriates were celebrating the kind of work their flexible career path offered. "I was hoping for some real hands-on experience," noted one young Norwegian health care worker in Nepal for a six-month position at a local hospital, "but I find all I do is fill out forms." Although she had a sense of humor about this situation, observing that her future job in Norway was likely to involve a great deal of paperwork as well, she had come to Nepal to escape such bureaucracy and really "meet the people." The types of work these short-term overseas workers were able to do were also limited: they lacked technical skills, language ability and knowledge of Nepal. Like their package expatriate predecessors, they were eager to distinguish themselves from the tourists, whom they resembled. The comparison was difficult to escape and exacerbated by a practice that several young Europeans discussed one afternoon at 1905. "It is great that she is here, and I get news from friends at home . . . but I have to go to work . . . she doesn't understand," began the complaint of a French woman whose friend was traveling around the world and staying with her in Kathmandu for several weeks. The rest of the group all seemed to have a story of friends who had seen their work engagement in Kathmandu as an opportunity for free lodging during their global travels. The intrusion of these guests was often balanced by the welcome of a new face into the small group. The narrow distinction between tourists and workers is seen in the story of one man who noted that his job in Kathmandu had come at the last minute, just as he was going to take off on a trip around the world during his gap year—"at least this way I get paid and free housing."

The skill of a former generation of expatriate workers was being replaced in part by these young voluntourists and short-term semi-skilled workers, but also by consultants. By 2012, many governments and aid agencies had given up on health care and literacy programs in favor of infrastructure- and enterprise-building projects. "Trade not aid" was the popular slogan, and the many failures of the political system in Nepal were being deemed intractable, by both Nepalis and foreigners. Programs of "democracy building" and "good governance" were being abandoned, and the hope was just to get more Nepalis in paid positions, either in Nepal or as migrant labor, thus precipitating a rise in social entrepreneurship and vocational training programs. The efficacy of these projects was being impacted by the new population of expatriates. "Sixty percent of our budget for the project goes to consultants," said one Nepali who had worked for several international agencies. He described how most of the projects contracted with companies from their home countries for supplies and spent the major part of their budgets on short-term contractors. "They get, like two thousand U.S. dollars a day—do you know how much that is in Nepal?" he continued, remarking that less than 10 percent of a project's budget these days seems to ever get to beneficiaries.

The Why of Change

The crowd at the 1905 farmers market, the significant number of foreign consultants at the Radisson Hotel's Corner Bar, the decreased presence of families at the American Recreational Club pool and the dominance of Nepalis on the board of the United Nations Women's Organization all point to a transformation in the population of expatriates working in Kathmandu. Yet the observation of a change in the demographic makeup and social venues of expatriates in Kathmandu is insufficient to explain why this change has happened. To what degree has the nature of expatriate labor also changed and how does it relate to the different people occupying what were once package expatriate jobs? Furthermore, what has caused these changes? Is this a case of flexible workers pursuing alternative career pathways, as predicted by labor sociologists, or are other transformations coming into play? To understand the related shifts in the nature of labor done by expatriates and the population of overseas workers, one must look at the structural and bureaucratic changes that have taken place in the understanding of overseas work, in the local situation of Nepal and in expatriate-sending countries. Finally, one must understand how wider shifts in labor and gender have had distinctive influences on what it means to be an expatriate in Nepal.

While the despatialized worker anticipated by both some globalization scholars and many in international human resources scholarship did not appear to in the numbers predicted, changes in international employment practices and the mobility of people and goods do play a role in the twenty-first-century transformation of Expatria. Even as they have been slow to arrive in Nepal, technologies like Skype that enable everyday connectivity with a family at home have begun to contribute to a willingness of potential workers to consider seeking jobs in Kathmandu. Furthermore, the expansion of the variety of employers sending workers to Nepal and other overseas locations—the general globalness of business (Ho 2005)—has brought forth more specialized service providers that reduce the dissonance of living abroad, especially for short periods. As both public and private employers have been pushed towards forms of measurable efficiency, the tendency has been for a diverse array of industries to utilize workers at two extremes of the labor scale—hyperskilled subcontracted experts and deskilled volunteers or nonprofessionals. Thus, whereas a previous generation of expatriate workers in Kathmandu had a generalized technical skill set that allowed them to work as engineering experts on a variety of projects in different countries, whether hydropower or road building, these long-term broadly skilled employees are less common today. In their place are highly paid consultants who specialize in very narrow concerns. Meanwhile, the day-to-day work in Nepal is carried out by a combination of local staffers and semi-volunteers from abroad who find working in the country of value in and of itself.

Underlying this new regime are also some transformations that escaped the calculations of human resources professionals. The poor job market for youth in many countries in the Global North produced a generation struggling to gain a foothold in their preferred profession, and many of these well-educated people find that a year or two of working in Nepal can provide both some resume filler and personal fulfillment, which they hope will facilitate a transition into more lucrative positions. Wars in Iraq and Afghanistan have contributed to the generation of the labor pool at the other end of the spectrum, producing a cohort of former military personnel or military contractors who have the social knowledge and technical skills to operate as consultants on technical projects. The privatization of formerly military tasks has not only caused the quick retirement of soldiers who find they can make more money doing the same job in the private sector, but also created an infrastructure to facilitate contracting and to connect these experts with short-term technical needs in many overseas locations. What has had to expand to make this form of labor possible is the bureaucratic infrastructure. The numbers of grant writers, personnel managers and accountants have grown in this system. These new positions often exist in the home country, rather than abroad, but are necessary to coordinate the work of those overseas. At times, former expatriates have found their jobs transformed from hands-on work to ones of oversight and management responsibilities. With the new hyperskilled and deskilled expatriate labor that has replaced previous mid-level middleman positions, more managerial coordination is required to keep track of the transient laborers, who are now at the extremes of skill and pay scales.

The instability of the formal government in Nepal throughout the 1990s and until the present created difficulties for those seeking to conduct business—including development—in the country. Although the bureaucratic class has remained more consistent in this period, the ever-changing leadership of the country frightened many home offices and curtailed investment of financial and human resources in the nation. Many longtime expatriates in Nepal noted that the changing governments had limited impact on their work, as they continued to avoid working though government channels and their daily contacts in the Nepali government ministries did not change as frequently as the national leadership. Nonetheless overseas businesses, viewing conditions from the metropole, feared the unstable climate and especially the Maoist parties. Although leaders of the Maoist parties proclaimed their support for foreign investment and preservation of private property when the party garnered the largest percentage of votes in the 2008 election, many looking at the situation from abroad were hesitant to invest. The placement of the Maoists on the U.S. Terrorist Exclusion list in 2004, which continued until September 2012, further exacerbated the anxiety of those seeking to do business in Nepal, especially those without a strong presence in the country already. The country was swept into the militarized framework of global terrorism, with short-term consultants predominating in what was perceived to be a high-risk location, while on the other hand adventurous youth found the danger an appeal. Meanwhile, the Nepali consultant class, which had long had a significant role particularly in the aid community, found themselves in greater demand as foreign experts declined in numbers and new organizations, such as election-monitoring NGOs, searched for local knowledge. On the one hand, everything about Nepal's expatriate population has changed; but on the other, in many ways the new population of foreigners and the political instability of the country have had less of an impact on the daily work of expatriates than one might expect. There is more bureaucratic labor, for more administration is required to manage this new style of foreign labor, resulting in more paperwork. In addition, many of the mediating roles of expatriates in Nepal have also expanded as the dissonance between on-the-ground life in Kathmandu and formal perceptions has grown. Despite the political and personnel shifts, aid projects largely continue on the same path, even as the overarching rhetorics shift from health to governance to entrepreneurship. Business as well continues, with the financial risks of enterprise in Nepal often overcome by the financial potential seen in this country, increasingly described not as a yam between two boulders, as has long been the platitude, but as a bridge between the expanding markets of India and China.

The decline of package expatriacy in Nepal, a condition I argue resulted from economics of the Global North, changing gender-labor alignments, militarization and local political tensions in Nepal, rather than the economic rationalities of international human resources, has changed the gender makeup of expatriate Kathmandu, but not in predicted ways. Because of the recent divide between hyperskilled and deskilled expatriates, a new and in many ways more stereotyping gender dynamic has emerged, with subcontractors incorporating a masculine dynamic often brought in from their military past and reinforced by their ability to remain isolated from local conditions (Hindman 2010). Meanwhile, the deskilled volunteers or semi-volunteers are designated to carework positions that are both feminized and given little financial accord, even when held by men. Thus, although a new global workforce was expected to bring both racial and gender diversity, it has further segregated the experts from the implementers.

The Future of Mediators in Kathmandu

While the population of expatriates in Kathmandu is changing, its mediating role continues and even expands as greater regulatory pressure is exerted from above and the career needs of overseas workers do not align with their employers' desires. Both the new and old types of expatriates in Nepal are asked to be implementers of neoliberalism and also find themselves its objects. Thus, while in their official positions these international workers promote bureaucratic rationality, in other contexts their own worth is diminished and their social lives are restricted by the application of rationalizing policies. There has been an expansion of professional programs in NGO and development management, especially in Europe (Lewis 2003; Dar and Cooke 2008; Hindman and Fechter 2011), resembling the expansion of international human resources education and scholarship that this book began with and perhaps threatening to engage in the same metropolitan and homogenizing gaze. The expatriate middlemen hold an underappreciated position as the front line in performing values like "good governance," "development" and "transparency" for a Nepali audience. They must act as marketers and exemplars of globalization's benefits as well as of certain best practices of business, but are also products of its negative repercussions, their unstable job environment moving toward deskilling and flexibility. This disjuncture between their formal message and their daily experience of insecurity is made invisible by the unbundling of epistemic practices and the everyday social life of a knowledge field (Knorr Cetina 1999: 6). The same workers charged with administering programs of structural adjustment and bureaucratization abroad, in their domestic lives find their every action subject to an "impersonal, individualized rationality," a "character of calculability" (Mitchell 2002: 80) as a result of the pursuits of efficiency in expatriate labor.

The development professionals, mid-career foreign service workers and business men in remote locations who were the central figures in the expatriate community in Kathmandu in the 1990s, as well as their consultant and volunteer successors, are frequently caught between the importance they are perceived to have in Nepal as representatives of a global market and their perception at home as transient representatives of a larger project. In Nepal, expatriates have great authority as representatives of a desired extra-regional world (Liechty 2003) and grandiose titles that seem to indicate their importance. They receive dictums from above that they are encouraged to represent as their own and are imbued with authority as representatives of "the developed world." Yet few are asked to view their role as transformative, to see themselves as workers engaged in active, creative translation of dialogues between "here" and "there." The betwixt and between nature of life abroad, far from home and yet making a home, is often seen in literature on displaced and mobile populations, yet expatriate between-ness in the present exceeds a geographical situation. The life of perpetual transitoriness, be it of location or job, impels expatriates to focus on a trajectory outside the mission of their employer. Some must continually be on the hunt for the next contract, others look to the "real job" that work in Nepal will give them a leg up towards; and the remaining package expatriates look to Expatria itself to give continuity to both their lives and their work. Thus, even though this is a story of expatriate lives and that which impinges upon them, it is also a story of networks, a point of view that enables one to see beyond the requirement that the expatriate, the "neoliberal system" and the target population be either active or passive, but instead to see this as "*concatenations of mediators* where each point can be said to fully act" (Latour 2005: 59). How different elements in this concatenation will influence others is unpredictable, but it seems unlikely that things will proceed as the central offices or metropolitan managers predict in their models.

The social and bureaucratic forms I have examined in this book point to the need to understand a global muddle that is impossible to describe in a simple language of flows and exchange (Tsing 2004). The producers and targets of global policy appear as one and the same, depending on perspective. While critical development theory, policy planners and cross-cultural exchange professionals presume a dyad of originating site and destination site, expatriates are precisely the location where this dualism breaks down. As long as one takes the perspective that globalization constitutes flows between an originating site and a receiving site, the important role of mediation is ignored; expatriates exist precisely at the moment of exchange and transform and are transformed as a part of their labor of translation. This misrecognition of the interstitial position and the active role of mediators has a potential to generate misunderstanding, as those focused on expatriates as employees shake their fists at workers exclaiming their inadequacy for the task, and local actors shout back that headquarters does not understand what is really happening on the ground. This is more than a story of understanding the local or the particular (and they are not always one and the same): it is a demand to see knowledge production as processual and even "cultural" in an effort to take technical expertise out of a black box and attend to the social production of global knowledge. Bureaucratic processes are often taken to be mechanistic and transparent; they are rather always intertwined with humans and their management, and for this reason are often riven by internal contradiction. In bureaucracies of global business and government, the gears sometimes grind themselves.

Reference Matter

Notes

Introduction

1. It is worth noting that such codifications of culture, nonetheless, have political power. The Janajati activists of the 1990s were using similar claims to make demands upon the state, as are contemporary Madhesi activists in Nepal (cf. Guneratne 2002; Gellner 2007; Hachhethu 2007; Shneiderman 2010).

2. Several other salient texts were also appearing about expatriates in this period, including a special issue of the journal *The Annals of the American Academy of Political and Social Sciences* (Lambert 1966) and the work of Ruth and John Useem on third culture kids (Useem and Useem 1967).

3. On the limits of anthropology's cultural relativism see Geertz, 1984.

4. For more on the intertwined definitions of the Nepali word *bikas* and the English word *development*, see Mary Des Chene, "In the Name of *Bikas*," *Studies in Nepali History and Society* 1: 2 (December 1996), as well as Pigg 1992.

5. Throughout, I use the phrase "permanent resident" to indicate a foreigner living in Nepal for a long time as a consequence of employment or out of some interest in the country.

6. For an extensive discussion of the distinction between mediating "between" and "among," see Oppenheim 2007.

7. For Latour, one of the major innovations of mediation as a category is the ability to recognize not just people but objects as mediators. Thus, the beakers and test tubes of the science laboratory are not mere tools—mere extensions of the human agent—but part of a network of actants with a role to play in the experiment at hand. This important aspect of a theory of mediators will emerge as the importance of bureaucratic forms and physical buildings come to play a role in the construction of the expatriate project, but for now, I focus exclusively on human actants and their mediations.

8. While I will use *Expatria* throughout the book, I intend the term always to exert a bit of disjuncture and even discomfort. The tension that should be apparent is between the self-perception held by a group about their coherence as an entity and the risk of naturalizing and romanticizing "community" (Joseph 2002).

Chapter 1

1. The closely related topic of the associations between colonialism, development and anthropology has attracted the attention of many scholars (see Asad 1973 and Escobar 1995 as some of the more subtle theorists), although here again, the focus is on outcomes and intent more than structure, although some authors do explore the institutional and, importantly, financial relationship between academic knowledge of the Other and market demands in colonialism and development (i.e., Escobar 1991; Cohn and Chatterjee 1994.)

2. Examples from the Nepal-based United Nations Women's Organization will be discussed in subsequent chapters. Examples for many organizations and countries exist online: e.g., the World Food Programme (http://www.wfp.org/welcom/undp/brf_nep.htm [accessed September 8, 1998]), eDiplomat (http://edip lomat.com/np/post_reports /pr_np.htm [accessed August 25, 2005]) and the Real Post Report: Nepal Series (http://www.talesmag.com/real-post-reports/all/nepal/kathmandu [accessed May 4, 2013]).

3. One dramatic moment in British colonial history in England when women and domestic concerns came into official view was the Indian Rebellion of 1857, during which concerns over the violation of British women and the future of domestic life for colonists was central to official policy and subsequent scholarship (cf. Hutchins 1967; Bayly 1989; Blunt 2000)

4. In the post-Rebellion period, the "British" life that many leaders sought to establish in India was seen as a counterpoint not just to India but also to England itself. Domestic economic and social instability, combined with reactions to the Rebellion at home, led to a shift in approach to India from one of reform to a reactionary attempt to build a new and purer Britain on the "blank" territory of India (Hutchins 1967: xi). This political shift is seen in the "hyper-English" mores that some sought to institute in British homes in India.

5. The events from 1950 to 1951 in Nepal have been discussed extensively by those with interest and expertise in national and diplomatic historical narratives (Mihaly 1965; Joshi and Rose 1966; Rose 1971; Burghart 1984) as well as by those discussing the frequently tense relationship with India and the Treaty of Peace and Friendship signed between the two countries just prior to the King's departure (Rose and Dial 1969; Ghimire 1992; Mishra 2004). I cannot offer a complete analysis or even description of these often-contested events. Instead, I read them against the grain, not to revise any given historical narrative but to look at its edges for transformations of bureaucracy and conceptualization that might have influenced the practice of international employment in the present.

6. It is worth noting that the United States was writing numerous "Point Four Agreements" during the early 1950s, nearly all containing the same boilerplate statements. Nepal's statement on personnel is unique, because at the time the United States had diplomatic relations with Nepal but no embassy or ambassadorial staff resident in Kathmandu. Other agreements signed during the same period (e.g., with Afghanistan) are able to rely on preexisting treaties whereby diplomatic employees can simply claim the same rights for aid personnel as for embassy staff.

7. The numbers of Indians, by citizenship, resident in Nepal, as well as Nepalis resident in India dwarfs all of these other forms of labor exchange. Even the issue of the geographic and ethnic lines between the two countries is a constant source of tension. The complexity of the relationship between India and Nepal, and the mutual, if uneven, exchange of labor and knowledge between the two countries is far beyond the scope of this book. There have recently been a number of books directly addressing the experience of Nepali laborers in India (Upreti 2003; Thieme 2006) as well as mention and popular accounts of the role of Indian businessmen and the trusted laborers they bring to Nepal with them (Subedi 1991). This cannot meaningfully be addressed here, although the reader should be aware of this numerically dominant, but tangential to this story, population of labor flowing across Nepal's southern border.

8. Dening's historical project and his investment in "beachcombers" (1980) is emblematic of the history of contact that I seek to generate here. I will avoid using his language of "culture-contact" or "cross-cultural" history because this same wording, as I subsequently discuss, becomes the verbiage of global employment. I find justification for the adoption of Dening's concepts without his language in his own observations that the labels "for what I do have come and gone" (1998: 170), even as he persisted in the desire to hold multiple perspectives on any given encounter.

9. http://www.shell.com/home/content/aboutshell/who_we_are/our_history /1960s_1980s/1960s_to_1980s_history_of_shell.html (accessed September 27, 2001).

10. As will be discussed in subsequent chapters, the degree to which companies actually use or benefit from a focus on "soft skills" versus the needs of the job is unclear. Furthermore, there is a suspicious conjunction between those doing research on the benefits of cross-cultural training and selection and those providing such services.

Chapter 2

1. In a 1998 article, Frank Dobbin and John Sutton attribute the development of a distinct human resources field to the need to comply with Civil Rights Act legislation and argue that because of a Reagan-era decline in attention to and enforcement of diversity policies and laws, HRM turned attention to more economically driven concerns (Dobbin and Sutton 1998). For more on the issue of diversity and business management, see Gordon 1995; 1996.

2. Shell Oil exemplifies the early company-centered approach to expatriate management, and its extensive resources for families as well as archives of expatriate wives' materials illustrate alternatives to the outsourced form of management, as discussed in Chapter 1 (Shell Ladies' Project 1993; Gordon 2008).

3. This test is also discussed in Hindman 2007a.

4. Despite the protestations of the test creators that personality tests are difficult to deceive, the practice seems common according to anecdotal evidence I have collected from expatriates. It is interesting to note that William Whyte—in *Fortune* magazine (1954) as well as in the appendix to *Organization Man* (1956) discussed in Chapter 4— presented guides on "How to Cheat on Personality Tests" (Whyte 1956: 449–56). In "The Fallacies of 'Personality' Testing," he presents a set of sample questions and reviews how various responses will be analyzed by administrators (Whyte 1954: 120–21).

5. In the concept of "structuration of affection," there are three key reference points I draw from: Raymond Williams's idea of "structures of feeling" (1961), Pierre Bourdieu's ideas of habitus and structure (1992) and contemporary queer theory, which questions the benefit of normativizing relations along heterogeneous paradigms (cf. Warner 1999).

6. The narrowness of expatriate families has been changing between the early years of foreign presence in Nepal and the present. Expatriates from a wider range of locations have been a significant presence in the post-2000 era, especially in aid work and UN positions. In addition, as discussed in Chapters 4 through 6, families are, after 2010, becoming outnumbered by single men, a phenomenon brought about by changing contracting and compensation structures.

7. http://www.transition-dynamics.com/expatfamily.html (accessed March 25, 2013).

Chapter 3

1. As will be discussed in the following chapter, those who anticipate a "strong globalization" will claim that the wide reach and inevitability of global processes will, eventually, make the world more homogeneous. While few contemporary researchers maintain this extreme position, claims about the dominance of English, the global availability of goods and the dominance of American cultural forms can be found. What I bring attention to here is that these positions are used as arguments against the need for expatriate labor itself by business scholars. These researchers use claims about a more diverse workplace, the ability to do everything virtually and the increasing speed at which people and things can be moved to suggest that the practice of resident expatriate employees is no longer necessary. The mechanisms of expatriate compensation I discuss here, such as hardship allowances and the market basket, are themselves in part contradictions of this claim and thus the reality of the distinction that expatriates are tasked with bridging is affirmed.

2. These stories of moving disasters were often the opportunity for one-upmanship, including the story of a mover who had packed the garbage in the garbage cans that then sat in a container ship for several months, or of the family whose storage goods were shipped to them overseas while the items they needed abroad went into storage.

3. As I discuss in Chapter 4, there is a newly emerging category of expatriates who are hired as independent contractors rather than as ongoing employees of a company. These workers also receive bonuses negotiated as part of the subcontracting arrangement, but these are often less specifically delineated supplements and are often seen by workers as a lump sum inducement to work abroad or in difficult conditions.

4. The State Department compensation system is distinct from a parallel Department of Defense system that governs overseas military personnel, although at times the two share data and regulations.

5. In addition to government and in-company compensation calculation processes, a specialization has emerged of compensation advisors—particularly for the complex expatriate pay packages and often in conjunction with other expatriate service providers. These private subcontractors offer to "reduce expatriate compensation costs without sacrificing comprehensiveness or competitiveness" (ORC Worldwide 2000) through recalculating expatriate pay packages. This is usually done through the sort of refiguration of the definition of an expatriate discussed in Chapter 4, rather than any new data

collection, as these companies often use U.S. government supplement tables and statistics. They cite the extensive research and history required to collect the data required as justification for such data mining.

6. This same quest for generating a single system with the intent of universal applicability that as a result of its generality ends up serving no one is also seen in the expatriate testing and training processes discussed in Chapters 2 and 4.

7. http://www.state.gov/documents/organization/84383.pdf (accessed September 25, 2001).

8. http://www.state.gov/documents/organization/89232.pdf (accessed September 25, 2001).

9. http://aoprals.state.gov/content.asp?content_id=134&menu_id=75 (accessed September 25, 2001).

10. http://aoprals.state.gov/content.asp?content_id=249&menu_id=81 (accessed September 25, 2001).

11. http://aoprals.state.gov/content.asp?content_id=172&menu_id=81 (accessed September 25, 2001). The policy responses are yes to the former, no to the latter.

12. College costs have been an important topic of conversation among expatriate families, as in addition to the rising costs of higher education, expatriates often face challenges meeting requirements for lower-cost options such as in-state tuition at state universities. Many Foreign Service families as well as the American Foreign Service Association have lobbied for regulations that exempt official overseas U.S. government employees from residency requirements—with some success. Yet the problem persists, especially with a declining number of direct employees and more families working indirectly for governments.

13. The ranking system for U.S. government Foreign Service jobs is different for the first two years of a worker's time, when she or he is more directly placed in a position. After this time, there are a series of exchanges in which employees are given a list of available positions; they then rank their preferences and explain why they ranked in a particular way. A good deal of attention is paid in these ranking essays to family concerns, which often trump employment considerations. Embassies then are able to select from professionals interested in a position. The conversations about postings and ranking are often precursors to the ranking essay, which sometimes is driven by family needs and desires. But in some cases the rhetoric of family needs is deployed to forward the professional aspirations of the employee.

14. In terms of absolute increase in the amount one receives in a biweekly paycheck, a 60 percent cost-of-living allowance and a 25 percent post differential could, depending on the employee's salary, add about the same amount, as the former is an additional percentage of spendable income while the latter is an addition to base salary.

15. The only time I can find Kathmandu receiving a cost-of-living allowance is during much of 2005. Several U.S. Mission employees mentioned its loss in conversations in 2007, but most thought that a 5 percent allowance had been common policy in Nepal. According to official statistics, the 5 percent allowance in 2005 was an anomaly, and yet the constant movement of people in and out means institutional memory of these changes can be quite erratic.

16. In talking with those responsible for completing these surveys, I learned that in locations where the COLA was substantial, officers were more diligent in completing the litany of data required, whereas in postings such as Nepal where it had little effect on employee salaries, there was some laxity in complying with these regulations.

17. http://aoprals.state.gov/content.asp?content_id=166&menu_id=81 (accessed July 7, 2008). LES is a Locally Engaged Staff member.

18. Behind this discussion is a difficult issue of race and gender, centered on long-term expatriate men who divorce a wife who had been a trailing spouse from a home country to marry a local woman. In conversations with expatriates, the issue of "foreign-born" wives was a contentious one and there was frequent talk of a divide between social groups of "first wives" and "second wives." The foreignness of wives was often proclaimed on the basis of race rather than knowledge of citizenship or place of birth.

19. In larger countries with greater numbers of expatriates, U.S. government employees often outsource these surveys to agencies specializing in international human resource consulting. Although this last path would seem to contradict the requirement that these reports reflect the actual consumption patterns of real American families, the requirement that forms must "[i]dentify the name of the Price Collector(s) and the agency assigned to or hired by" suggests that such delegation occurs regularly (DS-2020I). http://www.state.gov/documents/organization/80008.pdf (accessed July 7, 2008).

20. As noted elsewhere, in Nepal, the wage-laboring expatriate worker continues to be predominately male and families predominately heterosexual—thus the focus on wives as consumers.

21. http://www.state.gov/documents/organization/80008.pdf (accessed July 7, 2008).

22. For American expatriates, Tex-Mex food was a particular focus of discussion, both in Nepal and in other places I visited. One expatriate American noted that she was seeing a significant change in the world when burritos appeared on the menu at the snack bar of the American Recreational Club in Kathmandu.

23. *The Newcomers Guide* is of a genre common to many expatriate communities. Similar texts, usually produced by women's organizations, embassies or national clubs circulate in most cities with a significant population of foreign professionals.

24. This idea of an overlying map of spaces that allow people, particularly the privileged, a disconnected experience of proximate space is one that has provoked vociferous discussion among theorists of globalization. I use this concept mainly as an index to the critical literature on gated cities (Low 2003) and gentrification (Smith 2002). In invoking the idea of a discontiguous global, it is also important to make a distinction between a generic "floating global" and a particular expatriate mapping of both Kathmandu and of Expatria. The "floating global" is a contentious issue among social scientific theories of globalization. Theorists such as Jonathan Friedman (2008: 111) question the idea of globalization as a distinct actor and refute claims to a linear and systemic increasing of globalness. While I find much in his argument useful and representative, within the world of Expatria the novelty and particularity of globalization is a claim being produced by expatriates themselves. Once again, anthropology's critique has been ignored within the business world and the celebrations of globalization hold more weight than cautionary tales like Friedman's.

25. The amount of time and expertise devoted to expatriate compensation is detailed in Calvin Reynolds's article "Expatriate Compensation in Historical Perspective" (1997), in which he notes the complexity of this specialization and the wide number of logics that are utilized. In his concluding remarks, he makes a point salient to this book, observing that the quest for cost savings combined with the increasing convolution of compensation theories and calculations has caused many companies to outsource compensation evaluation, a strategy that business will find neglects the "true needs of the company," let alone the worker (31).

26. The production of normalcy as a mode of research in globalization is best seen in an article by Carla Freeman (2001) where she observes the production of universal theories of globalization as masculine while the local transformations and manifestations of this unmarked universal system are generally seen in ethnographies of women and children.

27. This issue of the codetermination of self and Other has been an important one at the intellectual intersection of anthropology and philosophy, including in the work of Hegel, Sartre, Lacan and Levinas, as well as in fields such as gender studies (Beauvoir 1974; Kristeva 1982; Butler 1990) and postcolonial studies (Fanon 1965; Said 1978; Bhabha 1994). While I find the critique that posits this dualism as too self-fulfilling and reductionist to be convincing (McClintock 1992; Pels 1997), nonetheless, I observe the strategic deployment of such dualisms emerging in the corporate approaches to diversity in the global marketplace.

28. Trouillot's underlying point is less about the unmarked than the homogenization of forms of alterity in contemporary manifestation of globalization. Rather than accepting this process of genericizing alterity, Trouillot calls for an interrogation of the process of generating "restrictive," that is, nonglobal, identities—an investigation that he concludes offers many pitfalls, but the threat of erasure generated by the illusion of the equivalence of all alterities, in his estimation, makes the potential removal of spaces of voice for the Other worthy of such drawbacks.

29. In a much more complex and conflicting setting, Michel-Rolph Trouillot argues for a very similar distinction in the rise and ultimate uselessness of collective historical apologies (Trouillot 2000). Here, he makes the distinction between states acting as agents dispensing compensation, a role that many have been willing to do, and the state acting as a subject to render a collective apology, an act that Trouillot finds previously rare, now more common, although such ritual apologies are more performative than transformative (Trouillot 2000: 177).

Chapter 4

1. The shifts in expatriate employment that I describe here echo those observed in less spatially dispersed forms of labor, namely the end of Fordist forms of labor and a rise in temporary contract work, which has recently given rise to a cluster of anthropological studies of precarity. Concern over the demise of Fordism presumes such practices as long-standing, normal and desirable, whereas in much of the world and in many historical moments precarity has been predominant (Neilson and Rossiter 2008). There is a need for reexamining a history of labor that does not presume precarity as negative

or unusual, as well as historicizing what stability might mean in a given situation. Yet, as has been noted here, expatriate labor before the early 2000s was fairly stable and contract driven, thus making these emergent practices appropriately considered as a form of precarity.

2. It is worth noting with some irony here that one of the key figures in the development of the "Japanese model" was himself an American expatriate. W. Edwards Deming began his work on quality control and efficiency in the United States, but it was not until his post–World War II involvement with Japanese executives that his ideas found a receptive audience. Thus, the importation of Japanese methods was in some small part a reimportation of ideas initially rejected by American government and business.

3. As should be clear, these revelations of errors in corporate thinking or neglect of a given approach reoccur, as a new generation "discovers" the mistakes of its predecessors—and then makes them again. It is worth remembering Shell Oil's pursuit of a local-manager-driven system in the 1960s or a turn to "local rule" as a technique of colonialism.

4. It is worth noting that the demise of the "traditional model" of employment, often traced back to Whyte's caricature, has great staying power even if only as an oppositional form. Dalton Conley's (2009) *Elsewhere, U.S.A.* uses Whyte's organization man as a contrast to what he sees as a new model of work and a more fluid relationship between work and leisure. Like many contemporary authors who use the organization man as a foil for their own theories, Conley remains a bit nostalgic, seeming to lament the passing of a more interdependent relationship of worker and employer even as he condemns it as an anachronism.

5. Anna Tsing (2009) presents a trenchant examination of these processes whereby companies are able to defer elements of their business that they would like to deny responsibility for and to claim others that are advantageous through strategic manipulation of the bounds of the company via subcontracting (Tsing 2009: 156). She refers to a set of practices by which organizations are able to accomplish both high levels of profit and low levels of legal, or other, responsibility as "supply chain capitalism" (149). Her concept effectively captures the set of activities I describe, but given that the focus here is on humans, the phrase offers the potential for confusion rather than clarification.

6. The first seems to be the 1999 Greenpoint Financial/Harris poll documenting freedom as the major motivator for the entrepreneur—similar studies seem to reappear on an annual basis.

7. Carla Freeman's "The 'Reputation' of Neoliberalism" (2007) offers a creative inflection of this problematic in examining the neoliberal use of *flexibility* and Caribbean understandings of "reputational flexibility" in ways that are contrastive, but which offer a generative friction (Tsing 2004) for Barbadian entrepreneurs and social theorists to rethink the cultural meanings of flexibility.

8. It is worth noting this as an example of the questionable methodology discussed by Anne-Wil Harzing in Chapter 2. The authors of this study note that too much attention has been focused on U.S.-based expatriates but then proceed to make wide conclusions about the state of expatriate employment based on a survey directed exclusively to workers at a few large companies in Germany.

9. There is a literature discussing this dilemma, creating a distinction between voluntary versus involuntary boundaryless workers (see, for example, Pang 2003 and Dany 2003).

Chapter 5

1. There is a long history of tension and hostility between Nepal and India as a result of numerous political and economic incidents, which is felt strongly by Nepal as a tiny nation between two large countries. In the 1990s and 2000s, labor tensions between the two countries were frequent topics of conversation, especially in concerns about the prominence of Indian businessmen in Kathmandu, the large numbers of Nepali girls drawn into prostitution in India and an influx of laborers from North India in the capital city.

2. Astute readers will note that this book does not in fact contain a chapter on Nepal. Rather like the story of John being seen as "close enough" to Nepali, the chapter on India was deemed "close enough" for at least one employer, further substantiating the rarity of "cultural specificity" for Nepal. One expatriate in Kathmandu found in a local bookstore a copy of *Culture Shock! Nepal* (Burbank 1998) that contained a culture-assimilator-like "Cultural Quiz" for Nepal (268–77). This survey lists a number of possible scenarios one might encounter as a foreigner in Nepal and a list of possible responses as well as a comment on the best reaction, very much like a cultural assimilator. The book also contains sections titled "An A-Z of Cultural Adjustments," "Dealing with Nepalis," and "Close Encounters." This book was known to very few expatriates in Kathmandu, in my experience.

3. This is putting aside the glaring predominance of gender and race as determining factors for the type of workers who come to be successful expatriates in Nepal, which I discuss elsewhere.

4. An episode of the television series *The Office* (United States), titled "Diversity Day," exemplifies this approach to addressing cultural difference in domestic worksites, suggesting that this approach has become so familiar as to appear in a mass-market venue.

5. One of the most interesting examples of using cross-cultural testing as a means to manage risk is in the selection of reality show contestants. Dr. Judith Meyers, one of the authors of the Cross-Cultural Adaptability Inventory, has worked with a number of reality shows to discern good candidates for reality programs.

6. While I find numerous discussions of the validity of culture assimilators that address how host nationals respond to trainees before and after assimilation, there is little discussion about the generation of assimilators or the way in which correct answers are determined. Brislin (1986: 218) mentions a process of confirming the correct answers with members of the "host or target culture." The originators of this method are vague in their description of how the questions are generated, describing questions generated from expatriates they knew, brainstorming of plausible answers, some library reading and a focus group with foreign students at the university (Fiedler, Mitchell, and Triandis 1971: 97–98).

7. This fruit-based trope is in wide circulation, with the soft exterior and hard interior of Americans contrasted to coconuts, with a hard outer shell, but the hard interior

of Americans is perceived as their true self, a character that has been attributed to most European countries and Japan as well. Occasionally, one can find other fruits brought into this analogy. I have been unable to find the source of this widely used cross-cultural training theme.

8. The *Global Relocation Trends 2009 Survey Report* is often discussed as a comprehensive poll of expatriate mobility and services, but it is worth noting that the survey is conducted by one of the largest expatriate services providers, GMAC Global Relocation Services, an organization with incentive to find value in the culture-general approach.

9. It is worth connecting these generalizations performed upon ethnographic data to the generalizations taken from business data that are discussed in Anne-Wil Harzing's work explored in Chapter 2. In a similar way to what Harzing notes, the national and historical contexts are ignored in favor of the ability to quantify, an approach that takes on distinct irony when one is creating data about differences, as in cross-cultural training.

10. On the "bazaar" as a form, see "Shopping in the Bazaar, Bizarre Shopping" (Hindman 2009a). The term "bazaar of cultures" gained prominence with its deployment in Alan Bloom's *The Closing of the American Mind*, where Bloom uses the image to critique what he saw as the perceived amorality of anthropology and the dangerous potential of extremes of cultural relativism (Bloom 1987: 33). While dismissive of Bloom's point (c.f. di Leonardo 1998: 40), I find the language of culture bazaars an effective evocation of exoticism, consumer orientation and structural symmetry of this type of event.

11. My lack of knowledge about this demonstrates one of the lacunae in this research, my focus mainly on English-speaking expatriates or Europeans who used English as a lingua franca for social occasions. The Japanese expatriate community participated in many of the social events that others did, but there were also many exclusively Japanese elements of Expatria for this population, including a Saturday Japanese language school for expatriate children, an informal commissary and a women's club. I was able to learn about these events through an English-speaking spouse of a Japanese official. Future research will have to take greater account of the growing influence of Asia, especially South Korea, Japan and China, in both development and business in Nepal, and the expatriate communities that emerge from this new population.

Chapter 6

1. The challenges of downloading material in Nepal have been addressed by many in the IT community in Kathmandu who are eager to help others search for workaround solutions to these blockages, both legally and illegally. For example, a discussion on the website of an enterprise that specializes in importing foreign goods to Nepal contained an extensive discussion of successes and failures in downloading to the Kindle. http://forum.harilo.com/How-to-register-the-Kindle-3G-wifi-from-Nepal-td1691687 .html (accessed February 24, 2012).

2. For example, Francesca Kelly, the editor of the *SUN*, took one element of the newsletter, the Real Post Report, online and later founded a website around this genre, Tales from a Small Planet (www.talesmag.com), for which she was the editor in chief until 2003 and now acts as an advisor. She also consults with expatriate management organizations.

3. It was not until 2008 that a similar forum was formed for Kathmandu. Currently, Kathmandu, Kathmandu (ktmktm.org) lists goods for sale by departing expatriates and household help recommendations as well as current events, and is largely intended for an audience of expatriates and long-term foreign residents. This forum perhaps reflects the increasing availability of Internet connections in Nepal as well as the more diverse and transient character of the community of overseas elite transnational laborers in Nepal.

4. Members of the staff at IRG (Integrated Resources Group) and Bailey&Partner Start-Up Services were helpful in sharing information about their organizations, the history of their development and their production of online services.

5. The author of this comment was a frequent participant in the group in the late 1990s and went on to form her own expatriate consulting company. Although she has since left work with expatriates, she continues as a business consultant on international issues.

6. The leader of this move to close Expat Spouses E-Groups was Betsy Burlingame, now the community leader of Expat Exchange, a position that she continues to hold. Burlingame is now also president of Burlingame Interactive, a broad-based provider of online community services assisting a diverse set of businesses. In addition, Burlingame also developed a (now-defunct) website offering domestic and international moving services that businesses could provide for their employees.

7. The promise of "worldwide" delivery was often far short of complete. It was often stipulated that such services could be provided only in North America, Europe and some parts of Asia. While many companies claimed they were expanding their global reach, most rarely attained anything like global coverage. The reality of global reach seemed similar to what Karen Ho describes as the "global" reach of finance companies— globally lucrative and profitable reach buttressed by a rhetoric of universality (Ho 2005).

8. In June 1999 the egroup "spouses-expat" was eliminated and participants were directed to subscribe to a similar service at Expat Exchange. Although many continued to post that month on familiar topics, the majority of postings were related to the move. A regular poster who expressed resistance to the move subsequently discussed her new business providing workshops for expatriate families as an alternative to the new website. Many expressed practical concerns about how to use what was a new technology to most: the familiar method of postings arriving as emails would be supplanted by a discussion board format that concerned some. There were quite a few posters concerned that the new venue would limit the topics, thus destroying the community that had been established. The last days of the group saw numerous protests and many participants seeking to re-form the group on other platforms. Several current venues for expatriate expression continue to bear the marks of such a transition: see, for example, the history presented at http://www.expatforums.org/ (accessed July 21, 2001).

9. This had changed by 2010 with the arrival of the earlier-discussed Kathmandu, Kathmandu group, which has become popular due both to the expanding availability of the Internet and the new character of overseas laborers in Nepal.

10. *Ke garne?* in Nepali means "What to do?" and thus could be an appropriate title for an informational calendar, although there is some humor that may be lost in trans-

lation, as *Ke garne?* is often part of a familiar Nepali phrase, *Ke garne? Jiban yestai cha* ("What to do? Such is life") that may capture a more cynical aspect of the phrase.

Conclusion

1. Nepal requires all businesses to be majority-owned by Nepalis, so many of these foreign-run businesses are either unregistered or co-owned with a Nepali who has varying degrees of daily involvement with the enterprise.

2. Blue plates on vehicles in Nepal often indicate cars used by diplomats or package expatriates, as they are attached to cars that have been brought into the country without the payment of import tax, and by law such vehicles can be used only by those who have official status. This echoes the Point Four Agreement and its discussion of special import regulations for official Americans.

Bibliography

Abu-Lughod, Janet. 1989. *Before European Hegemony.* New York: Oxford University Press.

Adas, Michael, ed. 1993. *Islamic and European Expansion.* Philadelphia: Temple University Press.

Adams, Kathleen, and Sara Dickey, eds. 2000. *Home and Hegemony: Domestic Service and Identity Politics in South and Southeast Asia.* Ann Arbor: University of Michigan Press.

Adams, Vincanne. 1996. *Tiger of the Snow and Other Virtual Sherpas.* Princeton: Princeton University Press.

———. 1998. *Doctors for Democracy: Health Professionals in the Nepal Revolution.* Cambridge: Cambridge University Press.

Adler, Nancy. 1986. *International Dimensions of Organizational Behavior.* Boston, MA: Kent.

———. 1994. "Women Managers in a Global Economy." *Training and Development* (April): 31–36.

Adler, Nancy, and Anne-Wil Harzing. 2009. "When Knowledge Wins: Transcending the Sense and Nonsense of Academic Rankings." *Academy of Management Learning and Education* 8 (1): 72–95.

Allard, Leigh Ann Collins. 1996. "Managing Globe-Trotting Expats." *Management Review* (May): 39–43.

Allen, Charles, ed. 1975. *Plain Tales from the Raj: Images of British India in the Twentieth Century.* New York: St. Martin's Press.

Anderson, Benedict. 1991. *Imagined Communities.* New York: Verso.

Anderson, John, ed. 1987. *Insight Guides: Nepal.* Singapore: APA Productions.

Andreason, Aaron. 2008. "Expatriate Adjustment of Spouses and Expatriate Managers: An Integrative Research Review." *International Journal of Management* 25 (2): 382–95.

Appadurai, Arjun. 1988. "Putting Hierarchy in its Place." *Cultural Anthropology* 3 (1): 36–49.

———. 1996. *Modernity at Large: Culture Dimensions of Globalization*. Minneapolis: University of Minnesota Press.

———. 2006. *Fear of Small Numbers: An Essay on the Geography of Anger*. Durham, NC: Duke University Press.

Appiah, Kwame Anthony. 1992. "The Postcolonial and the Postmodern." In *My Father's House*, 137–57. New York: Oxford University Press.

Archer, John. 1997. "Colonial Suburbs in South Asia, 1700–1850, and the Spaces of Modernity." In *Visions of Suburbia*, edited by Roger Silverstone, 26–54. London: Routledge.

Arthur, Michael. 1996. "Introduction: The Boundaryless Career as New Employment Principle. In *The Boundaryless Career*, edited by M. Arthur and D. Rousseau, 3–20. New York: Oxford University Press.

Arthur, Michael, Kerr Inkson, and Judith Pringle. 1991. *New Careers: Individual Action and Economic Change*. London: Sage Books.

Arthur, Michael, and Denise Rousseau, eds. 1996. *The Boundaryless Career: A New Employment Principle for a New Organizational Era*. New York: Oxford University Press.

Asad, Talal, ed. 1973. *Anthropology and the Colonial Encounter*. New York: Humanities Press.

———. 1993. *Genealogies of Religion: Discipline and Reasons of Power in Christianity and Islam*. Baltimore: Johns Hopkins University Press.

Augé, Marc. 1995. *Non-Places: An Introduction to an Anthropology of Supermodernity*. Translated by John Howe. New York: Verso.

Axtell, Roger, ed. 1993. *Do's and Taboos Around the World*. New York: Wiley.

Bailey, Susan F. 1983. *Women and the British Empire: An Annotated Guide to Sources*. New York: Garland.

Baker, Ted, and Howard Aldrich. 1996. "Prometheus Stretches: Identity, Knowledge Cumulation, and Multi-Employer Careers." In *The Boundaryless Career*, edited by M. Arthur and D. Rousseau, 132–49. New York: Oxford University Press.

Ballantine, Henry. 1895. *On India's Frontier or Nepal: The Gurkhas' Mysterious Land*. New York: J. Selwin Tait and Sons.

Ballhatchet, Kenneth. 1980. *Race, Sex and Class under the Raj*. New York: St. Martin's Press.

Banai, Moshe, and Wes Harry. 2004. "Boundaryless Global Careers: The International Itinerants." *International Studies of Management and Organization* 34 (3): 96–120.

Barr, Pat. 1976. *The Memsahibs*. London: Secker and Warburg.

Barth, Fredrik. 1969. *Ethnic Groups and Boundaries*. Boston, MA: Little, Brown.

Bayly, C. A. 1989. *Imperial Meridian: The British Empire and the World, 1780–1830*. New York: Longman.

Beauvoir, Simone de. (1952) 1974. *The Second Sex*. Translated and edited by H. M. Parshley. New York: Vintage.

Beaverstock, Jonathan. 2002. "Transnational Elites in Global Cities: British Expatriates in Singapore's Financial District." *Geoforum* 33: 525–38.

———. 2005. "Transnational Elites in the City: British Highly-Skilled Inter-Company Transferees in New York City's Financial District." *Journal of Ethnic and Migration Studies* 31 (2): 245–68.

Beer, M., B. Spector, P. R. Lawrence, D. Q. Mills, and R. E. Walton. 1984. *Managing Human Assets*. New York: Free Press.

Benjamin, David, ed. 1995. *The Home: Words, Interpretations, Meanings, and Environments*. Brookfield, MA: Ashgate.

Berman, Marshall. 1988. *All that Is Solid Melts into Air: The Experience of Modernity*. New York: Penguin Books.

Bhabha, Homi K., ed. 1990. *Nation and Narration*. New York: Routledge.

———. 1994. *The Location of Culture*. London: Routledge.

———. 1997. "Postscript: Bombs Away in Front-line Suburbia." In *Visions of Suburbia*, edited by Roger Silverstone, 298–303. London: Routledge.

Bhawuk, Dharm, and Richard Brislin. 2000. "Cross-cultural Training: A Review." *Applied Psychology: An International Review* 49 (1): 162–91.

Birkett, Dea. 1992. "The "White Woman's Burden" in the White Man's Grave." In *Western Women and Imperialism*. Bloomington: Indiana University Press.

Bissell, William. 2005. "Engaging Colonial Nostalgia." *Cultural Anthropology* 20 (2): 215–48.

Bista, Dor Bahadur. 1994. *Fatalism and Development: Nepal's Struggle for Modernization*. Calcutta: Orient Longman.

Bjerregaard, Toke, Jakob Lauring, and Anders Klitmøller. 2009. "A Critical Analysis of Intercultural Communication Research in Cross-cultural Management: Introducing Newer Developments in Anthropology." *Critical Perspectives on International Business* 5 (3): 207–28.

Black, J. Stewart. 1992. "Coming Home: The Relationship of Expatriate Expectations with Repatriation Adjustment and Job Performance." *Human Relations* 45 (2): 177–92.

Black, J. Stewart, Hal Gregersen, and Mark Mendenhall. 1992. *Global Assignments: Successfully Expatriating and Repatriating International Managers*. San Francisco: Jossey-Bass.

Blaut, J. M. 1992. *1492: The Debate on Colonialism, Eurocentrism and History*. Trenton, N.J.: Africa World Press.

———. 1993. *The Colonizer's Model of the World: Geographical Diffusionism and Eurocentric History*. New York: Guilford Press.

Bloom, Alan. 1987. *The Closing of the American Mind*. New York: Simon and Schuster.

Blunt, Alison. 2000. "Embodying War: British Women and Domestic Defilement in the Indian 'Mutiny,' 1857–8." *Journal of Historical Geography* 26 (3): 403–28.

———. 2005. *Domicile and Diaspora: Anglo-Indian Women and the Spatial Politics of Home*. Malden, MA: Blackwell.

Bolles, Richard. (1970) 1989. *What Color Is Your Parachute?* Berkeley, CA: Ten Speed Press.

Bourdieu, Pierre. 1984. *Distinction: A Social Critique of the Judgments of Taste*. Translated by Richard Nice. Cambridge, MA: Harvard University Press.

———. (1977) 1992.. *Outline of a Theory of Practice*. Translated by Richard Nice. Cambridge: Cambridge University Press.

Brennan, Denise. 2004. *What's Love Got to Do with It? Transnational Desires and Sex Tourism in the Dominican Republic*. Durham, NC: Duke University Press.

Brennan, Timothy. 1997. *At Home in the World: Cosmopolitanism Now*. Cambridge, MA: Harvard University Press.

Brewster, Chris, and Juana Pickard. 1994. "Evaluating Expatriate Training." *International Studies in Management and Organization* 24 (3): 18–27.

Brislin, Richard. 1986. "A Culture General Assimilator: Preparation for Various Types of Sojourns." *International Journal of Intercultural Relations* 10: 215–34.

Brown, Hilton, ed. 1948. *The Sahibs: The Life and Ways of the British in India as Recorded by Themselves*. London: William Hodge and Company.

Buettner, Elizabeth. 2004. *Empire Families: Britons and Late Imperial India*. New York: Oxford University Press.

———. 2006. "Cemeteries, Public Memory and Raj Nostalgia in Postcolonial Britain and India." *History and Memory* 18 (1): 5–42.

Burawoy, Michael. 2000. "Introduction: Reaching for the global." In *Global Ethnography: Forces, Connections, and Imaginations in a Postmodern World*, by Michael Burawoy et al., 1–40. Berkeley: University of California Press.

Burbank, Jon. 1998. *Culture Shock! Nepal*. Portland, OR: Graphic Arts Center.

Burghart, Richard. 1984. "The Formation of the Concept of Nation-State in Nepal." *Journal of Asian Studies* 44 (1): 101–25.

———. 1993. "The Political Culture of Panchayat Democracy." In *Nepal in the Nineties*, edited by M. Hutt, 1–13. Delhi: Oxford University Press.

Burke, Timothy. 1996. *Lifebuoy Men, Lux Women: Commodification, Consumption, and Cleanliness in Modern Zimbabwe*. Durham, NC: Duke University Press.

Burton, Antoinette. 1994. *Burdens of History: British Feminists, Indian Women and Imperial Culture*. Chapel Hill: University of North Carolina Press.

———. 2003. *Dwelling in the Archive*. New York: Oxford University Press.

Büscher, M., J. Urry, and K. Witchger. 2010. *Mobile Methods*. New York: Routledge.

Butcher, Jim, and Peter Smith. 2010. "'Making a Difference': Volunteer Tourism and Development." *Tourism and Recreation Research* 35 (1): 27–36.

Butler, Judith. 1990. *Gender Trouble: Feminism and the Subversion of Identity*. New York: Routledge.

Calhoun, Craig, ed. 1992. *Habermas and the Public Sphere*. Cambridge, MA: MIT Press.

Caligiuri, Paula, and Wayne Cascio. 1998. "Can We Send Her There? Maximizing the Success of Western Women on Global Assignments." *Journal of World Business* 33 (4): 394–416.

Callan, Hilary, and Shirley Ardener, eds. 1984. *The Incorporated Wife*. London: Croom Helm.

Callaway, Helen. 1987. *Gender, Culture and Empire: European Women in Colonial Nigeria*. Chicago: University of Illinois Press.

Carr, Nicholas. 2011. *The Shallows: What the Internet Is Doing to Our Brains*. New York: Norton.

Cernea, Michael. 2003. "For a New Economics of Resettlement: A Sociological Critique of the Compensation Principle." *International Social Science Journal* 175: 37–45.

Chakrabarty, Dipesh. 1992. "Postcoloniality and the Artifice of History: Who Speaks for 'Indian' Pasts?" *Representations* 37: 1–26.

———. 2000. *Provincializing Europe: Postcolonial Thought and Historical Difference.* Princeton: Princeton University Press.

———. 2002. *Habitations of Modernity.* Chicago: University of Chicago Press.

Chambers, Deborah. 1997. "A Stake in the Country: Women's Experiences of Suburban Development." In *Visions of Suburbia,* edited by Roger Silverstone, 86–107. London: Routledge.

Chatterjee, Partha. 1986. *Nationalist Thought and the Colonial World.* Minneapolis: University of Minnesota Press.

———. 1993. *The Nation and Its Fragments: Colonial and Postcolonial Histories.* Princeton: Princeton University Press.

Chaudhuri, K. C. 1960. *Anglo-Nepalese Relations: From the Earliest Times of the British Rule in India till the Gurkha War.* Calcutta: Modern Book Agency.

Chaudhuri, Nupur. 1988. "Memsahibs and Motherhood in Nineteenth-Century Colonial India." *Victorian Studies* (Summer): 517–35.

———. 1992. "Shawls, Jewelry, Curry, and Rice in Victorian Britain." In *Western Women and Imperialism,* edited by Nupur Chaudhuri and Margaret Strobel, 231–46. Bloomington: Indiana University Press.

———. 1994. "Memsahibs and their Servants in Ninetheenth-century India." *Women's History Review* 3 (4): 549–60.

Chaudhuri, Nupur, and Margaret Strobel, eds. 1992. *Western Women and Imperialism.* Bloomington: Indiana University Press.

———. 1992. "Introduction." In *Western Women and Imperialism: Complicity and Resistance,* edited by Nupur Chaudhuri and Margaret Strobel, 1–18. Bloomington: Indiana University Press.

Chauhan, R. S. 1971. *The Political Development in Nepal 1950–1970.* New Delhi: Associated Publishing House.

Chin, Christine. 1998. *In Service and Servitude: Foreign Female Domestic Workers and the Malaysian "Modernity" Project.* New York: Columbia University Press.

Cieraad, Irene, ed. 1999. *At Home: An Anthropology of Domestic Space.* Syracuse: Syracuse University Press.

Clarke, Alison. 1997. "Tupperware: Suburbia, Sociality and Mass Consumption." In *Visions of Suburbia,* edited by Roger Silverstone, 132–60. London: Routledge.

———. 1999. *Tupperware, the Promise of Plastic in 1950s America.* Washington: Smithsonian Institution Press.

Clifford, James. 1997. *Routes: Travel and Translation in the Late Twentieth Century.* Cambridge, MA: Harvard University Press.

Clifford, James, and George Marcus, eds. 1986. *Writing Culture: The Poetics and Politics of Ethnography.* Berkeley: University of California Press.

Cohen, Erik. 1977. *Expatriate Communities.* London: Sage.

Cohn, Bernard. 1987. *An Anthropologist among the Historians and Other Essays.* New York: Oxford University Press.

———. 1996. *Colonialism and Its Forms of Knowledge.* Princeton: Princeton University Press.

Cohn, Bernard S., and Piya Chatterjee. 1994. "Colonial Knowledges/Imperial Outreach:

World War II and the Invention of Area Studies in the United States." Paper presented at the Historical Sociology Workshop, University of Chicago.

Conley, Dalton. 2009. *Elsewhere, U.S.A.: How We Got from the Company Man, Family Dinners, and the Affluent Society to the Home Office, BlackBerry Moms, and Economic Anxiety.* New York: Pantheon Press.

Coontz, Stephanie. 1992. *The Way We Never Were: American Families and the Nostalgia Trap.* New York: Basic Books.

Coronil, Fernando. 2001. "Toward a Critique of Globalcentrism: Speculations on Capitalism's Nature." In *Millennial Capitalism and the Culture of Neoliberalism*, edited by Jean Comaroff and John L. Comaroff, 63–87. Durham, NC: Duke University Press.

Cramer, Tim. 1995. "A Profile of American Expatriates on Assignment." Master's thesis, Loyola University, Chicago.

Dammann, Nancy. 1995. *We Tried: Government Service in India and Nepal.* Sun City, AZ: Social Change Press.

D'Andrea, A., L. Ciolfi, and B. Gray. 2011. "Methodological Challenges and Innovations in Mobilities Research." *Mobilities* 6 (2): 149–60.

Dany, Françoise. 2003. "'Free actors' and Organizations: Critical Remarks about the New Career Literature, Based on French Insights." *International Journal of Human Resource Management* 14 (5): 821–38.

Dar, S., and B. Cooke. 2008. *The New Development Management.* New York: Zed Books.

Dávila, Arlene. 2001. *Latinos, Inc.: The Marketing and Making of a People.* Berkeley: University of California Press.

Deleuze, Gilles, and Félix Guattari. 1987. *A Thousand Plateaus.* Translated by Brian Massoni. Minneapolis: University of Minnesota Press.

Dening, Greg. 1980. *Islands and Beaches: Discourses on a Silent Land.* Chicago: Dorsey Press.

———. 1998. "Writing, Rewriting the Beach." *Rethinking History* 2 (2): 143–72.

Denslow, Lanie. 2006. *World Wise: What to Know Before You Go.* New York: Fairchild.

Department of Tourism, Ministry of Commerce and Industry, His Majesty's Government of Nepal. 1972. *Nepal Tourism Master Plan.* Kathmandu: HMG.

Des Chene, Mary. 1991. "Relics of Empire: A Cultural History of the Gurkhas, 1815–1987." PhD dissertation, Stanford University.

———. 1996. "In the Name of *Bikās.*" *Studies in Nepali History and Society* 1 (2): 259–70.

Deshpande, Satish P., and Chockalingam Viswesvaran. 1992. "Is Cross-Cultural Training of Expatriate Managers Effective: A Meta Analysis." *International Journal of Intercultural Relations* 16: 295–310.

DeVita, Philip R., and James Armstrong, eds. 1993. *Distant Mirrors: America as a Foreign Culture.* Belmont: Wadsworth.

di Leonardo, Micaela. 1998. *Exotics at Home: Anthropologies, Others, American Modernity.* Chicago: University of Chicago Press.

Diver, Maud. 1909. *The English Woman in India.* Edinburgh: William Blackwood.

Dobbin, Frank, and John R. Sutton. 1998. "The Strength of a Weak State: The Rights Revolution and the Rise of Human Resources Management Divisions." *American Journal of Sociology* 104 (2): 441–76.

Doig, Desmond. 1995. *Look Back in Wonder*. New Delhi: HarperCollins.

Douglas, Mary. 1966. *Purity and Danger: An Analysis of Concepts of Pollution and Taboo*. New York: Routledge.

———. 1993. "The Idea of a Home: A Kind of Space." In *Home: A Place in the World*, edited by Arien Mack, 261–81. New York: New York University Press.

Dower, John. 1986. *War without Mercy*. New York: Pantheon Books.

———. 1999. *Embracing Defeat: Japan in the Wake of World War II*. New York: Norton.

Dowling, P. J., and R. S. Schuler. 1990. *International Human Resource Management*. Boston, MA: PWS-Kent.

Dudden, Alexis. 2006. *Japan's Colonization of Korea: Discourse and Power*. Honolulu: University of Hawaii Press.

Durkheim, Emile. 1995. *Elementary Forms of Religious Life*.Translated bt Karen E. Fields. New York: Free Press.

Eaton Consulting Group. 2002. "Cross-Cultural Training: Candidate Selection/Assessment." http://www.eatonconsultinggroup.com/training/candidates.html (accessed June 14, 2003).

Edwards, Michael. 1988. *The Sahibs and the Lotus: The British in India*. London: Constable.

Ehrenreich, Barbara, and Deirdre English. 1978. *For Her Own Good: 150 Years of the Experts' Advice to Women*. New York: Doubleday.

Ehrenreich, Barbara, and Arlie Hochschild, eds. 2002. *Global Women: Nannies, Maids, and Sex Workers*. New York: Henry Holt.

Einsiedel, Sebastian von, D. Malone, and S. Pradhan, eds. 2012. *Nepal in Transition: From People's War to Fragile Peace*. New York: Cambridge University Press.

Engelhardt, Tom. 1995. *The End of Victory Culture: Cold War America and the Disillusioning of a Generation*. New York: Basic Books.

Engels, Friedrich. (1884) 1978. "The Origin of the Family, Private Property and the State." In *The Marx-Engels Reader*. Second edition, edited by R. Tucker, 734–59. New York: Norton.

England, Paula. 2005. "Emerging Theories of Care Work." *Annual Review of Sociology* 31: 381–99.

Enloe, Cynthia. 1983. *Does Khaki Become You?* Boston, MA: South End Press.

———. 1990. *Bananas, Beaches and Bases*. Berkeley: University of California Press.

Escobar, Arturo. 1995. *Encountering Development*. Princeton: Princeton University Press.

Fabian, Johannes. 1983. *Time and the Other: How Anthropology Makes Its Object*. New York: Columbia University Press.

Fanon, Frantz. 1965. *A Dying Colonialism*. Translated by Haakon Chevalier. New York: Grove Press.

———. 1968. *The Wretched of the Earth*. Translated by Constance Farrington. New York: Grove Press.

Farwell, Byron. 1984. *The Gurkhas*. London: Norton.

Fechter, Anne-Meike. 2007. *Transnational Lives: Expatriated in Indonesia*. Farnham, UK: Ashgate.

Ferguson, James. 1994. *The Anti-Politics Machine: "Development," Depoliticization and Bureaucratic Power in Lesotho*. Minneapolis: University of Minnesota Press.

———. 1999. *Expectations of Modernity*. Berkeley: University of California Press.

———. 2006. *Global Shadows: Africa in the Neoliberal World Order*. Durham, NC: Duke University Press.

Ferguson, Niall. 2004. *Colossus: The Rise and Fall of the American Empire*. New York: Penguin Books.

Fiedler, Fred, Terence Mitchell, and Harry Triandis. 1971. "The Culture Assimilator: An Approach to Cross-Cultural Training." *Journal of Applied Psychology* 55 (2): 95–102.

Fischer, Claude. 1999. "Comment on 'Anxiety': Compensation in Social History." *Journal of Social History* 33 (1): 143–45.

Fisher, James. 1986. *Trans-Himalayan Traders*. Berkeley: University of California Press.

———. 1990. *Sherpas: Reflections on Change in Himalayan Nepal*. Berkeley: University of California Press.

———. 1997. *Living Martyrs: Individuals and Revolution in Nepal*. New York: Oxford University Press.

Flanagan, John. 1954. "The Critical Incident Technique." *Psychological Bulletin* 51 (4): 327–58.

Flemming, Leslie A. 1992. "A New Humanity: American Missionaries' Ideals for Women in North India, 1870–1930." In *Western Women and Imperialism*, edited by Nupur Chaudhuri and Margaret Strobel, 191–206. Bloomington: Indiana University Press.

Fletcher, Joyce, and Lotte Bailyn. 1996. "Challenging the Last Boundary: Reconnecting Work and Family." In *The Boundaryless Career*, edited by M. Arthur and D. Rousseau, 256–67. New York: Oxford University Press.

Fondas, Nanette. 1996. "Feminization at Work: Career Implications." In *The Boundaryless Career*, edited by M. Arthur and D. Rousseau, 282–93. New York: Oxford University Press.

Forster, Nick. 1992. "International Managers and Mobile Families: The Professional and Personal Dynamics of Trans-National Career Pathing and Job Mobility in the 1990s." *International Journal of Human Resource Management* 3 (3): 605–21.

———. 1997. "'The Persistent Myth of High Expatriate Failure Rates': A Reappraisal." *International Journal of Human Resource Management* 8 (4): 414–33.

Forster, Nick, and Mette Johnsen. 1996. "Expatriate Management Policies in UK Companies New to the International Scene." *International Journal of Human Resource Management* 7 (1): 177–205.

Foster, Robert J. 2008. *Coca-Globalization: Following Soft Drinks from New York to New Guinea*. New York: Palgrave MacMillan.

Foucault, Michel. 1973. *The Order of Things: An Archaeology of the Human Sciences*. New York: Random House.

———. 1979. *Discipline and Punish: The Birth of the Prison*. Translated by Alan Sheridan. New York: Vintage Books.

———. 2008. *The Birth of Biopolitics*. Edited by M. Senellart. Translated by Graham Burchell. New York: Palgrave Macmillan.

Fox, Richard, and Barbara King, eds. 2002a. *Anthropology Beyond Culture*. New York: Berg.

———. 2002b. "Introduction: Beyond Culture Worry." In *Anthropology Beyond Culture*, edited by Richard Fox and Barbara King, 1–20. New York: Berg.

Frank, Thomas. 2000. *One Market Under God.* New York: Anchor Books.

Fraser, Nancy. 1990. "Rethinking the Public Sphere: A Contribution to the Critique of Actually Existing Democracy." *Social Text* 25/26: 56–80.

Freeman, Carla. 2000. *High Tech and High Heels in the Global Economy.* Durham, NC: Duke University Press.

———. 2001. "Is Local: Global as Feminine: Masculine? Rethinking the Gender of Globalization." *Signs* 26 (4): 1007–37.

———. 2007. "The 'Reputation' of Neoliberalism." *American Ethnologist* 34 (2): 252–67.

Freeman, Kimberly, and Jeffrey Kane. 1995. "An Alternative Approach to Expatriate Allowances: An 'International Citizen.'" *The International Executive* 37 (3): 245–59.

Friedman, Jonathan. 2008. "Global Systems, Globalization, and Anthropological Theory." In *Frontiers of Globalization Research: Theoretical and Methodological Approaches*, edited by Ino Rossi, 109–32. New York: Springer.

Friedman, Thomas. 2005. *The World is Flat: A Brief History of the Twenty-First Century.* New York: Farrar, Straus and Giroux.

Frost, Robert L. 1993. "Machine Liberation: Inventing Housewives and Home Appliances in Interwar France." *French Historical Studies* (Spring): 103–30.

Fujikura, Tatsuro. 1996. "Technologies of Improvement, Locations of Culture: American Discourses of Democracy and 'Community Development' in Nepal." *Studies in Nepali History and Society* 2 (1): 271–311.

Fukuda, K., John Chu, and Priscilla Chu. 1994. "Wrestling with Expatriate Family Problems." *International Studies of Management and Organization* 24 (3): 36–47.

Furber, Holden. 1948. *John Company at Work.* Cambridge, MA: Harvard University Press.

Fussell, Paul. 1989. *Wartime: Understanding and Behavior in the Second World War.* New York: Oxford University Press.

Gabaccia, Donna. 2002. "As American as Budweiser and Pickles? Nation-Building in American Food Industries." In *Food Nations*, edited by W. Belasco and P. Scranton, 175–93. New York: Routledge.

Galbraith, John Kenneth. 1958. *The Affluent Society.* Boston, MA: Houghton Mifflin.

Gammel, C. David. 2000. "Cross-cultural Training and International Business Assignments." http://www.highcontext.com/Articles/srp/TableofContents.php (accessed September 27, 2001).

Gartrell, Beverly. 1984. "Colonial Wives: Villains or Victims?" In *The Incorporated Wife*, edited by Hillary Callan and Shirley Ardener, 165–85. London: Croom Helm.

Geertz, Clifford, ed. 1963. *Old Societies and New States: The Quest for Modernity in Asia and Africa.* New York: Free Press of Glencoe.

———. 1984. "Distinguished Lecture: Anti-Relativism." *American Anthropologist* 86 (2): 263–78.

Gellner, David. 1992. *Monk, Householder, and Tantric Priest.* New Delhi: Cambridge University Press.

———. 2007. "Ethnicity and Inequality in Nepal." *Economic and Political Weekly* 42 (20): 1823–28.

Gellner, David, Joanna Pfaff-Czarnecka, and John Whelpton, eds. 1997. *Nationalism and*

Ethnicity in a Hindu Kingdom: The Politics of Culture in Contemporary Nepal. Amsterdam: Harwood.

Ghosh, Amitav. 1994. *In an Antique Land.* New York: Random House.

Ghosh, Suresh Chandra. 1970. *The Social Condition of the British Community in Bengal, 1757–1800.* Leiden: Brill.

Gill, Stephen. 2008. *Power and Resistance in the New World Order.* Second edition. New York: Palgrave Macmillan.

Gilly, Mary. 1995. "The Consumer Acculturation of Expatriate Americans." *Advances in Consumer Research* 22: 506–10.

GMAC Global Relocation Services. 2009. *Global Relocation Trends 2009 Survey Report.* Woodridge, IL: GMAC Global Relocation Services.

Goffman, Erving. 1986. *Frame Analysis: An Essay on the Organization of Experience.* Boston, MA: Northeastern University Press.

Gordon, Avery. 1995. "The Work of Corporate Culture: Diversity Management." *Social Text* 44: 3–30.

———. 1996. "Multiculturalism's Unfinished Business." In *Mapping Multiculturalism,* edited by Avery F. Gordon and Christopher Newfield, 76–115. Minneapolis: University of Minnesota Press.

Gordon, Leonie. 2008. "The Shell Ladies' Project: Making and Remaking Home." In *Gender and Family among Transnational Professionals,* edited by A. Coles and A. Fechter, 21–39. New York: Routledge.

Gray, John. 1992. "Driving in a Soft City: Trafficking in Images of Identity and Power on the Roads of Kathmandu." In *Anthropology of Nepal: Peoples, Problems and Processes,* edited by Michael Allen, 147–59. Kathmandu: Mandala Book Point.

Green, Nancy. 2009. "Expatriation, Expatriates, and Expats: The American Transformation of a Concept." *American Historical Review* 114 (2): 307–28.

Gregersen, Hal, and Linda Stroh. 1997. "Coming Home to the Arctic Cold: Antecedents to Finnish Expatriate and Spouse Repatriation Adjustment." *Personnel Psychology* 50: 635–54.

Gregory, Steven. 1998. "Globalization and the 'Place' of Politics in Contemporary Theory: A Commentary." *City and Society* 10 (1): 47–64.

Gregson, Jonathan. 2002. *Massacre at the Palace.* New York: Hyperion.

Grewal, Inderpal. 2011. "Humanitarian Citizenship and Race: Katrina and the Global War on Terror." Talk at the Rapoport Center for Human Rights and Justice, University of Texas at Austin.

Grove, Cornelius, and Willa Hallowell. 1996. "Cost Effective Expatriate Training." *International Insight* (Summer): 414–18.

———. 1997. "The Trailing Family: An Overlooked Key to a Successful Relocation." *Benefits and Compensation Solutions* (February): 203.

———. 2002. "Expatriate Candidate Assessment Solutions." http://www.grovewell-expat.com/assess-expat-candidate.html (accessed October 12, 2001).

———. n.d. "An Assessment of Assessment Instruments for Expat Candidate Selection." http://www.grovewell.com/pub-expat-assess2.html (accessed October 12, 2001).

Guneratne, Arjun. 2002. *Many Tongues, One People: The Making of Tharu Identity in Nepal.* Ithaca: Cornell University Press.

Gupta, Akhil. 1998. *Postcolonial Developments: Agriculture in the Making of Modern India.* Durham, NC: Duke University Press.

———. 2012. *Red Tape: Bureaucracy, Structural Violence and Poverty in India.* Durham: Duke University Press.

Gupta, Anirudha. 1993. *Politics in Nepal 1950–1960.* Delhi: Kalinga Publications.

Habermas, Jürgen. 1995. *The Structural Transformation of the Public Sphere: An Inquiry into a Category of Bourgeois Society.* Translated by T. Burger. Cambridge, MA: MIT Press.

Hachhethu, Krishna. 2007. "Madhesi Nationalism and Restructuring the Nepali State." Paper presented at international seminar, Constitutionalism and Diversity in Nepal, Centre for Nepal and Asian Studies, Tribhuvan University http://www.uni-bielefeld .de/midea/pdf/Hachhethu.pdf (accessed May 4, 2013).

Hacking, Ian. 1999. *The Social Construction of What?* Cambridge, MA: Harvard University Press.

———. 2002. *Historical Ontology.* Cambridge, MA: Harvard University Press.

Hagen, Toni. 1994. *Building Bridges to the Third World.* Delhi: Book Faith India.

Hall, Douglas. 1976. *Careers in Organizations.* Pacific Palisades, CA: Goodyear Publications.

———. 2004. "The Protean Career: A Quarter-Century Journey." *Journal of Vocational Behavior* 64: 1–13.

Hall, Edward T. 1959. *The Silent Language.* Garden City, NY: Doubleday.

———. (1967) 1977. *Beyond Culture.* Garden City, NY: Anchor Books.

———. 1992. *An Anthropology of Everyday Life: An Autobiography.* New York: Doubleday.

Handler, Richard. 1988. *Nationalism and the Politics of Culture in Quebec.* Madison: University of Wisconsin Press.

Handler, Richard, and Eric Gable. 1997. *The New History in an Old Museum.* Durham, NC: Duke University Press.

Handler, Richard, and Jocelyn Linnekin. 1984. "Tradition, Genuine or Spurious." *Journal of American Folklore.* 97: 273–90.

Hangen, Susan. 2010. *The Rise of Ethnic Politics in Nepal: Democracy in the Margins.* New York: Routledge.

Harper, Richard. 2000. "The Social Organization of the IMF's Mission Work: An Examination of International Auditing." In *Audit Cultures,* edited by M. Strathern, 21–53. London: Routledge.

Harris, Hilary, and Chris Brewster. 1999. "The Coffee-Machine System: How International Selection Really Works." *International Journal of Human Resource Management* 10 (3): 488–500.

Harrison, J. Kline. 1992. "Individual and Combined Effects of Behavior Modeling and the Cultural Assimilator in Cross-Cultural Management Training." *Journal of Applied Psychology* 77 (6): 952–62.

Harrison, Roger, and Richard Hopkins. 1967. "The Design of Cross-Cultural Training:

An Alternative to the University Model." *The Journal of Applied Behavioral Science* 3 (4): 431–60.

Harvey, David. 1990. *The Condition of Postmodernity*. Cambridge, MA: Blackwell.

Harzing, Anne-Wil K. 1995. "The Persistent Myth of High Expatriate Failure Rates." *International Journal of Human Resource Management* 6 (2): 457–74.

———. 2002. "Are Our Referencing Errors Undermining Our Scholarship and Credibility? The Case of Expatriate Failure Rates." *Journal of Organizational Behavior* 23: 127–48.

Harzing, Anne-Wil, and Claus Christensen. 2004. "Expatriate Failure: Time to Abandon the Concept?" *Career Development International* 9 (5): 616–26.

Harzing, Anne-Wil, and Joris Van Ruysseveld, eds. 1995. *International Human Resource*. London: Sage.

Haslberger, Arno, and Chris Brewster. 2008. "The Expatriate Family: An International Perspective." *Journal of Managerial Psychology* 23 (3): 324–46.

Hawley, Kevan. 2001. "Proactive International Human Resources Management." http://www.expatprep.com/library (accessed March 15, 2013).

Hayward, D. G. 1975. "Home as an Environmental Concept and Psychological Concept." *Landscape* 20 (1): 2–9.

Hein, Laura. 2003. "War Compensation: Claims against the Japanese Government and Japanese Corporations for War Crimes." In *Politics of the Past: On Reparing Historical Injustices*, edited by John Torpey, 127–47. Lanham, MD: Rowman and Littlefield.

Hendry, Chris, and Andrew Pettigrew. 1990. "Human Resource Management: An Agenda for the 1990's." *International Journal of Human Resource Management* 1 (1): 17–44.

Henry, Edwin R. 1965. "What Business Can Learn from Peace Corps Selection and Training." *Personnel* 42 (4): 17–25.

Hepburn, Sharon. 1995. "The Case of the Missing Trekker." In *Anthropology of Nepal: Peoples, Problems and Processes*, edited by Michael Allen, 448–59. Kathmandu: Mandala Book Point.

———. 1997. "To See the World: Vision, Tourism, Anthropological Practice, and Ethnic Politics in Nepal." PhD dissertation, Cornell University.

Hindman, Heather. 2002. "The Everyday Life of American Development in Nepal." *Studies in Nepali History and Society* 7 (1): 99–136.

———. 2007a. "Outsourcing Difference: Expatriate Training and the Disciplining of Culture." In *Deciphering the Global: Its Scales Spaces and Subjectivities*, edited by Saskia Sassen, 155–77. New York: Routledge.

———. 2007b. "Shopping for a Hypernational Home: How Expatriate Women in Kathmandu Labour to Assuage Fear." In *Gender and Family among Transnational Professionals*, edited by A. Coles and A. Fechter, 41–61. New York: Routledge.

———. 2009a. "Shopping in the Bazaar/Bizarre Shopping: Culture and the Accidental Elitism of Expatriates in Kathmandu, Nepal." *The Journal of Popular Culture* 42 (4): 663–79.

———. 2009b. "Cosmopolitan Codifications: Elite, Expatriates and Difference in Kathmandu, Nepal." *Identities: Global Studies in Culture and Power* 16: 249–70.

———. 2010. "Performing Security in Nepal's Little America: Bureaucracy and its Malcontents." *Bodhi* 4 (1): 1–17.

———. 2011. "The Hollowing Out of Aidland: Subcontracting and the New Development Family in Nepal." In *Inside the Everyday Lives of Development Workers*, edited by Heather Hindman and Anne-Meike Fechter, 169–91. Sterling, VA: Kumarian Press.

Hindman, Heather, and Anne-Meike Fechter. 2011. "Introduction." In *Inside the Everyday Lives of Development Workers*, edited by Heather Hindman and Anne-Meike Fechter, 1–19. Sterling, VA: Kumarian Press.

Ho, Karen. 2005. "Situating Global Captialisms: A View from Wall Street Investment Banks." *Cultural Anthropology* 20 (1): 68–96.

Hobsbawm, Eric. 1983. "Introduction: Inventing Traditions." In *The Invention of Tradition*, edited by Eric Hobsbawm and Terence Ranger, 1–14. New York: Cambridge University Press.

Hobsbawm, Eric, and Terence Ranger, eds. 1983. *The Invention of Tradition*. New York: Cambridge University Press.

Hochschild, Arlie. 1989. *The Second Shift*. New York: Avon Books.

Höfer, András. 1979. *The Caste Hierarchy and the State in Nepal*. Innsbruck: Wagner.

Hofstede, Geert. 2001. *Culture's Consequences: Comparing Values, Behaviors, Institutions, and Organizations Across Nations*. Second edition. Thousand Oaks, CA: Sage Publications.

Hofstede, Geert, and Michael Hoppe. 2004. "An Interview of Geert Hofstede." *The Academy of Management Executive* 18 (1): 75–79.

Hoftun, Martin. 1993. "The Dynamics and Chronology of the 1990 Revolution." In *Nepal in the Nineties*, edited by M. Hutt, 14–27. Delhi: Oxford University Press.

Hommers, Wilfried, and Norman H. Anderson. 1991. "Moral Algebra of Harm and Recompense." In *Contributions to Information Integration Theory*. Vol. 2: *Social*, edited by Norman H. Anderson, 101–34. London: Psychology Press.

Hopkins, A. G. 1976. "Imperial Business in Africa Part II. Interpretations." *Journal of African History* 17 (2): 267–90.

Howes, David, ed. 1996. *Cross-Cultural Consumption: Global Markets: Local Realities*. New York: Routledge.

"HRFocus Special Report on Expatriate Management." 1998. *HRFocus* 75 (3): S11.

Hull, Mathew. 2012. *Government of Paper: The Materiality of Bureaucracy in Urban Pakistan*. Berkeley: University of California Press.

Husain, Asad. 1970. *British India's Relations with the Kingdom of Nepal*. London: George Allen and Unwin.

Hutchins, Francis G. 1967. *The Illusion of Permanence: British Imperialism in India*. Princeton: Princeton University Press.

Hutt, Michael, ed. 2004. *Himalayan People's War: Nepal's Maoist Rebellion*. Bloomington: Indiana University Press.

Hyam, Ronald. 1990. *Empire and Sexuality: The British Experience*. New York: St. Martin's Press.

Ivy, Marilyn. 1995. *Discourses of the Vanishing: Modernity Phantasm Japan.* Chicago: University of Chicago Press.

Iyer, Pico. 1998. "The New Business Class." *New York Times Magazine–Late Edition,* March 8.

———. 2000. *The Global Soul: Jet Lag, Shopping Malls, and the Search for Home.* New York: Knopf.

Jayawardena, Kumari. 1995. *The White Woman's Other Burden.* New York: Routledge.

Johnson, Spencer. 1998. *Who Moved My Cheese?* New York: G.P. Putnam's Sons.

Joseph, Miranda. 2002. *Against the Romance of Community.* Minneapolis: University of Minnesota Press.

Joshi, Bhuwan Lal, and Leo E. Rose. 1966. *Democratic Innovations in Nepal: A Case Study of Political Acculturation.* Berkeley: University of California Press.

Kane, Jeffrey, and Kimberly Freeman. 1997. "A Theory of Equitable Performance Standards." *Journal of Management* 23 (1): 37–58.

Kaplan, Caren. 1996. *Questions of Travel.* Durham, NC: Duke University Press.

———. 2002. "Transporting the Subject: Technologies of Mobility and Location in an Era of Globalization." *Publications of the Modern Language Association of America* 117 (1): 32–42.

Kaplan, Caren, Norma Alarcon, and Minoo Moallem, eds. 1999. *Between Women and Nation: Nationalism, Transnational Feminisms, and the State.* Durham, NC: Duke University Press.

Kaplan, Robert. 1997. "Was Democracy Just a Moment?" *Atlantic Monthly* (December): 55–80.

Kaufman, Bruce. 2008. *Managing the Human Factor: The Early Years of Human Resource Management in American Industry.* Ithaca, NY: Cornell University Press.

Kauppinen, Marja. 1993. *Expatriate Adjustment.* Helsinki: HSE Press.

Keats, John. 1956. *The Crack in the Picture Window.* Cambridge, MA: The Riverside Press.

Kelley, Colleen, and Judith Meyers. 1995. *Cross Cultural Adaptability Inventory: Manual.* Minneapolis: National Computer Systems.

Kelly, John D., and Martha Kaplan. 2001. *Represented Communities.* Chicago: University of Chicago Press.

Kennard, E. A. 1948. "Cultural Anthropology and the Foreign Service." *American Foreign Service Journal* (November): 18–19, 42, 44.

Kern, Stephen. 1983. *The Culture of Time and Space, 1880–1918.* Cambridge, MA: Harvard University Press.

Khadka, Narayan. 2000. "U.S. Aid to Nepal in the Cold War Period: Lessons for the Future." *Pacific Affairs* 73 (1): 77–95.

Kincaid, Dennis. (1938) 1973. *British Social Life in India, 1608–1937.* London: Routledge and Kegan Paul.

King, Anthony. 1997. "Excavating the Multicultural Suburb: Hidden Histories of the Bungalow." In *Visions of Suburbia,* edited by Roger Silverstone, 55–85. London: Routledge.

Knorr Cetina, Karin. 1999. *Epistemic Cultures: How Sciences Make Knowledge*. Cambridge, MA: Harvard University Press.

Kobrin, Stephen J. 1988. "Expatriate Reduction and Strategic Control in American Multinational Corporations." *Human Resources Management* 27 (1): 63–75.

Kozloff, Barry. 1996. "Assessing Expatriate Selection." *Relocation Journal* (February). http://relojournal.com/feb96/exsel.htm (accessed November 8, 2002).

Kristeva, Julia. 1982. *Powers of Horror: An Essay on Abjection*. Translayed by Leon S. Roudiez. New York: Columbia University Press.

Lambert, Richard, ed. 1966. "Americans Abroad." *The Annals of the American Academy of Political and Social Sciences* 368, special issue.

Landon, Percival. 1928. *Nepal*. Two vols. London: Constable.

Lang, Gretchen. 2004. "Cross-cultural Training: How much Difference does it Really Make?" *New York Times*, January 24.

Lanier, Jaron. 2010. *You Are Not a Gadget: A Manifesto*. New York: Alfred Knopf.

Lascher, Edward Jr., and Michael Powers. 2004. "September 11 Victims, Random Events, and the Ethics of Compensation." *American Behavioral Scientist* 48 (3): 281–94.

Latour, Bruno. 1987. *Science in Action*. Cambridge, MA: Harvard University Press.

———. 1993. *We Have Never Been Modern*. Translated by Catherine Porter. Cambridge, MA: Harvard University Press.

———. 2005. *Reassembling the Social: An Introduction to Actor-Network-Theory*. Oxford: Oxford University Press.

Lawoti, Mahendra, and Anup Pahari, eds. 2010. *The Maoist Insurgency in Nepal: Revolution in the Twenty-First Century*. London: Routledge.

Lebeau, Vicky. 1997. "The Worst of All Possible Worlds?" In *Visions of Suburbia*, edited by Roger Silverstone, 280–97. London: Routledge.

Lederer, William J., and Eugene Burdick. 1958. *The Ugly American*. New York: Norton.

Lee, Hung-Wen. 2007. "Factors that Influence Expatriate Failure: An Interview Study." *International Journal of Management* 24 (3): 403–13.

Lee, Lee W. 2001. "Employee Compensation." In *Encyclopedia of Business and Finance*, 295–99. New York: Macmillan Reference Group.

Lefebvre, Henri. (1947) 1991. *Critique of Everyday Life*. Translated by John Moore. New York: Verso.

Leuchtag, Erika. 1958. *Erika and the King*. New York: Coward-McCann.

Lévinas, Emmanuel. 1998. *Entre Nous: On Thinking-of-the-Other*. Translated by Michael B. Smith and Barbara Harshav. New York: Columbia University Press.

———. 1999. *Alterity and Transcendence*. Translated by Michael B. Smith. New York: Columbia University Press.

Levine, Philippa, ed. 2004. *Gender and Empire*. New York: Oxford University Press.

Levitt, Steven D., and Stephen J. Dubner. 2005. *Freakonomics*. New York: HarperCollins.

Levitt, Theodore. 1983. "The Globalization of Markets." *Harvard Business Review* 61 (3): 92–102.

Levy, Robert I. 1992. *Mesocosm: Hinduism and the Organization of a Traditional Newar City in Nepal*. Delhi: Motilal Banarsidass Publishers.

Lewis, David. 2003. "Theorizing the Organization and Management of Non-Governmental Development Organizations." *Public Management Review* 5 (3): 325–44.

Lewis, Richard. 1996. *When Cultures Collide: Leading Across Cultures.* Boston, MA: Nicholas Brealey.

Li, Lan, and E. Tse. 1998. "Antecedents and consequences of expatriate satisfaction in the Asian Pacific." *Tourism Management* 19 (2): 135–43.

Liechty, Mark. 1994. "Fashioning Modernity in Kathmandu: Mass Media, Consumer Culture, and the Middle Class in Nepal." PhD dissertation, University of Pennsylvania.

———. 1997. "Selective Exclusion: Foreigners, Foreign Goods, and Foreignness in Modern Nepali History." *Studies in Nepali History and Society* 2 (1): 5–68.

———. 2003. *Suitably Modern: Making Middle-Class Culture in a New Consumer Society.* Princeton: Princeton University Press.

———. 2005a. "Building the Road to Kathmandu: Notes on the History of Tourism in Nepal." *Himalaya* 24 (1–2): 19–28.

———. 2005b. "Carnal Economies: The Commodification of Food and Sex in Kathmandu." *Cultural Anthropology* 20 (1): 1–38.

———. 2010. *Out Here in Kathmandu: Modernity on the Global Periphery.* Kathmandu: Martin Chautari Press.

Lifton, Robert. 1968. "Protean Man." *Partisan Review* 7 (6): 13–27.

Linton, Ralph. 1950. "An Anthropologist Looks at Point Four." *American Perspective* 4: 113–22.

Locke, John K. S.J. 1980. *Karunamaya: The Cult of Avalokitesvara-Matsyendranath in the Valley of Nepal.* Kathmandu: Sahayogi Press.

Low, Setha. 2003. *Behind the Gates: Life, Security, and the Pursuit of Happiness in Fortress America.* New York: Routledge.

Luhrman, T. M. 1989. *Persuasions of the Witch's Craft.* Cambridge, MA: Harvard University Press.

Lynd, Robert, and Helen Merrell Lynd. 1929. *Middletown: A Study in Contemporary American Culture.* New York: Harcourt, Brace and Company.

Lyons, Mike. 1992. "History of the Hash Disorganization." http://half-mind.com/Hashing/who.php (accessed March 8, 2012).

MacCannell, Dean. (1976) 1989. *The Tourist: A New Theory of the Leisure Class.* New York: Schocken.

Mack, Arien, ed. 1993. *Home: A Place in the World.* New York: New York University Press.

MacMillan, Margaret. 1988. *Women of the Raj.* New York: Thames and Hudson.

Magazine Intercultures. n.d. "Culture Does Not Exist: An Interview with Geert Hofstede." *Magazine Intercultures* 2 (3). http://www.international.gc.ca/cfsi-icse/cil-cai/magazine/v02n03/1-3-eng.asp (accessed Dec. 12, 2001).

Malabari, Phiroze. 1910. *Bombay in the Making.* London: T. Fisher Unwin.

Maldonado, Julie. 2009. "Putting a Price-Tag on Humanity: Development-Forced Displaced Communities' Fight for More than Just Compensation." *Hydro Nepal* 4: 18–20.

Malinowski, Bronislaw. (1944) 1969. *A Scientific Theory of Culture and Other Essays.* New York: Oxford University Press.

———. (1922) 1984. *Argonauts of the Western Pacific*. Prospect Heights, IL: Waveland Press.

Malkki, Liisa. 1992. "National Geographic: The Rooting of Peoples and the Territorialization of National Identity Among Scholars and Refugees." *Cultural Anthropology* 7 (1): 24–44.

———. 1994. "Citizens of Humanity: Internationalism and the Imagined Community of Nations." *Diaspora* 3 (1): 41–68.

———. 1995a. *Purity and Exile*. Chicago: University of Chicago Press.

———. 1995b. "Refugees and Exile: From 'Refugee Studies' to the National Order of Things." *Annual Review of Anthropology* 24: 495–523.

Mandell, Nikki. 2002. *The Corporation as Family: The Gendering of Corporate Welfare, 1890–1930*. Chapel Hill: University of North Carolina Press.

Marcus, George. 1995. "Ethnography In/Of the World System: The Emergence of Multi-Sited Ethnography." *Annual Reviews in Anthropology* 24: 95–117.

Marsh, Margaret. 1990. *Suburban Lives*. New Brunswick: Rutgers University Press.

Martin, Emily. 1994. *Flexible Bodies*. Boston, MA: Beacon Press.

Marx, Karl. (1932) 1964. *The Economic and Philosophic Manuscripts of 1844*. Edited with an Introduction by Dirk J. Struik. Translated by Martin Milligan. New York: International Publishers.

Maurer, Bill. 2008. "Implementing Empirical Knowledge in Anthropology and Islamic Accountancy." In *Global Assemblages: Technology, Politics, and Ethics as Anthropological Problems*, edited by Aihwa Ong and Stephen Collier, 214–31. Malden, MA: Blackwell.

Mauss, Marcel. (1925) 1954. *The Gift: Forms and Functions of Exchange in Archaic Societies*. Translated by Ian Cunnison. London: Cohen and West.

Mayerhofer, Helene, Linley Hartmann, and Anne Herbert. 2004. "Career Management Issues for Flexpatriate International Staff." *Thunderbird International Business Review* 46 (6): 647–66.

McCarthy, Patrick. 2007. "Boundaryless Career: Is There a Disparity between Theory, Practice and Worker Desire in Relation to Older Workers?" PhD dissertation, Department of Business and Enterprise, Swinburne University, Melbourne.

McClintock, Anne. 1992. "The Angel of Progress: Pitfalls of the Term 'Post-Colonialism.'" *Social Text* 31/32: 84–98.

———. 1995. *Imperial Leather: Race, Gender and Sexuality in the Colonial Conquest*. New York: Routledge.

McCracken, Janet. 2001. *Taste and the Household: The Domestic Aesthetic and Moral Reasoning*. Albany: State University of New York Press.

McDonald, Maryon. 2000. "Accountability, Anthropology and the European Commission." In *Audit Cultures*, edited by M. Strathern, 106–312. London: Routledge.

McDougall, John. 2009. "IBM Offers to Move Laid Off to India." *Information Week*, February 2.

McEnaney, Laura. 2000. *Civil Defense Begins at Home: Militarization Meets Everyday Life in the Fifties*. Princeton: Princeton University Press.

McGranahan, Carole. 2006. "Tibet's Cold War: The CIA and the Chushi Gangdrug Resistance, 1956–1974." *Journal of Cold War Studies* 8 (3): 102–30.

McNeill, William. 1989. *The Age of Gunpowder Empires, 1450–1800.* Washington, DC: American Historical Association.

———. 1993. "The Age of Gunpowder Empires, 1450–1800." In *Islamic and European Expansion: The Forging of a Global Order,* edited by Michael Adas, 103–40. Philadelphia: Temple University Press.

McNulty, Yvonne, and Phyllis Tharenou. 2004. "Expatriate Return on Investment: A Definition and Antecedents." *International Studies of Management and Organization* 34 (3): 68–95.

Mead, Margaret. 1965. *And Keep Your Powder Dry: An Anthropologist Looks at America.* New York: William Morrow and Company.

Meerman, Mariji. 2001. *Chain of Love.* Documentary film, VHS. Brooklyn, NY: First Run Icarus Films.

Metcalfe, Rhoda. 1998. "Ties that Bind: A US Firm Strives to Keep Globe-Trotting Expatriates and Their Families Happy." *Business Latin America,* May 25, 7.

Mickelson, Joan. 1978. "British Women in India: 1757–1857." PhD dissertation, University of Michigan.

Mierow, Dorothy. 1997. *Thirty Years in Pokhara.* Kathmandu: Pilgrims Book House.

Mihaly, Eugene Bramer. 1965. *Foreign Aid and Politics in Nepal: A Case Study.* London: Oxford University Press.

Miller, Daniel. 1995. "Consumption and Commodities." *The Annual Review of Anthropology* 24: 141–61.

Miller, Edwin. 1973. "The International Selection Decision: A Study of Some Dimensions of Managerial Behavior in the Selection Decision Process." *The Academy of Management Journal* 16 (2): 239–52.

Miller, J. Hillis. 2000. "Humanistic Discourse and the Others." *Surfaces* 4: 1–18.

Miner, Horace. 1956. "Body Rituals among the Nacirema." *American Anthropologist* 58: 503–7.

Ministry of Defense (Great Britain). 1965. *Nepal and the Gurkhas.* London: Her Majesty's Stationery Office.

Minor, Shirley. 1986. "Differences in Morale Between Standard and Career Expatriate Teachers in the Department of Defense Schools in the Philippines." PhD dissertation, Oklahoma State University.

Mishra, Rabindra. 2004. "India's Role in Nepal's Maoist Insurgency." *Asian Survey* 44 (5): 627–46.

Misra, Joya, Jonathan Woodring, and Sabine N. Merz. 2006. "The Globalization of Care Work: Neoliberal Economic Restructuring and Migration Policy." *Globalizations* 3 (3): 317–32.

Mitchell, Timothy. 1991. *Colonising Egypt.* Berkeley: University of California Press.

———. 2002. *Rule of Experts: Egypt, techno-politics, modernity.* Berkeley: University of California Press.

Moffatt, Michael. 1989. *Coming of Age in New Jersey.* New Brunswick: Rutgers University Press.

Mohanty, Chandra, A. Russo, and L. Torres, eds. 1991. *Third World Women and the Politics of Feminism*. Bloomington: Indiana University Press.

Moran, Peter. 2004. *Buddhism Observed: Travellers, Exiles and Tibetan Dharma in Kathmandu*. London: Routledge.

Morris, John. 1963. *A Winter in Nepal*. London: Rupert Hart-Davis.

Morrison, Terri, Wayne Conaway, and George Borden. 1994. *Kiss, Bow, or Shake Hands: How to Do Business in Sixty Countries*. Holbrook, MA: Adams Publishing.

Motzafi-Haller, Pnina. 2002. *Fragmented Worlds, Coherent Lives: The Politics of Difference in Botswana*. Westport: Bergin and Garvey.

Mueller, Adele. 1986. "The Bureaucratization of Feminist Knowledge: The Case of Women in Development." *Resources for Feminist Research* 15 (1): 36–38.

Mullan, Catherine. 1993. "Growing Old in Spain—the Problems of the Elderly British Expatriate Community in Spain." *International Journal of Geriatric Psychiatry* 8: 1015–17.

Munton, Anthony, and Nick Forster. 1990. "Job Relocation: Stress and the Role of the Family." *Work and Stress* 4 (1): 75–81.

Myers, Ramon, and M. Peattie. 1984. *The Japanese Colonial Empire*. Princeton: Princeton University Press.

Nash, Dennison. 1970. *A Community in Limbo: An Anthropological Study of an American Community Abroad*. Bloomington: Indiana University Press.

Nelson, Laura C. 2000. *Measured Excess: Status, Gender, and Consumer Nationalism in South Korea*. New York: Columbia University Press.

Nielsen, Bjarke. 2011. "UNESCO and the 'Right' Kind of Culture: Bureaucratic Production and Articulation." *Critique of Anthropology* 31 (4): 273–92.

Neilson, Brett, and Ned Rossiter. 2008. "Precarity as a Political Concept, or Fordism as Exception." *Theory, Culture and Society* 25 (7–8): 51–72.

Northey, W. Brook, and C. J. Morris. 1974. *The Gurkhas: Their Manners, Customs and Country*. Delhi: Cosmo Publications.

Nowicka, Magdalena. 2007. "Mobile Locations: Construction of Home in a Group of Mobile Transnational Professions." *Global Networks* 7 (1): 69–86.

Oakes, Guy. 1994. *The Imaginary War: Civil Defense and American Cold War Culture*. New York: Oxford University Press.

Ogura, Kiyoko. 2001. *Kathmandu Spring: The People's Movement of 1990*. Lalitpur, Nepal: Himal Books.

Onesto, Li. 2005. *Dispatches from the People's War in Nepal*. London: Pluto Press.

Ong, Aihwa. 1993. "On the Edge of Empires: Flexible Citizenship among Chinese in Diaspora." *positions* 1 (3): 745–78.

———. 1996. "Cultural Citizenship as Subject-Making." *Current Anthropology* 37 (5): 737–62.

———. 1999. *Flexible Citizenship: The Cultural Logics of Transnationality*. Durham, NC: Duke University Press.

———. 2006. *Neoliberalism as Exception: Mutations in Citizenship and Sovereignty*. Durham, NC: Duke University Press.

Onta, Pratyoush. 1996. "Ambivalence Denied: The Making of *Rastriya Itihas* in Panchayat Era Textbooks." *Contributions to Nepalese Studies* 23 (1): 213–54.

——. 2004. "Democracy and Duplicity: The Maoists and Their Interlocutors in Nepal." In *Himalayan People's War*, edited by Michael Hutt, 136–51. Bloomington: Indiana University Press.

Oppenheim, Robert. 2007. "Actor-Network Theory and Anthropology After Science, Technology, and Society." *Anthropological Theory* 7 (4): 471–93.

ORC Worldwide (Organization Resources Counselors, Inc.). 2000. *Location Evaluation Report. Hardship Ratings.* Sample document, Tallinn, Estonia. New York: Organization Resources Counselors, Inc.

Ortner, Sherry B. 1974. "Is Female to Male as Nature Is to Culture?" In *Women, Culture and Society*, edited by M. Rosoldo and L. Lamphere, 67–88. Stanford: Stanford University Press.

——. 1989. *High Religion*. Princeton: Princeton University Press.

——. 1995. "Resistance and the Problem of Ethnographic Refusal." *Comparative Studies in Society and History* 37 (1): 173–93.

——. 1999. *Life and Death on Mt. Everest.* Princeton: Princeton University Press.

Pang, Mary. 2003. "Boundaryless Careers? The (In)voluntary (Re-)actions of Some Chinese in Hong Kong and Britain." *International Journal of Human Resource Management* 14 (5): 809–20.

Parreñas, Rhacel Salazar. 2001. *Servants of Globalization: Women, Migration, and Domestic Work.* Stanford, CA: Stanford University Press.

Pascoe, Robin. 1992. *Culture Shock! A Wife's Guide.* Singapore: Times Books International.

——. 1993. *Culture Shock! A Parent's Guide.* Portland: Graphic Arts.

Pateman, Carole. 1988. *The Sexual Contract.* Stanford, CA: Stanford University Press.

Patterson, Orlando. 1993. "Slavery, Alienation, and the Female Discovery of Personal Freedom." In *Home: A Place in the World*, edited by Arien Mack, 159–88. New York: New York University Press.

Peace Corps. 1999. *Culture Matters: Trainer's Guide.* Washington, DC: Peace Corps Information Collection and Exchange.

Peissel, Michel. 1966. *Tiger for Breakfast: The Story of Boris of Kathmandu.* New Delhi: Time Books International.

Pels, Peter. 1997. "The Anthropology of Colonialism: Culture, History, and the Emergency of Western Governmentality." *Annual Reviews in Anthropology* 26: 163–83.

Pelton, Robert Young. 2007. *Licensed to Kill: Hired Guns in the War on Terror.* New York: Random House.

Pemble, John. 1971. *The Invasion of Nepal.* Oxford: Clarendon Press.

Pendergrast, Mark. 1993. *For God, Country and Coca-Cola: The Unauthorized History of the Great American Soft Drink and the Company that Makes It.* New York: Charles Scribner's Sons.

Peters, Katherine. 2000. "Moving Violations." *Government Executive* (February): 33–38.

Petryna, A., A. Lakoff, and A. Kleinman, eds. 2006. *Global Pharmaceuticals: Ethics, Markets, Practices.* Durham, NC: Duke University Press.

Philipps, Lisa. 2008. "Silent Partners: The Role of Unpaid Market Labor in Families." *Feminist Economics* 14 (2): 37–57.

Pigg, Stacy Leigh. 1992. "Inventing Social Categories Through Place: Social Representations and Development in Nepal." *Comparative Studies in Society and History* 34 (3): 491–513.

Piper, Maggie. 2009. "A Side Note." *United Nations Women's Organization Newsletter* (March): 3.

Pletch, C. 1981. "The Three Worlds or the Division of Social Scientific Labour 1950–1975." *Comparative Studies in Society and History* 23: 565–90.

Pokharel, Gopal, A. Shakya, and B. Dahal, eds. 2009. *Foreign Policy of Nepal*. Kathmandu: Institute for Foreign Affairs.

Poole, Michael. 1990. "Editorial: Human Resource Management in an International Perspective." *International Journal of Human Resource Management* 1 (1): 1–15.

Posey, Darrell. 1990. "Intellectual Property Rights and Just Compensation for Indigenous Knowledge." *Anthropology Today* 6 (4): 13–16.

Potter, David M. 1954. *People of Plenty: Economic Abundance and the American Character*. Chicago: University of Chicago Press.

Potthast-Jukeit, Barbara. 1997. "The History of Family and Colonialism." *The History of the Family: An International Quarterly* 2 (2): 115–21.

Poudel, Keshab. 2003. "Kathmandu's Architectural Heritage." *ECS Nepal*, September.

Povinelli, Elizabeth. 2002. *The Cunning of Recognition: Indigenous Alterities and the Making of Australian Multiculturalism*. Durham, NC: Duke University Press.

Power, Michael. 1997. *The Audit Society: Rituals of Verification*. New York: Oxford University Press.

Pringle, Judith, and Mary Mallon. 2003. "Challenges for the Boundaryless Career Odyssey." *International Journal of Human Resource Management* 14 (5): 839–53.

Procida, Mary A. 2002. *Married to the Empire: Gender Politics and Imperialism in India, 1883–1947*. Manchester, UK: Manchester University Press.

Puck, Jonas, Markus Kittler, and Christopher Wright. 2008. "Does It Really Work? Re-Assessing the Impact of Pre-Departure Cross-Cultural Training on Expatriate Adjustment." *International Journal of Human Resource Management* 19 (12): 2182–97.

Pugh, Allison J. 2002. "From 'Compensation' to 'Childhood Wonder': Why Parents Buy." Working Paper 39. Center for Working Families, University of California, Berkeley.

———. 2009. *Longing and Belonging: Parents, Children, and Consumer Culture*. Berkeley: University of California Press.

———. 2011. "Consumption as Care and Belonging: Economies of Dignity in Children's Daily Lives." In *At the Heart of Work and the Family*, edited by Anita Ilta Garey and Karen Hansen, 217–28. New Brunswick, NJ: Rutgers University Press.

Radcliffe-Brown, A. R. (1952) 1965. *Structure and Function in Primitive Society*. New York: The Free Press.

Raeper, William, and Martin Hoftun. 1992. *Spring Awakening: An Account of the 1990 Revolution in Nepal*. New Delhi: Viking.

Rapaille, Clotaire. 2006. *The Culture Code: An Ingenious Way to Understand Why People Around the World Live and Buy as They Do*. New York: Broadway Books.

Reddy, Deepa. 2007. "Good Gifts for the Common Good: Blood and Bioethics in the Market of Genetic Research." *Cultural Anthropology* 22 (3): 429–72.

Reed, Adam. 2006. "Documents Unfolding." In *Documents: Artifacts of Modern Knowledge*, edited by A. Riles, 158–78. Ann Arbor: University of Michigan Press.

Reed, David. 1993. *Nepal: The Rough Guide.* New York: Penguin Books.

Regmi, D. R. 1975. *Modern Nepal.* Two vols. Calcutta: Firma K.L. Mukhopadhyay.

Reynolds, Calvin. 1997. "Expatriate Compensation in Historical Perspective." *Journal of World Business* 32 (2): 118–32.

Richards, David. 1996. "Strangers in a Strange Land: Expatriate Paranoia and the Dynamics of Exclusion." *International Journal of Human Resource Management* 7 (2): 553–71.

Riesman, David. 1950. *The Lonely Crowd: A Study of the Changing American Character.* New Haven: Yale University Press.

Riles, Annelise, ed. 2006a. *Documents: Artifacts of Modern Knowledge.* Ann Arbor: University of Michigan Press.

———. 2006b. "Introduction: In Response." In *Documents: Artifacts of Modern Knowledge*, edited by A. Riles, 1–38. Ann Arbor: University of Michigan Press.

Rizer, George. 1996. *The McDonaldization of Society.* London: Pine Forge Press.

Robinson, Jennifer. 1991. *Native and Newcomer.* Berkeley: University of California Press.

Rodman, Margaret. 2001. *Houses far from Home: British Colonial Space in the New Hebrides.* Honolulu: University of Hawai'i Press.

Rogers, Everett, William Hart, and Yoshitaka Miike. 2002. "Edward T. Hall and the History of Intercultural Communication: The United States and Japan." *Keio Communication Review* 24: 3–26.

Rose, Kenneth. 2001. *One Nation Underground: The Fallout Shelter in American Culture.* New York: New York University Press.

Rose, Leo E. 1960. "The Role of Nepal and Tibet in Sino-Indian Relations." PhD dissertation, University of California, Berkeley.

———. 1971. *Nepal: Strategy for Survival.* Berkeley: University of California Press.

Rose, Leo E., and Roger Dial. 1969. "Can a Ministate Find True Happiness in a World Dominated by Protagonist Powers? The Nepal Case." *Annals of the American Academy of Political and Social Science* 386: 89–101.

Rose, Leo E., and Margaret W. Fisher. 1970. *The Politics of Nepal: Persistence and Change in an Asian Monarchy.* Ithaca: Cornell University Press.

Rose, Lisle A. 1999. *The Cold War Comes to Main Street: America in 1950.* Wichita: University Press of Kansas.

Rosin, Hanna. 2010. "The End of Men." *Atlantic Monthly,* (July/August): 56–72.

Ross, Kristin. 1999. *Fast Cars, Clean Bodies.* Cambridge: MIT Press.

Rouse, Roger. 1991. "Mexican Migration and the Social Space of Postmodernism." *Diaspora* 1 (1): 8–23.

Roy, Arundhati. 1999. *The Greater Common Good.* Bombay: India Book Distributor.

Rybczynski, Witold. 1986. *Home: A Short History of an Idea.* New York: Penguin Books.

Sachs, Wolfgang, ed. 1992. *The Development Dictionary: A Guide to Knowledge as Power.* London: Zed Books.

Sackmann, Sonja, and Margaret Phillips. 2004. "Contextual Influences on Culture Research: Shifting Assumptions for New Workplace Realities." *International Journal of Cross Cultural Management* 4 (3): 370–90.

Sahlins, Marshall. 1974. *Stone Age Economics.* New York: Aldine De Gruyter.

———. 1981. *Historical Metaphors and Mythical Realities.* Ann Arbor: University of Michigan Press.

Said, Edward. 1978. *Orientalism.* New York: Pantheon.

Salzinger, Leslie. 2003. *Genders in Production: Making Workers in Mexico's Global Factories.* Berkeley: University of California Press.

Sanwal, B. D. 1965. *Nepal and the East India Company.* New York: Asia Publishing House.

Sartre, Jean-Paul. 1963. *Search for a Method.* Translated by Hazel E. Barnes. New York: Vintage.

Sassen, Saskia. 1991. *The Global City: New York, London, Tokyo.* Princeton: Princeton University Press.

———. 1998. *Globalization and Its Discontents: Essays on the New Mobility of People and Money.* New York: The New Press.

———. 2006a. *Cities in a World Economy.* Third edition. Thousand Oaks, CA: Pine Forge Press.

———. 2006b. *Territory, Authority, Rights: From Medieval to Global Assemblages.* Princeton: Princeton University Press.

Satyal, Yajna Raj. 1988. *Tourism in Nepal—A Profile.* Varanasi: Nath Publishing House.

Schell, Orville. 2000. *Virtual Tibet: Searching for Shangri-La from the Himalayas to Hollywood.* New York: Metropolitan Books.

Schneider, Susan, and Kazuhiro Asakawa. 1995. "American and Japanese Expatriate Adjustment: A Psychoanalytic Perspective." *Human Relations* 48 (10): 1109–27.

Schwab, Raymond. 1984. *The Oriental Renaissance.* Translated by Gene Patterson-Black and Victor Reinking. New York: Columbia University Press.

Scott, David. 1999. *Refashioning Futures: Criticism after Postcolonality.* Princeton: Princeton University Press.

———. 2004. *Conscripts of Modernity: The Tragedy of Colonial Enlightenment.* Durham, NC: Duke University Press.

Scott, James C. 1998. *Seeing Like a State: How Certain Schemes to Improve the Human Condition Have Failed.* New Haven: Yale University Press.

Scott, Robert E. 1997. *Expatriate Adjustment and Performance: A Research Report.* Abilene, TX: Integrated Resources Group.

Seddon, David. 1993. "Democracy and Development in Nepal." In *Nepal in the Nineties,* edited by M. Hutt, 28–47. Delhi: Oxford University Press.

Segal, Howard. 1985. *Technological Utopianism in American Culture.* Chicago: University of Chicago Press.

Sen, Tansen. 2006. "The Travel Records of Chinese Pilgrims Faxian, Xuanzang, and Yijing." *Education About Asia* 11 (3): 24–33.

Sennett, Richard, and Jonathan Cobb. 1972. *The Hidden Injuries of Class.* New York: Norton.

Sewell, William H. Jr. 2005. *Logics of History: Social Theory and Social Transformation.* Chicago: University of Chicago Press.

Shah, Saubhagya. 2000. "Service or Servitude? The Domestication of Household Labor in Nepal." In *Home and Hegemony*, edited by K. Adams and S. Dickey, 87–118. Ann Arbor: University of Michigan.

Shah, Sheeba. 2010. *Facing my Phantoms.* New Delhi: Rupa.

Shell Ladies' Project. 1993. *Life on the Move.* The Hague: Shell Ladies' Project.

———. 1996. *Life Now.* The Hague: Shell Ladies' Project.

Shell Outpost Survey. 1993. *Summary of Findings.* The Hague: Shell B.V.

Shilling, Marvina. 1993. "Avoid Expatriate Culture Shock." *HRMagazine* (July): 58–63.

Shneiderman, Sara. 2010. "Are the Central Himalayas in Zomia?" *Journal of Global History* 5 (2): 289–312.

Shrestha, Aditya Man. 1999. *Bleeding Mountains of Nepal.* Kathmandu: Ekta Books.

Shrestha, Nanda R. 1997. *In the Name of Development: A Reflection on Nepal.* Kathmandu: Educational Enterprises.

Silverstone, Roger, ed. 1997. *Visions of Suburbia.* London: Routledge.

Singer, Peter. 2008. *Corporate Warriors: The Rise of the Privitized Military Industry.* Ithaca: Cornell University Press.

Skerry, Christa A., Kerry Moran, and Kay M. Calavan. 1991. *Four Decades of Development: The History of U.S. Assistance to Nepal, 1951–1991.* Kathmandu: United States Agency for International Development.

Slotkin, Richard. 1992. *Gunfighter Nation: The Myth of the Frontier in Twentieth Century America.* New York: Atheneum.

Smith, Adam. (1904) 1976. *The Wealth of Nations.* Chicago: University of Chicago Press.

Smith, Dorothy. 1975. "Women, the Family and Corporate Capitalism." *Berkeley Journal of Sociology* 20: 55–90.

Smith, Neil. 2002. "New Globalism, New Urbanism: Gentrification as Global Urban Strategy." *Antipode* 34 (3): 434–57.

Smith, Valene L., ed. 1989. *Hosts and Guests: The Anthropology of Tourism.* Philadelphia: University of Pennsylvania Press.

Søderberg, Anne-Marie, and Nigel Holden. 2002. "Rethinking Cross Cultural Management in a Globalizing Business World." *International Journal of Cross Cultural Management* 2 (1): 103–21.

Solomon, Charlene. 1996. "Expats Say: Help Make Us Mobile." *Personnel Journal* (July): 47–52.

Spigel, Lynn. 1992. *Make Room for TV.* Chicago: University of Chicago Press.

Spivak, Gayatri Chakravorty. 1987. *In Other Worlds.* New York: Methuen.

Stahl, Günter K., E. Miller, and R. Tung. 2002. "Toward the Boundaryless Career: A Closer Look at the Expatriate Career Concept and the Perceived Implications of an International Assignment." *Journal of World Business* 37 (3): 216–27.

Stalder, Felix. 2000. Review of *Pandora's Hope: Essays on the Reality of Science Studies*, by Bruno Latour. *The Information Society* 16 (3): 245–47.

Stark, Herbert Alick. (1926) 2007. *Hostages to India.* London: Simon Wallenburg Press.

Steel, F. A., and G. Gardiner. 1890. *The Complete Indian Housekeeper and Cook.* Edinburgh: Frank Murry.

Stewart, Kathleen. 1996. *A Space on the Side of the Road.* Princeton: Princeton University Press.

———. 2012. "Precarity's Forms." *Cultural Anthropology* 27 (3): 518–25.

Stewart, Susan. 1993. *On Longing: Narratives of the Miniature, the Gigantic, the Souvenir, the Collection.* Durham, NC: Duke University Press.

Stocking, George W. Jr., ed. 1986. *Malinowski, Rivers, Benedict and Others: Essays on Culture and Personality.* Madison, WI: University of Wisconsin Press.

Stoddart, Susan. 1980. "The Search of an Ideal Multicultural Environment: An Ethnography of Two Overseas American Schools." PhD dissertation, Michigan State University.

Stoler, Ann Laura. 1989. "Rethinking Colonial Categories: European Communities and the Boundaries of Rule." *Comparative Studies in Society and History* 31 (1): 134–61.

———. 2002. *Carnal Knowledge and Imperial Power: Race and the Intimate in Colonial Rule.* Berkeley: University of California Press.

Stopford, John. 1974. "The Origins of British-Based Multinational Manufacturing Enterprises." *The Business History Review* 48 (3): 303–35.

Strathern, Marilyn. 1988. *The Gender of the Gift.* Berkeley: University of California Press.

———, ed. 2000a. *Audit Cultures: Anthropological Studies in Accountability, Ethics and the Academy.* London: Routledge.

———. 2000b. "New Accountabilities: Anthropological Studies in Audit, Ethics and the Academy." In *Audit Cultures*, edited by M. Strathern, 1–18. London: Routledge.

———. 2006. "Bullet-Proofing: A Tale from the United Kingdom." In *Documents: Artifacts of Modern Knowledge*, edited by A. Riles, 181–205. Ann Arbor: University of Michigan Press.

Strobel, Margaret. 1991. *European Women and the Second British Empire.* Bloomington: Indiana University Press.

Stroh, Linda, and Jeanne Brett. 1996. "The Dual-Earner Dad Penalty in Salary Progression." *Human Resource Management* 35 (2): 181–201.

Stuart, Karen. 1992. "Teens Play a Role in Moves Overseas." *Personnel Journal* (March): 72–78.

Subedi, Bhim Prasad. 1991. "International Migration in Nepal: Towards an Analytical Framework." *Contributions to Nepalese Studies* 18 (1): 83–102.

Suyin, Han. (1958) 1999. *The Mountain Is Young.* New Delhi: Rupa and Company.

Swaak, Reyer. 1995. "Expatriate Failures: Too Many, Too Much Cost, Too Little Planning." *Compensation and Benefits Review* 27: 47–55.

———. 1997. "Examining Hardship, Danger and Other Incentive Allowances." Executive report. *Relocation Journal and Real Estate News,* excerpted by www.frankallen.com.

Takeuchi, Riki, and John Hannon. 1996. *Antecedents of Expatriate Spouse Adjustment: An Analysis of Japanese Spouses in the United States.* West Lafayette, IN: Center for International Business Education and Research.

Thapa, Deepak, and Bandita Sijapati. 2005. *A Kingdom Under Siege: Nepal's Maoist Insurgency, 1996–2004.* London: Zed Books.

Thapa, Netra B. 1996. *A Short History of Nepal.* Kathmandu: Ratna Pustak Bhandar.

Thieme, Susan. 2006. *Social Networks and Migration: Far West Nepalese Labour Migrants in Delhi.* Münster: Lit Verlag.

Thomas, David, and Brian Toyne. 1995. "Subordinates' Responses to Cultural Adaptation by Japanese Expatriate Managers." *Journal of Business Research* 32: 1–10.

Thomas, Nicholas. 1994. *Colonialism's Culture: Anthropology, Travel and Government.* Princeton: Princeton University Press.

Thomas, William, ed. 1974. *American Education Abroad.* New York: Macmillan.

Thompson, E. P. 1966. *The Making of the English Working Class.* New York: Vintage Books.

———. 1967. "Time, Work-Discipline, and Industrial Capitalism." *Past and Present* 38: 56–97.

Tichy, Noel M. 1988. "Setting the Global Human Resource Management Agenda for the 1990s." *Human Resources Management* 27 (1): 1–18.

Tixier, Maud. 1996. "Cultural Adjustments Required by Expatriate Managers Working in the Nordic Countries." *International Journal of Manpower* 17 (6/7): 19–42.

Tocqueville, Alexis de. (1840) 2000. *Democracy in America.* Chicago: University of Chicago Press.

Torbiörn, Ingemar. 1982. *Living Abroad.* New York: Wiley.

Tornikoski, Christelle. 2011. "Expatriate Compensation: A Total Reward Perspective." PhD dissertation, University of Vaasa, Finland.

Townsend, Janet, Gina Porter, and Emma Mawdsley. 2002. "The Role of the Transnational Community of Non-Governmental Organizations: Governance or Poverty Reduction?" *Journal of International Development* 14: 829–39.

Tremayne, Soraya. 1984. "Shell Wives in Limbo." In *The Incorporated Wife,* edited by H. Callan and S. Ardener, 120–34. London: Croom Helm.

Triandis, Harry. 1972. *The Analysis of Subjective Culture.* New York: Wiley Interscience.

———. 1977. "Theoretical Framework for Evaluation of Cross-Cultural Training Effectiveness." *International Journal of Intercultural Relations* 1 (4): 19–45.

Trollope, Joanna. 1983. *Britannia's Daughters: Women of the British Empire.* Oxford: Hutchinson.

Trompenaars, Fons, and Charles Hampden-Turner. 1998. *Riding the Waves of Culture: Understanding Diversity in Global Business.* Second edition. New York: McGraw-Hill.

Trouillot, Michel-Rolph. 1995. *Silencing the Past: Power and the Production of History.* Boston, MA: Beacon Press.

———. 2000. "Abortive Rituals: Historical Apologies in the Global Era." *Interventions* 2 (2): 171–86.

———. 2002. "Adieu, Culture: A New Duty Arises." In *Anthropology Beyond Culture,* edited by R. Fox and B. King, 37–60. New York: Berg.

———. 2003. *Global Transformations: Anthropology and the Modern World.* New York: Palgrave Macmillan.

Tsing, Anna. 2004. *Friction: An Ethnography of Global Connection.* Princeton, NJ: Princeton University Press.

———. 2009. "Supply Chains and the Human Condition." *Rethinking Marxism* 21 (2): 148–76.

Tuker, Francis. 1957. *Gorkha: The Story of the Gurkhas of Nepal.* London: Constable and Company.

Tuladhar, Bhushan. 1996. "Kathmandu's Garbage: Simple Solutions Going to Waste." *Studies in Nepali History and Society* 1 (2): 365–93.

Tuladhar, Daman R. 1980. *Contemporary Nepal.* Varanasi: Deepak Press.

Tung, Rosalie. 1982. "Selection and Training Procedures of U.S., European, and Japanese Multinationals." *California Management Review* 25 (1): 57–71.

Turkle, Sherry. 2011. *Alone Together.* New York: Basic Books.

UN-Nepal. 1996. "Living Conditions in Nepal." ms. Kathmandu: United Nations Development Programme.

UNWO (United Nations Women's Organization of Nepal). 1998. *1998 Newcomers Guide to Kathmandu.* Karen Corbett, update. Kathmandu: UNWO.

U.S. Census Bureau. 1990. "State of Residence in 1990 by State of Birth." http://landview.census.gov/population/socdemo/migration/90pob.txt (accessed September 8, 2002).

U.S. Department of State. 1949. "Point Four: Cooperative Program for Aid in the Development of Economically Underdeveloped Areas." Washington, DC: Department of State.

———. 1951. "Point Four General Agreement for Technical Cooperation Between the Government of the United States of America and the Government of Nepal." In *United States Treaties and Other International Agreements,* Vol. 2, part 1, 489–93. Washington, DC: Government Printing Office.

———. 2001. "Post(Hardship) Differential Allowance." http://www.state.gov/m/a/als/faq/1828.htm (accessed September 21, 2001).

———. 2002a. "Compensation of American Government Employees in Foreign Countries." http://www.state.gov/m/a/als/qtrpt/2002/9248.htm (accessed September 21, 2002).

———. 2002b. "Table 1. Indexes of Living Costs Abroad." http://www.state.gov/m/a/als/qtrpt/2002/10651.htm (accessed September 21, 2002).

Upreti, B. C. 2003. *The Marginal Migrants: A Study of Nepali Emigrants in India.* Delhi: Kalinga Publications.

Urry, John. 2007. *Mobilities.* London: Palgrave.

Useem, John, and Ruth Useem. 1967. "The Interfaces of a Binational Third Culture: A Study of the American Community in India." *Journal of Social Issues* 23: 130–43.

Valcour, P. Monique, and Pamela Tolbert. 2003. "Gender, Family and Career in the Era of Boundarylessness: Determinants and Effects of Intra- and Inter-Organizational Mobility." *International Journal of Human Resource Management* 14 (5): 768–87.

Vance, Charles, and Peter Smith Ring. 1994. "Preparing the Host Country Workforce for Expatriate Managers: The Neglected Other Side of the Coin." *Human Resource Development Quarterly* 5 (4): 337–52.

Veblen, Thorstein. 1904. *The Theory of Business Enterprise.* New York: Charles Scribner's Sons.

———. 1932. *The Engineers and the Price System.* New York: Viking Press.

———. 1934. *The Theory of the Leisure Class.* New York: Modern Library.

Verdery, Katherine. 1996. *What Was Socialism, and What Comes Next?* Princeton: Princeton University Press.

Wallock, Leonard. 1991. "The Myth of the Master Builder." *Journal of Urban History* 17 (4): 339–63.

Walsh, Judith. 2004. *Domesticity in Colonial India: What Women Learned When Men Gave Them Advice.* Lanham, MD: Rowman and Littlefield.

Walsh, Katie. 2006. "British Expatriate Belongings: Mobile Homes and Transnational Homing." *Home Cultures* 3 (2): 123–44.

———. 2007. "'It Got Very Debauched, Very Dubai!' Heterosexual Intimacy Amongst Single British Expatriates." *Social and Cultural Geography* 8 (4): 507–33.

Ward, Stuart, ed. 2001. *British Culture and the End of Empire.* New York: Palgrave.

Ware, Vron. 1992. *Beyond the Pale: White Women, Racism and History.* London: Verso.

Warner, Michael. 1999. *The Trouble with Normal: Sex, Politics, and the Ethics of Queer Life.* Cambridge, MA: Harvard University Press.

———. 2002. "Publics and Counterpublics." *Public Culture* 14 (1): 49–90.

Watkins, Evan. 1995. Introduction. *Social Text* 44: 1–2.

Watson, James L. 1997. "Introduction: Transnationalism, Localization, and Fast Foods in East Asia." In *Golden Arches East: McDonald's in East Asia,* edited by James L. Watson, 1–28. Stanford: Stanford University Press.

———, ed. 1997. *Golden Arches East: McDonald's in East Asia.* Stanford: Stanford University Press.

Weber, Max. (1968) 1978. *Economy and Society.* Vol. 2, edited by G. Roth and C. Wittich. Berkeley: University of California Press.

———. (1930) 1992. *The Protestant Ethic and the Spirit of Capitalism.* Translated by Talcott Parsons. New York: Routledge.

Weiner, Annette. 1976. *Women of Value, Men of Renown.* Austin: University of Texas Press.

Whelpton, John. 1983. *Jang Bahadur in Europe.* Kathmandu: Sahayogi Press.

———. 2005. *A History of Nepal.* Cambridge: Cambridge University Press.

Whyte, William Foote. 1943. *Street Corner Society: The Social Structure of an Italian Slum.* Chicago: University of Illinois Press.

Whyte, William H. Jr. 1954. "The Fallacies of 'Personality' Testing." *Fortune* (September): 117–21.

———. 1956. *The Organization Man.* Garden City, NY: Doubleday Anchor Books.

Wilk, Richard. 1995. "Learning to Be Local in Belize: Global Systems of Common Difference." In *Worlds Apart,* edited by D. Miller, 110–33. New York: Routledge.

Wilkins, Mira. 1974. *The Maturing of Multinational Enterprise: American Business Abroad from 1914–1970.* Cambridge, MA: Harvard University Press.

Williams, Brakette F., ed. 1996. *Women out of Place: The Gender of Agency and the Race of Nationality.* New York: Routledge Press.

Williams, Raymond. 1961. *The Long Revolution.* New York: Columbia University Press.

Wilson, Kathleen, ed. 2004. *A New Imperial History: Culture Identity and Modernity in Britain and the Empire, 1660–1840.* New York: Cambridge University Press.

Wilson, Samuel, and L. Peterson. 2002. "The Anthropology of Online Communities." *Annual Review of Anthropology* 31: 449–67.

Winichakul, Tongchai. 1994. *Siam Mapped: A History of the Geo-Body of a Nation*. Honolulu: University of Hawaii Press.

Wittgenstein, Ludwig. (1953) 2001. *Philosophical Investigations*. Oxford: Blackwell.

Wolf, Eric. 1982. *Europe and the People without History*. Berkeley: University of California Press.

Wood, Hugh B. 1987. *Nepal Diary*. Tillamook, OR: American Nepal Education Foundation.

Wood, Hugh B., and Bruno Knall. 1962. *Educational Planning in Nepal and Its Economic Implications*. Kathmandu: UNESCO Mission to Nepal.

Yang, Hyunah. 1997. "Revisiting the Issue of Korean 'Military Comfort Women': The Question of Truth and Positionality." *Positions* 5 (1): 51–71.

Yang, Mayfair. 1994. *Gifts, Favors, and Banquets: The Art of Social Relationships in China*. Ithaca: Cornell University Press.

Young, Robert. 1995. *Colonial Desire: Hybridity in Theory, Culture and Race*. New York: Routledge.

Zelizer, Viviana. 2007. *The Purchase of Intimacy*. Princeton: Princeton University Press.

Žižek, Slavoj. 1989. *The Sublime Object of Ideology*. New York: Verso.

———. 1992. *Everything You Always Wanted to Know about Lacan: (But Were Afraid to Ask Hitchcock)*. New York: Verso.

———. 1996. *The Indivisible Remainder*. New York: Verso.

———. 1999. *The Ticklish Subject: The Absent Centre of Political Ontology*. New York: Verso.

Index

Page numbers followed by f, t, or n refer to figures, tables, and endnotes, respectively.

process by families, 60–61; by Peace
Corps, 55; personality tests for,
58–61, 225n4. *See also* cross-cultural
training (CCT); international human
resources management (IHRM)
Selection Research International, 59
self-employment. *See* career forms,
international; contractors and
subcontractors
seminars, cross-cultural, 151
Sepoy Rebellion (1857, India), 29–30
service provision and providers: application of research by, 54; confusing
mix of, 151, 201; demographic
changes as challenge for, 69; family
failure and, 51–52; on Internet,
185–86; newcomers' needs for
finding, 105, 110, 190; outsourcing,
unintended consequences of, 65–66;
personality testing by, 60; quantification and, 42
Shah, Prithvi Naryan, 32
Shell Ladies' Project, 179
Shell Oil Company, 40–43, 178, 225n2,
230n3
Shiva's Slaves motorcycle club, 175
shopping. *See* consumption
short-term contracts. *See* career forms,
international; contractors and
subcontractors
Shruti, Princess, 164
sightseeing, 139, 203. *See also* tourism
and tourists
single men: blame placed on, 99; in
British India, 28, 30; growing demographic of, 68–69; rise in number of,
in Kathmandu, 135, 212
social networks, organizations, and
sociality: avocation-oriented groups,
70, 173–75, 196–201; carework and
distance issues, 201; compensation
structures and advice and, 95;
globalization and, 176; Internet-based,
176–78, 179–89; movement and

following networks, 9; Newcomers
Coffees, 13–14; newsletters, 178–79;
predeparture training and, 152;
retirement and, 175–76; shopping and
consumption patterns and, 104–7,
109–11; short-term expatriates and
hotel microcommunities, 201–4;
small-town feeling, 11; UNWO and
AWON, 102, 104, 174, 189–96. *See also*
work-leisure dichotomy and work-life
balance
South Asian Inter-Scholastic Association
(SAISA), 199–200
spouses. *See* trailing spouses; women
Spouses' Underground Newsletter (*SUN*),
179, 232n2
Stahl, Gunter, 134
State Department. *See* U.S. State Department and Foreign Service
stereotypes, cultural, 149, 152–54, 157
Sterling Club (British Embassy Club),
173–74, 198
structuration of affection, 62, 226n5
Subaltern Studies, 27
suburban lifestyle in colonial India, 30–
31. *See also* enclavic cosmopolitanism
successfulness of expatriates: "buying,"
81; corporate policies vs. everyday
life and, 63; cultural competency
and, 147–48; culture and, 147–48,
160; family success vs., 67; flexibility and, 125, 137; gender, race, and,
231n3; homemaking and, 78; IHRM
scholarship and, 54; internal, 130–31;
personality tests, selection process,
and, 58–61; rationalization and, 201;
trailing spouses and, 66. *See also* family failure discourse
summers, family decisions on, 71
Summit Hotel, Kathmandu, 1, 1f, 106f, 107
SUN (*Spouses' Underground Newsletter*),
179, 232n2
supplementary instruction allowances,
94–95

276 Index

supply chain capitalism, 230n5

Tales from a Small Planet website, 232n2
technology. *See* Internet technology
telephone service, criticism of, 122
Terrorism, War on, 216
Tex-Mex food, 102–3, 228n22
Thamel, 38, 102, 139, 203
Thanksgiving, 163
Tiger for Breakfast (Peissel), 34
time-space compression, 112, 198
tourism and tourists: expatriates distin-
    guished from tourists, 7–8, 137–38;
    expectations of, 38–39; guests,
    intrusion of, 213; Kathmandu tourist
    geography and dynamics, 37–38;
    religious, 38; short-term expatriates
    and, 203, 213
trailing spouses: Internet and, 179, 187;
    male, 73, 136; as subsidiary, 72;
    unpaid labor of, 62, 74–76. *See also*
    women
training, cultural. *See* cross-cultural
    training (CCT)
travel narrative displays, cultural, 167
Triandis, Harry, 155
Tribhuvan, King of Nepal, 33, 44
Trompenaars, Fons, 153
Trouillot, Michel-Rolph, 229nn28–29
Truman, Harry, 36
Tsing, Anna, 230n5
Tung, Rosalie, 134

UN Day, 162
United Nations, 165
"United Nations utopia," 171. *See also*
    horizontal symmetries, political and
    cultural
United Nations Women's Organization
    (UNWO), 104, 174, 189–95
United States: early relations with Nepal,
    34; governmental expectations, prob-
    lem of, 35; post-WWII investment
    in Nepal, 44; Thanksgiving holiday,

163; Truman's Point IV program, 36,
    44, 224n6
"university model," 150
unmarkedness, 115
unpaid market labor, 62, 66, 74, 75
U.S. State Department and Foreign
    Service: college costs and, 227n12;
    compensation system as benchmark,
    90–91; Defense Department and,
    226n4; Office of Allowances, 91;
    ranking system for jobs, 227n13; reg-
    ulatory documents (FAM, FAH, and
    DSSR), 91–95; survey requirements
    (LPQ and RPS) and documentary
    processes, 98–102
U.S. Technical Cooperation Mission to
    Nepal, 34, 35, 36

violence, 10, 46–47, 137, 202
volunteer work, 75

Weber, Max, 47
We Tried (Dammann), 34–36
Whyte, William, 129–30, 225n4, 230n4
Wilk, Richard, 160, 169
Williams, Raymond, 226n5
women: boundaryless careers and,
    136–37; career concerns, 74–75;
    colonial India and, 28–31, 192; "com-
    pany wives," 74; homemaking and,
    76–80; hostess expectations, 72–73;
    local or "foreign-born" wives, 71,
    99–100, 193–94, 228n18; purifica-
    tion missions of, 82; "Shell wives," 41;
    Web-based entrepreneurship by, 187.
    See also trailing spouses
women's clubs: Active/American Women
    of Nepal (AWON), 102, 189; decline
    of, 189, 201–4; Newcomers Coffees,
    13–14; United Nations Women's
    Organization (UNWO), 104, 174,
    189–95. *See also* social networks,
    organizations, and sociality
Wood, Hugh, 34–35